The Films of Sherlock Holmes

THE FILMS OF
SHERLOCK HOLMES

by
Chris Steinbrunner
and
Norman Michaels

CITADEL PRESS   SECAUCUS, N.J.

To our loving parents

DAVE M. AND FRITZIE MICHAELS

JOSEF AND MARIA STEINBRUNNER

ACKNOWLEDGEMENTS

Many, many Sherlockians opened their treasures of rare materials to help the research and the reconstructions found in this book, but we must especially thank Peter Blau, Robert Watson Douty, John Cocchi, Ray Cabana, Jr., William K. Everson, Richard Katz, Jon Lellenberg, Tyke Niver, Donald Novorsky, and the Baker Street Cinematograph, as well as the pioneering groundwork done by the Priory Scholars.

First edition
Copyright © 1978 by Chris Steinbrunner and Norman Michaels
All rights reserved
Published by Citadel Press
A division of Lyle Stuart Inc.
120 Enterprise Ave., Secaucus, N.J. 07094
In Canada: George J. McLeod Limited
Don Mills, Ontario
Manufactured in the United States of America by
Halliday Lithograph, West Hanover, Mass.
Designed by A. Christopher Simon

Library of Congress Cataloging in Publication Data

Steinbrunner, Chris.
 The films of Sherlock Holmes.

 Includes index.
 1. Sherlock Holmes films. 2. Doyle, Arthur
Conan, Sir, 1859-1930—Film adaptations.
I. Michaels, Norman, joint author. II. Title.
PN1995.9.S5S7   791.43'0909'351   78-15511
ISBN 0-8065-0599-0

Contents

Introduction

. . . The place is a room in Baker Street, somewhere on the edge of eternity. It is a room endlessly the same, yet it has changed shape and perspective a hundred different times, across a hundred films, while outside on the fogbound street one hears the clatter of horse-drawn carriages, modern motor cars, the footfalls of Victorian villains and Nazi spies. Sherlock Holmes lives in this room, his features blurred and changing with the visages of some of the greatest actors of our time. The greatest detective of literature has become the super-sleuth of the screen: there have been more films devoted to his adventures than any other cinematic hero. He is the most popular motion picture detective of all time.

This book is a lighthearted chronicle of that screen career. It is a study in atmospheres. For the reason Sherlock Holmes, Film Detective, has endured may well be because of the trappings, both Victorian and beyond, which surround him and Watson across six decades on the screen. Or perhaps it is the challenge of the role. As many great actors have played Holmes as Hamlet on the screen—indeed, a good many more—and in these pages you will meet them all. As well, you will meet the troubled baronets and the frightened clients, the Scotland Yard men and master criminals, the regents and the riffraff who peopled the world of the great detective . . . that twilight, gaslit, sinister world that is forever Sherlock's London. That world—gloriously unreal—was well caught in the films of Sherlock Holmes, a rich and bizarre tapestry comprising some of the best mystery motion pictures ever made. This book is its history.

Early Holmes

Alwin Neuss as a Danish Sherlock Holmes.

The earliest Holmesian film takes us back to the very swirling mists of the cinema's beginning. *Sherlock Holmes Baffled,* filmed as early as 1900 (though officially copyrighted in February of 1903) in the New York rooftop studio of the American Mutoscope and Biograph Company, is a primitive humorous vignette showing the great detective, in dressing gown, outwitted by a sack-carrying burglar who has climbed into his Baker Street rooms—though finally turning the tables on the intruder. Crude in its quick telling (the film lasts but a minute) and built around the burglar's "trick" disappearance in the manner of Melies' stop-camera movie "magic," the film did nothing much to exploit and develop the image of the great detective—then still at the height of his first literary popularity—but it did introduce Sherlock Holmes to the screen.

In the beginning years, in the infant film industries of America and Europe, uncertain dramas and outright pastiches involving Holmes-like figures abounded. In *The Adventures of Sherlock Holmes,* a Vitagraph film released in 1905, we identify our first Sherlock: American actor Maurice Costello. *Sherlock Holmes and the Great Murder Mystery* (1908) mingles Conan Doyle's creation with Edgar Allan Poe: much like Dupin in the Rue Morgue, Holmes deduces (at the behest of his old college friend, Watson) that it was a gorilla escaped from a ship which has committed the murder for which a young man is about to be hanged. This one-reel film may be the first to make full use of the detective's ratiocinative powers.

The Scandinavian countries have always loved mysteries; their first Sherlockian series began in 1908! The Nordisk film company of Copenhagen

Stage poses of Gillette in the role of Sherlock Holmes. The film was very closely based on the stage production. Gillette lights the cigar to elude his captors in the classic Stepney Gas Chamber scene.

first presented—in *Sherlock Holmes I Livesfare (Sherlock Holmes Risks His Life)*—the detective pitted against both the evil Professor Moriarty and Raffles, the thief created by Conan Doyle's brother-in-law. Other Danish Holmesian films followed, and Sherlockian attempts in other European countries as well: Germany produced a 1915 version of *Der Hund von Baskervilles,* with a screenplay by Richard Oswald, one of the more important influences on Germanic cinema; a wildly melodramatic series of adventures which took audiences far beyond the boundaries of the original story. (There were other Teutonic Holmeses as well.) Much closer to the original sources were the British-made series done by the Franco-British Eclair Company, and starring Georges Treville as Holmes in adaptations of "The Speckled Band," "Silver Blaze," and six other stories. There were also carefully treated English versions of *A Study in Scarlet* and *The Valley of Fear*. The more irreverent American film companies, meanwhile, concentrated on a period of outrageous parodies and spoofs, including a D. W. Griffith–directed series of Mack Sennett comedies (*Trailing the Counterfeiter,* etc.), and mysteries trading on the now-famous name—*The Sherlock Holmes Girl* and *Sureluck Jones, Detective* among many. (Even Buster Keaton in *Sherlock Jr.,* in the next decade, was to daydream himself as the great detective.) In 1914 Carl Laemmle's fledgling Universal Pictures was to begin an association with Holmes that was really only to flourish three decades later; for the studio Francis Ford (older brother of director John) was both to direct and star—as Holmes—in a version of *A Study in Scarlet.*

The first "official" Sherlock Holmes to reach the screen was the incredible performance by the American actor who was firmly and happily associated with the role through decades of playing him on the stage: William Gillette (1853–1937). More than any of the actors before him, Gillette translated the Conan Doyle figure before him into flesh and blood. First on stage and then on screen, Gillette *was* Sherlock Holmes. He was the first of that select and distinguished group of actors who gave themselves totally to the role, submerging and even surrendering their very identities to nourish the legend of Holmes.

Although filmed in 1916, the celebrated stage play on which the Essanay motion picture was based—with more than a decade and a half of touring steadily—had already had profound influences. Gillette, though not the first actor to impersonate the detective, both as player and playwright

showed how *well* Holmes *could* be dramatized. The romantic subthreads he added were a short-lived experiment, though authorized by Conan Doyle himself (Holmes's feverish courting of Alice Faulkner at the finale was a concession to the love-inspired heroisms of the popular melodrama of that day), but many of the foundations which Gillette the stage architect designed became visual traditions. Even though Gillette moved from stage Holmes to film Holmes only some sixteen years after debuting in the role, his pioneering dramatization gave a formula, a basis, even for those Holmes films which came before his, and certainly all the films to come after.

Gillette was over sixty when playing the detective on the screen, and *Moving Picture World* in its May, 1916 review strikes an unknowingly poignant note: "A few more years and it would have become impossible for Mr. Gillette to take the part with the physical vigor that would recall his best efforts of the old days to his international admirers, and at the same time would leave in comparatively permanent form his Sherlock Holmes for the delight of future generations." Alas, no print of this film still exists. Gillette's play seems in the 1970s to be achieving even greater popularity, but his performance on the screen is lost to us.

Gratifyingly, a vast body of Sherlockian film *does* still exist, and this book will concentrate primarily on recreating the performances and the drama that still remain on view, visualizing for the reader some of the rarer as well as some of the more beloved Sherlocks that have strode confidently across the screen, magnifying glass or pipe in hand, piercing the darkest mysteries and righting the wrongs on the world. We shall follow his cinematic trail.

From the film itself, Gillette confronts Ernest Manpani as Moriarty.

The Silents of Eille Norwood

A dramatic night scene from Norwood's *Hound of the Baskervilles.*

One actor was to make an impressive—but now alas almost forgotten—contribution to the Sherlockian cinema in England during the final decade of the silent screen. Eille Norwood (1861–1948) had a modest career mainly on the stage when he was chosen to portray the great detective presented by a British film company called Stoll. In the brief time from 1921 to 1923 Norwood was to play Sherlock Holmes in more motion pictures than any other actor—forty-seven in all.

Actually all but two of these films were much less than feature length: "shorts" lasting about twenty minutes each. But as the treatments were close adaptations of the Conan Doyle stories, this worked out rather well; the cases fitted the twenty-minute format easily, with no need to pad the material out to feature length. (Similarly, Stoll at the same time adapted a series of Sax Rohmer's magazine stories of Fu Manchu equally effectively.)

Norwood was almost sixty when he first appeared as Holmes, yet his acceptance was astonishing. Sir Arthur Conan Doyle was very pleased with his portrayal, and was often quoted as having said Norwood "has that rare quality which can only be described as glamour, which compels you to watch an actor even when he is doing nothing. His wonderful impersonation of Holmes has amazed me." Doyle was also very impressed with the Stoll film productions, declaring them his favorite, and went to considerable trouble to make sure the company would have the rights to dramatize all the Holmes stories.

For his part, Norwood, a serious and sober actor, studied his character closely, and tried to give

11

Eille Norwood as Sherlock Holmes in *The Sign of Four*. Note the almost Satanic trimming of hairline and eyebrows.

Norwood as Holmes (note the colorful dressing gown) and Isobel Elsom as Mary Morstan in *Sign*.

depth and dimension to the great detective. "My idea of Holmes is that he is absolutely quiet. Nothing ruffles him but he is a man who intuitively seizes on points without revealing that he has done so, and nurses them up with complete inaction until the moment when he is called upon to exercise his wonderful detective powers. Then he is like a cat—the person he is after is the only person in all the world, and he is oblivious of everything else till his quarry is run to earth." Obviously, the actor has done more than a surface analysis of his role! Indeed, in his effort to take over the part completely he even learned how to finger a violin.

Norwood also excelled in the art of makeup. Not only could he with wax and wig change himself into totally another person, he also knew how to make those subtle facial changes which can significantly transform the appearance. It was in this way, by rearranging his hairstyle and slightly shortening his eyebrows, he first impersonated Holmes and impressed the director Maurice Elvey, who was to helm most of the Stoll series and, indeed, was over many decades one of England's leading creators of cinematic thrills. (It was Elvey, who had worked with Norwood in another film the year before, who suggested to Stoll that Norwood would be excellent in the part.)

In the forty-seven films, Norwood was frequently called upon to portray Holmes in a variety of disguises, and he relished creating a gallery of old women, lascars, clergymen, sea captains, and other colorful eccentric types. The *Picture Show* magazine for April of 1924 was to report that "makeup has become quite a hobby with him. Whenever he has any spare time, which is not very often, he will practice various forms of makeup. The eye of the camera is very searching, but Mr. Norwood can now afford to laugh at the lens, for he has so perfected his knowledge of makeup that when he dons a wig or faked eyebrows they look as though they belong to him, and not as the camera often makes such things appear—more false even than they are. Sometimes, when he has arrived on the studio set, made up for the part he is to portray, he has not been recognized by those with whom he has been working for days on end." (Lon Chaney, working in Hollywood during the same period, was receiving similar notices in the press.)

Continuing, the article noted that "at one time it was practically impossible to wear a bald pate [toupee] before the camera without showing a line where it joined the forehead. Such an effect did not satisfy Mr. Norwood, and he spent some considerable time contriving a new and original bald pate that did not show any joins. If you saw him as a Nonconformist minister in one of the first Sherlock Holmes films, you will have seen him wearing this bald head." Such was Norwood's dedication to the minutiae of the Holmesian *persona*.

But Norwood's contribution was not limited to facial change; he was an excellent actor and an excellent *mime,* bringing Sherlockian riches even to the silent screen. In a format which centered much of its impact on a detective's exposition, Norwood was able enough to bring color and dash even to a medium without a voice.

Norwood (with Hubert Willis as his Watson) made three series of Sherlock Holmes short films from 1921 to 1923. Each series—they were called "The Adventures of Sherlock Holmes," "The Further Adventures of Sherlock Holmes" and "The Last Adventures of Sherlock Holmes"— contained fifteen films apiece, each closely taken from the Conan Doyle stories. Additionally, two features were also made: *The Hound of the Baskervilles* in 1922, and *The Sign of Four* in 1923. The portrait these films presents of a vanished London has great charm: it is not, of course, a Victorian London but rather the city in the nineteen twenties, a city of motor cars and telephones, for the detective is mildly contemporized (and actually, readers of that decade felt Holmes still belonged to their time instead of being a turn-of-the-century figure). But despite this mild and almost unobtrusive updating, the rendering of Sherlock is accurate, the mood very much on target, and the adaptations (despite the necessity of title cards rather than spoken words) both well done and absolutely straight.

Very few Eille Norwood films still exist today, so instead of detailed expositions it may be better to convey fragments of mood and incident. In *The Dying Detective,* the very first short, we have an interesting view of a richly cluttered Baker Street chamber, fascinating books and test tubes everywhere. Holmes, in an effort to trap the poisoner Culverton Smith, visits him in disguise but is detected. He is ushered out of Smith's home at gunpoint, but mutters this parting shot: "As sure as my name is Sherlock Holmes, *I'll get you yet."* Opening a package containing a spring needle, Holmes is stricken; Watson comes back from a trip to find him dying. "Keep back, Watson, I've got Tampanule fever—invariably contagious and horribly fatal." Of course, it is only a trap for Smith, and in the final scene, Sherlock—who has starved for three days to look properly deathly—tackles

Norwood here looks surprisingly like Dracula!

Holmes and Watson (wielding chair) flank "the most dangerous man in London"; Charles Augustus Milverton—with gun.

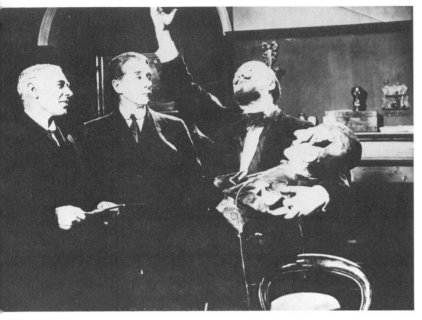

Once more a bust is smashed standing in for the detective.

While Norwood looks properly intense, his hat is set at a rakish angle.

"another tough proposition," a bird from Mrs. Hudson.

In *The Devil's Foot,* we are treated to an idyllic vacation on the Cornwall cliffs with Holmes and Watson, with the doctor saying to his friend (via title card): "Don't forget, Holmes, you're here for a rest. Thank goodness there won't be any work for you here." To which Holmes replies, "One never knows, my dear Watson." Naturally they soon discover dead bodies around a card table—and themselves barely escape a terrible poison emitted by smoke billowing from a lamp shield.

In *The Man with the Twisted Lip* we catch a lovely glimpse of London's Picadilly Circus as it existed in the twenties, with carts, horses and motor cars passing. Watson is sent by a friend's wife to an opium den near the docks to rescue her husband—"a dangerous mission down to the depths of London's underworld." There he finds Holmes, in disguise as a lascar, with Oriental mustache and black crepe hair—makeup which we later see him removing in elaborate close-up. And at the finale, when "beggar" Neville St. Claire is reunited with his wife, we are touched as both Holmes and Watson turn away, gazing steadily out the window, as the couple embrace.

So few of the Stoll series of Sherlock Holmes exist to be studied to this day that our glimpses of Eille Norwood are annoyingly incomplete and tantalizing. He was a towering Sherlock Holmes.

We cannot part from Norwood without noting that many of the original films he made are in the possession of the British Film Institute, but need transfering from their deteriorating nitrate material to safety stock. This work must be done soon, or the nitrate will crumble away and the films—the only copies known to exist in the world—will be lost for all time. Happily there now is a group called the Baker Street Cinematograph, a scion society of the Baker Street Irregulars, which is trying to preserve these treasures. Persons wishing to aid the Cinematograph in this preservation work can contact the society by writing the authors in care of the publisher of this book.

A gallery of Sherlockian disguises—
all of them Norwood.

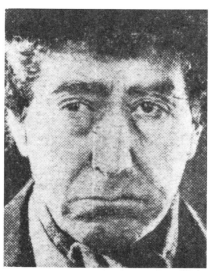

Sherlock Holmes

JOHN BARRYMORE

An aristocratic portrait pose of Barrymore as Holmes.

Goldwyn Pictures, 1922. Screenplay by Marion Fairfax and Earle Brown from the play by William Gillette and the stories by Sir Arthur Conan Doyle. Produced by E. J. Godsol. Directed by Albert Parker.

CAST

Sherlock Holmes, John Barrymore; *Moriarty,* Gustav von Seyffertitz; *Dr. Watson,* Roland Young; *Alice Faulkner,* Carol Dempster; *Forman Wells,* William Powell; *Madge Larabee,* Hedda Hopper; *Prince Alexis,* Reginald Denny; *Count von Stalberg,* David Torrence; *James Larabee,* Anders Randolf; *Craigin,* Louis Wolheim; *Sid Jones,* Percy Knight; *Rose Faulkner,* Peggy Bayfield; *Alf Bassick,* Robert Schable; *Billy,* Jerry Devine; *Inspector Gregson,* John Willard.

The first important Holmes of the 1920s American cinema was a great stage and screen thespian,

John Barrymore. Already reaching forty, already a successful theatrical star, already familiar to screen melodrama as the portrayer of *Raffles* in 1917, John Barrymore of the well-known profile was to be cast as an even better-known profile.

The casting of Barrymore was mainly the inspiration of the young and enthusiastic actor-director Albert Parker. (Michael Pointer in his *The Sherlock Holmes File* quotes Parker as seeing Barrymore on stage and convincing him to play Holmes: "He didn't want to do the film. I had to talk him into it. He didn't like the part, because it was such a trademark. . . ." At that time Parker had little else besides enthusiasm, and certainly not the rights to the property; he then rushed to Chicago where William Gillette was touring in the play *Sherlock Holmes* and made the deal.) The film was a prestige one, under the banner of Samuel Goldwyn, with extensive exterior location shooting in London locales. Until very recently it was a lost film.

Historian William K. Everson tells of the recovery of this important Barrymore film in his *Rediscovery* series in the February 1976 issue of *Films In Review*. "A few years ago, all that existed of this film were rolls and rolls of negative sections, in which every take—not every sequence, but every *take*—was jumbled out of order, with only a few single-frame flash titles for guidance." The task of putting the film together seemed herculean. "However, with the limited help of the film's director, Albert Parker, who remembered but little of the film's continuity and who died while the reconstruction work was in progress, British film-maker and historian Kevin Brownlow *did* piece it together, replaced titles, and generally made sense out of an impossible jigsaw. The result is one of the most painstaking recovery jobs ever. . . ."

Everson, who is perhaps the most astute observer of our film heritage alive today, goes on to be critical of the film, calling it a bland misuse of potentially exciting material despite its London location work, too often falling back to dialogue-heavy dependence on the Gillette play. It is a fair comment, but there is much in the film to interest the Sherlockian still. And Barrymore—though some claimed he was more interested during the

Barrymore wanders down an East India Dock street in his pursuit of "the most evil man in London."

filming in an upcoming stage commitment as Hamlet, or worse, on benders throughout—gives his own flair to the Holmesian image, a fascinating Byronic intonation.

The production gloss of actual London sequences—*and* actual days of shooting in Switzerland—displayed some of the film's care and budget. The casting, too, was given close attention. British newcomer Roland Young made his screen debut as Watson (he was, interestingly, a few years younger than Barrymore); Barrymore was later to recall amusedly that he assisted the green actor with his role throughout the shooting, only afterwards realizing that his Watson had quietly, cunningly stolen all their scenes together. Carol Dempster, the D. W. Griffith actress, was Holmes's romantic interest, true to the Gillette play. Like most of the cast, she was a short person; there was some concern over Barrymore's lack of Holmesian height. William Powell, who was to become Philo Vance in a later decade, portrayed a thief who is a Holmesian ally. Two players were to pursue literary careers: Hedda Hopper, who was Moriarty's cohort, and Madge Larabee, who later deserted acting for gossip. John Willard, a young, lean Inspector Gregson, was the actor-author of the most sensational stage melodrama of the time, *The Cat and the Canary.*

But the most important casting was giving the role of Moriarty to hawk-visaged German actor Gustav von Seyffertitz, who deservedly received second billing. (As a matter of fact, the film was released under the title *Moriarty* in England.) Splendidly melodramatic, von Seyffertitz articulated the Professor's great villainy with unrestrained fervor. Barrymore capitalized on his resemblance (in profile) to the actor by disguising himself as Moriarty in the climax of Gillette's play.

The celebrated William Gillette stage play, already enjoying several decades of success, was more or less faithfully translated to the screen, the only serious departure being the addition of a prologue clumsily attempting to add personal motivation to Holmes's struggle against Moriarty. The film—after a title warning us that "Life is infinitely strange"—begins with an overhead view of the city of London, a "vast whirlpool where eddy the conflicting forces of good and evil." In Limehouse, the most evil quarter of the metropolis, Moriarty sits as a spider, plotting crimes, "his blood cold as a corpse." The evil genius's shadow falls over Cambridge, where young Prince Alexis (Reginald Denny) is falsely accused of stealing athletic funds. Another young student, Watson, recalls, "There's a fellow in my year" who dabbles in mysteries, and might help clear the royal name. And that's how we meet Sherlock Holmes.

We see him first wandering aimlessly down

A pensive Holmes—and we have a view of his living quarters.

Holmes battles his way out of the villains' den.

The detective quizzes Billy about the note he has received.

country lanes, recording philosophical observations in a notebook. Stumbling, he is nearly over-run by a pony cart driven by an extraordinarily beautiful girl, Alice Faulkner, who stirs his heart. Turning his attention to the school theft, he traces its perpetrator—Moriarty—to a Limehouse joss-house, and has his first confrontation with the mastermind. "It is a world of strange complexities—love and monstrous evil." Holmes gropes for his place in the scheme of things. He has recognized the enormous wickedness in Moriarty, and vows to devote his life to ridding the world of him.

Some years later we are in Baker Street (an authentic London exterior, not Baker Street but a view along Torrington Square; at least looking like a straight thoroughfare rather than the curving lane simulated in later Hollywood films). Holmes has become a consulting detective, and Alice Faulkner re-enters his life. Her sister Rose—who has committed suicide in Switzerland—had written some letters to Prince Alexis which Moriarty is using for blackmail. The letters are in the possession of the Professor's minions, the Larabees. Holmes hopes to trap Moriarty, using the letters as bait. And from then on we are upon the familiar turf of the William Gillette play.

Much of the stage's unfolding dialogue, alas, serves to slow the pace of the silent, titled film. There are surprisingly few visual highspots. Even the Stepney gas chamber scene (in the theater version the climax of the second act), with its darting cigar and sleight-of-hand misdirection, fails to stun. And, strangely, many of the crackling lines in the final confrontation between detective and criminal are dropped. Even Holmes's recitation of his faults to Alice Faulkner is minimized. We are, however, granted this final, potent exchange, just before the end credits:

MORIARTY: You do not think that this is the end?
HOLMES: I rather hoped so, Moriarty. I start on my honeymoon tomorrow.

The detective's arrest of Moriarty would hopefully lead to the "clearing up of over forty mysteries," but it was only puzzling to the *New York Times* reviewer: "Holmes says that the time has come when he can arrest Moriarty, but no one knows why . . . You have to take his word for it. It's nothing the spectator can follow." (5/8/22) The critic also thought the film confused Holmes the lover with Holmes the detective.

Generally, however, the reviews nationwide were

Two incidents from the scene in which Holmes gets the better of his arch-foe.

Who is under that rather obviously false nose? It is Moriarty disguised as a cabman, captured by Holmes in the final scene of the film.

favorable, relishing "the creepy kind of thrills" the film provided, and lauding Barrymore's portrayal, which in one comment "thoroughly humanized" the Conan Doyle creation. "Sherlock Holmes could have had no more enthusiastic or sympathetic interpreter," gushed the Toledo *Blade,* also pleased that Holmes brings to justice a criminal band guilty of scores of gruesome crimes "without one of the crimes being shown. Only one shot is fired during the whole picture and that hits no one. It is a remarkable picture." (10/23/22)

Somewhat skittishly, Mae Tinee in the Chicago *Tribune* questioned the happy ending, the absence of Sherlock's drug indulgences. "There *would* have been a needle and there *wouldn't* have been a honeymoon if Rex Ingram had filmed *Sherlock Holmes.* He'd have fought the censors tooth and nail and stuck to the story. Oh, well—" It was not her only cogent observation. "Don't you think the adventures of Sherlock Holmes should be issued either as a serial or a series of pictures? The Conan Doyle stories contain a wealth of material. . . ."

John Barrymore stands pensively by the Thames in a pre-production photo—shot before he shaved off his moustache for the role.

22

The Return of Sherlock Holmes

CLIVE BROOK

A Paramount Picture, 1929. Screenplay by Garrett Ford and Basil Dean based on "The Dying Detective" and "His Final Bow" by Sir Arthur Conan Doyle. Directed by Basil Dean.

CAST

Sherlock Holmes, Clive Brook; *Dr. Watson,* H. Reeves-Smith; *Mary Watson,* Betty Lawford; *Captain Longmore,* Charles Hay; *Roger Longmore,* Phillips Holmes; *Colonel Moran,* Donald Crisp; *Professor Moriarty,* Harry T. Morey; *Sergeant Gripper,* Hubert Druce.

The first Sherlock Holmes film of the sound era also introduced a fresh new player—the distinguished British actor, Clive Brook. Then in his early forties, Brook was already a screen veteran; among the dozens of films in which he appeared were *A Tale of Two Cities,* von Sternberg's *Underworld,* and, in early 1929, Paramount's spectacular *Four Feathers.* David Selznick, then head of production at Paramount, thought to cast under-contract Brook as Sherlock Holmes because he felt the actor looked like the detective (Brook disagreed). Arrangements were made with the Doyle estate, and a plot was concocted to bring Holmes out of retirement into the modern world of 1929. The gentle updating, which had Holmes come to the rescue of Watson's grown daughter (!), also reactivated a Professor Moriarty as ruthless as ever—not to mention an equally malevolent Colonel Moran. All were trapped within the confines of a transatlantic ocean liner, a useful device when dealing with the restrictions of primitive sound pickup and the

The artist's representation of Holmes makes him look far younger than a detective supposedly in retirement—and his relationship with the girl other than merely the daughter of an old friend. Note the phrase "thrillingly active, talking..."

An early ad for the film announces Paramount star Evelyn Brent for the role which ultimately went to Betty Lawford.

stage background of new director Basil Dean (who later was to return to his own country to craft a number of distinguished British films). Dean collaborated on the screenplay with Garrett Ford, a melodrama specialist who in the next few years would work on the scenarios of both *Frankenstein* and *Dracula*. It was a good group . . . and something of a hybrid film.

Brook certainly was the most urbane of all the Holmesian imitators; he was the very image of imperial solidity, dubbed the Rock of Gibraltar by Adolph Zukor, and "the perfect Englishman" by the American press. His portrayal of Holmes wisely did not neglect the detective's foibles and eccentricities. He was surrounded by familiar, competent faces. H. Reeves-Smith, who like Brook had a long career on the British and American stage appearing opposite such stars as Ethel Barrymore and Nazimova, was of necessity an older Watson—being the heroine's father—playing a paternal role novel to Doyle enthusiasts. Phillips Holmes, the young hero, had come straight from college to the Paramount studios to be groomed as a leading man; three years later he was to star in Dreiser's *An American Tragedy.* Villains Moriarty and Moran were both played by screen veterans: Harry T. Morey was often a Paramount heavy, and Donald Crisp's career extended back to D. W. Griffith (he was, for instance, the murderous prizefighter in *Broken Blossoms*).

The film, interestingly enough, sought to widen Holmes's appeal by bringing the detective out of his London surroundings to America; indeed, at the climax, just as Holmes and Moriarty confront one another on the transatlantic liner as it docks in New York, the actual skyscrapers of the 1929 Manhattan skyline can be seen from the deck. (This was fairly easy to achieve, as the motion picture was shot at Paramount's old Astoria Studios in the Long Island City section of New York, and location shooting was done on piers and ships.) *The Return of Sherlock Holmes* predated both Basil Rathbone's trip to America in *Sherlock Holmes in Washington* and Rathbone's shipboard mystery feature, *Pursuit to Algiers.*

Return gives us a Professor Moriarty who is head of an international "radio-tapping" ring, supercriminals using illicit information to plot huge capers. The film begins as Moriarty is eliminating one of his associates who has developed pangs of conscience—eliminating him with a cigarette case from which a deadly needle can protrude, prepared for him by Colonel Moran (who in this film

The face peering at us on the right is the Austrian violinist and shipboard magician, actually Holmes under a wig.

doubles as both a doctor and a poison expert!). The victim is Captain Longmore, but before the poison fully does its work the dying man sends for his son Roger, and puts him in pursuit of both his murderer and a confession he has written telling "everything." The chase leads Roger aboard a transatlantic liner on which Moran is serving as ship's doctor; the youth is drugged and kidnapped as the ship—"fastest on the ocean"—sails for America via Cherbourg, and his disappearance causes the police to suspect him of his father's murder. Because he is engaged to Dr. Watson's daughter, Mary, the distraught girl appeals to her father's old friend—who has been living in retirement on a bee farm for a number of years—to clear Roger's name. Sherlock Holmes agrees (he looks none the worse for his seclusion: in sideburns, an old-fashioned lounge suit, and smoking a monstrously large pipe), and, suspecting that the lad must somehow be aboard Moran's liner he—with Watson and Mary—manages to board it in France for the Atlantic crossing.

Moriarty is among the passengers, establishing his headquarters on the boat, working with the radio operator in tapping "the international telephone circuit" for the sort of information which leads to world power.

Holmes, in order to sleuth effectively, disguises himself as an Austrian violinist with the ship's orchestra—complete with wig and octagonal glasses! In an after-dinner gala, he is called upon to perform sleight-of-hand tricks for the passengers in the salon: he tears a hundred-pound note to pieces and then returns it whole to its owner. Sitting in the audience and impressed with this ma-

gician's flashiness, Professor Moriarty rather dimwittedly hands him the all-important Longmore confession envelope so he can do the same. Naturally Holmes palms the real confession, replacing it with blank paper and proceeding with the trick.

Having the confession is not enough, however; the falsely accused Roger must be found. Holmes therefore adopts a second disguise, that of a humble "boots" steward, so that he can paint the heels of Moran's shoes with a phosphorescent solution and track down his secret cabin. He rescues Roger just in time to prevent his murder, but his identity is revealed to Moriarty—and the two sit down to a leisurely dinner of oysters, caviar and lobster! An amiable Moriarty proffers Holmes his cigarette case—with the secret needle. The agile-wristed detective, in this film certainly expert in legerdemain, pretends to be pricked—and reworks a page from Doyle's "The Dying Detective." Moriarty, remarkably easy to fool for a master criminal, is apprehended by a fresh-looking Holmes as the liner docks in New York. The film ends with what was becoming a classic exchange.

WATSON: Amazing, Holmes.
HOLMES: Elementary, my dear Watson, elementary.

Because of the new technical problems encountered in shooting a movie with sound, the filmmakers had some rough moments. Basil Dean, whose association with Brook had been in British stage ventures, was occasionally out of his depth as a sound-film director. Four-walled sets for the shipboard sequences proved impractical (there was

no place to put the sound recording equipment), and in order to film a dock sequence at the Astoria studio a complete loading winch had to be transferred there to supply off-screen creaking noises!

Nevertheless, the public accepted the talking Holmes, and Clive Brook was to portray the great detective twice again—first in a brief but very funny send-up (along with Philo Vance and Fu Manchu) in *Paramount on Parade,* and then in a feature for another studio—a new-image, younger and even sexy Holmes, not uniting other lovers but having a romance of his own!

Holmes (Clive Brook), pipe in hand, converses with Watson (H. Reeves-Smith) on deck; this location shot—where the detective would have his ultimate confrontation with Moriarty—shows the New York skyline dimly in the background. It is real.

Brook as himself and as Holmes.

Paramount on Parade
HOLMES SEQUENCE

Clive Brook sneers at William Powell (as Philo Vance).
Both are in their characteristic dress.

Paramount Pictures, 1930.

A galaxy of Paramount stars perform in a feature-length series of sketches and musical numbers designed as a revue primarily but also a salute to the studio. Eleven Paramount directors guide such acts as Maurice Chevalier and Evelyn Brent in a mock Apache dance, and Clara Bow joined by forty Marines in singing "I'm True to the Navy Now." Interestingly, both Clive Brook and William Powell were at that time working for Paramount, the former as Sherlock Holmes and the latter as S. S. Van Dine's urbane detective Philo Vance, and the studio was filming a Fu Manchu series (with Warner Oland) closely based on the Sax Rohmer books. It was an engaging and novel idea to combine all three melodrama figures in a single outrageous routine.

In a bantering prologue to the skit, Brook, Powell, Oland and Eugene Pallette (who had portrayed police sergeant Heath in the Philo Vance films) each confess to comedian Jack Oakie in the studio commissary that they are about to do "a mystery play written especially for me." Oakie takes all this in with a bemused grin; interestingly, while Pallette is sitting with a girl and Powell is flirting with *two* girls, Oland is at a table by himself and Brook is smoking a pipe with another man. When the drama begins, Fu Manchu has just murdered a "foreign devil" in some sort of Chinatown temple and confesses to Sergeant Heath, regarding the corpse: "He doubted I was a murderer so I killed the disbeliever." Just as Heath puts handcuffs on a surprisingly compliant Fu, "the honorable" Philo Vance—in top hat and tails—jumps out of an Egyptian coffin. How does Heath know Fu was the killer? Actually, the victim was stabbed and shot, and Heath explains he found the Chinese mastermind with both a knife and a gun in his hand. "But aren't you, Sergeant, just a trifle premature? For instance, you haven't once mentioned the word 'psychology.'" Heath snorts at this.

VANCE: But you can't expect me to admit Dr. Fu committed this murder without my at least eliminating all the other suspects.

FU MANCHU: When Fu Manchu is pleased to commit a murder, there *are* no other suspects.

VANCE: There *must* be other suspects. There are *always* other suspects.

Enter Sherlock Holmes.

"My dear Watson," the detective intones (we never see to whom he is speaking), "there are four men in this room, one of whom does not move. He is obviously not asleep. As he is not asleep, he was obviously murdered." He moves towards Vance.

"My name is Holmes, Sherlock." He too refuses to believe Fu Manchu guilty. The enraged Oriental, with Heath's gleeful cooperation, pulls a gun and shoots Philo Vance in the backside—he falls over dead—and then puts a bullet through Holmes's wrist and then his heart. Sherlock lowers himself rather effetely to the floor, the first time he has died on screen.

HEATH: Hey, that's neat.

FU MANCHU: I had to do it. It was the only way I could convince them I was a murderer.

So saying, Fu Manchu ends the farce on a surrealist note by literally flying away . . . after toppling the bodies of both Sherlock and Vance through trapdoors. A score of bobbies come to arrest Heath for murder, while the "corpse" which opened the act (it turns out to be Jack Oakie) turns to the audience with a grimace to say: "It's a mystery play—written especially for *me*."

The Speckled Band

RAYMOND MASSEY

A portrait shot, making the actor look thoughtful and older.

British and Dominions Studios, 1931. Screenplay by W. P. Lipscomb. Based on the story by Sir Arthur Conan Doyle. Produced by Herbert Wilcox. Directed by Jack Raymond.

CAST

Sherlock Holmes, Raymond Massey; *Dr. Watson,* Athole Stewart; *Dr. Grimesby Rylott,* Lyn Harding; *Helen Stoner,* Angela Baddeley; *Mrs. Staunton,* Nancy Price; *Mrs. Hudson,* Marie Ault; *Rodgers,* Stanley Lathbury; *Builder,* Charles Paton; *Violet,* Joyce Moore.

This interesting version of the Conan Doyle story—one of the most memorable mystery short stories in the language—is a comfortably paced version of a stage adaptation that had been a London success a few years earlier, which not only translated well to the screen but to the new medium of the *talking* screen. The director, Jack Raymond, had already become a competent craftsman, and later in the decade was to show himself equally facile with comedy and Edgar Wallace; in *The Speckled Band* he is helped considerably in the establishing of a heavily gothic, Germanic mood by the shadowy camerawork of Freddy Young, which is both brooding and superb. The mood is helped too by the playing of the actor taking on the role of Holmes, Raymond Massey in his screen debut.

Then in his mid-thirties, Massey had been a Canadian-born actor long active on the British stage; Holmes was his first screen part, and he gives an interesting portrayal of the detective. (He

"... The speckled band..." The dying Violet (Joyce Moore) whispers this message to her sister Helen Stoner (Angela Baddeley) as Dr. Grimesby Rylott (Lyn Harding) looks on. Some of the Germanic atmosphere of this scene can be perceived.

A ferocious, snarling Rylott taunts Sherlock Holmes, who stands his own (Raymond Massey).

is very much the film player from then on, memorable in the next few years in J. B. Priestley's *The Old Dark House* and H. G. Wells's *Things to Come,* and even as such notable Americans as Abraham Lincoln and abolitionist John Brown.) He is slightly more meditative than incisive, but achieves a poignancy seldom demonstrated by the detective on screen. As Jon Lellenberg notes in the *Baker Street Cinematograph,* Massey is cerebral, somewhat cynical, perhaps a bit modern in his attitudes, but very much his own Holmes—with no resort at all to the usual props of deerstalker and calabash.

Athole Stewart gives a fairly stock portrayal of a balding Watson, and Angela Baddeley is a wondrously frail heroine some four decades before her triumph in *Upstairs, Downstairs.* But for sheer villainy Lyn Harding as Dr. Grimesby Rylott (changed a bit from "Roylott," which is the way Conan Doyle spelled the name) could not easily be surpassed. He had played the role first in the stage version, and clearly no one else was thought of for the role. Twitching, glowering, conspiring, threatening, he is a master; one can certainly believe why his stepdaughter is terrified of him and recoils at his ministrations. Harding was to continue a happy association with Sherlockian villainy through the decade, appearing as Arthur Wontner's Moriarty. Already established as a screen heavy and heavyweight, he is, in the film's opening cast lineup, given credit *first, above* Massey as Holmes!

The Speckled Band opens with Violet Stoner's scream, and her death, in the misty, night-shrouded manor house of Grimesby Rylott, the girl's menacing stepfather. There is an inquest the next day, at which Dr. Watson is to testify; he is a friend of the dead girl's sister ("It's a great help to have a friend," the heroine confides) and knew Rylott's late wife in India. Rylott has strange Indian servants who carry out his every order, and sinister gypsies are camped on the grounds outside— Violet's dying words were "the speckled band..." The situation is mysterious enough for Watson's friend Sherlock Holmes to take a hand, and we travel to Baker Street.

Curiously, the house number is not 221-B but 107, and there are other, far more startling changes. Baker Street is "computerized"— in a 1931 version of up-to-the-minute efficiency. The anteroom to Holmes's study is filled with secretaries, stenographers, intercoms and automated filing systems. Watson, entering the room, is greeted by the clacking of office machinery and a sobbing assistant.

WATSON: Hello, what's the matter with you?

MISS PRINGLE: That machine you brought in, Dr. Watson. It's supposed to give details of every criminal case, and the whereabouts of every criminal at any given date. You know how I worked to get it complete. And *now*—

WATSON: What's wrong?

HOLMES (*entering*): I keep correcting it, that's all.

MISS PRINGLE: Mr. Holmes, it isn't fair. No machine can give you *everything*.

HOLMES: No, my dear. That's why I shall keep on using this old brain of mine.

Clearly, Holmes is the triumph of mind over machine, the super-computer. "I like a machine, Watson. It keeps me up to the mark!"

As Watson outlines the case to Holmes, the various members of the Rylott household under discussion are superimposed on the scene—an interesting directorial touch. Then, even more interestingly, Holmes informs Watson that his entire narrative has been recorded over an intercom, testimony to be used later in the investigation of the case. Seemingly, Baker Street's rooms are as routinely bugged as, later, the White House Oval Room!

Events move swiftly. Helen Stoner has decided to marry, so her fortune may slip through her stepfather's fingers unless he acts. Rylott has the celebrated confrontation with an unperturbed Holmes at Baker Street. The gypsies have returned to the Surrey countryside, and some restoration work being done in the Rylott house has forced Helen to temporarily move into her dead sister's room. Tension builds.

Indeed, it is the heavy atmosphere of the film that makes it tingle. The Germanic atmosphere of the house, the incredibly real-looking tinkers and their caravans add a sinister touch. Rylott moves purposefully down a country lane in a Victorian pony cart, while the heroine's suitor roars about in a sports car—and both exist without question in the Holmesian 1930s.

Sherlock, disguised as a workman, finds a dog-whip in Helen's sleeping quarters; that night he, Watson and the girl await the film's climax. In the next room, Rylott and his flute-playing Indian servant cast satanic shadows against the wall. Through a ventilator shaft they force "the dead-

In the film's epilogue, Watson (Athole Stewart) disturbs Holmes at his test tubes with news of Helen's marriage—causing the detective to reflect on the absence of romance in his own ordered existence.

liest snake in India," but Holmes drives it back, and Rylott becomes its victim: we hear his scream.

There is an interesting epilogue at Baker Street. Holmes, disheveled in a dressing gown, is making a chemical experiment as a dapper Watson enters in formal wear; he is going to Helen Stoner's wedding.

WATSON: Why don't you come along?
HOLMES: Not in my line, Watson .... Give them my congratulations—or perhaps condolences.
WATSON: Rubbish. We all come to it, my dear fellow, we all come to it. (exits laughing)

Holmes, alone with his thoughts, stares straight at the camera and mutters with utter pathos, "Not all, my dear Watson ... Not all ..." Giving a sigh of resignation, he flips on the intercom; we hear Miss Pringle's voice say: "Yes, Mr. Holmes?"

HOLMES: Have you added the details of Dr. Rylott's affair to the datum? Put them with cases concluded.

Few of the Sherlock Holmeses of the screen were allowed to show so much human feeling—and despair.

The test tubes and Bunsen burners of Holmes's laboratory are only dimly seen in this advertising display, but the Holmes we see, though pensive, looks quite youthful.

THE SPECKLED BAND

Raymond Massey as

Sherlock Holmes

BY
SIR ARTHUR CONAN DOYLE

FICTION'S GREATEST DETECTIVE RE-LIVES!

The exploits of the famous Sherlock Holmes and the inimitable Dr. Watson are vividly portrayed in this gripping mystery film.

THE STORY

The sole source of Dr. Rylott's income is the fortune of his stepdaughters, and he plots and schemes to secure it. One night a band of gipsies encamps near the house and Helen Stonor's elder sister dies under mysterious circumstances. The only clue to the mystery are her last words—"Band . . . . . speckled."
In spite of the untoward happenings the coroner's jury returns a verdict of "Death from natural causes." Helen confides her suspicion to Dr. Watson.
Watson, reporting to Sherlock Holmes, appears satisfied ; the great detective, however, is uneasy.
Twelve months later it is the eve of Helen's marriage and Dr. Rylott realises that his income is slipping from him. By a curious coincidence the gipsies return, and after a night of terror, Helen goes to Baker Street and invokes the aid of Sherlock Holmes.
The wizard of Baker Street takes up the case and saves Helen from the evil plot hatched by Dr. Rylott.

HIRING SERVICE

This film can now be shown in schools, clubs, hotels, universities, societies, or in any hall in any part of the country, at a moderate cost inclusive of sound reproduction equipment and operator.
Other films to form a complete programme are also available.
For prices and other information, application should be made to:

The Hound of the Baskervilles

ROBERT RENDEL

Gaumont British Picture Corporation, 1931. A Gainsborough Picture. Dialogue by Edgar Wallace. Produced by Michael Balcon. Scenario and direction by V. Gareth Gundrey.

CAST

Sherlock Holmes, Robert Rendel; *Dr. Watson,* Frederick Lloyd; *Sir Henry Baskerville,* John Stuart; *Stapleton,* Reginald Bach; *Beryl,* Heather Angel; *Dr. Mortimer,* Wilfred Shure; *Sir Hugo,* Sam Livesey; *Mrs. Laura Lyons,* Elizabeth Vaughn; *Mrs. Barrymore,* Sybil Jane; *Cartwright,* Leonard Hayes; *Barrymore,* Henry Hallett; *The Hound of the Baskervilles,* Champion Egmund of Send.

The first screen presentation of the *Hound* in the talking era was done by a small British studio.

Gainsborough Pictures had conducted a poll in a film magazine to learn which film audiences most wished them to make, and the Conan Doyle mystery novel was the choice. The Islington studio, then eight years old, placed the project under the supervision of the young and dynamic Michael Balcon, who had joined them only a year before (this was the beginning of a distinguished career in motion pictures; three years later he was to chart *The Thirty-nine Steps* with Alfred Hitchcock), and a flawed but interesting Holmesian film was to result. Alas, this version of *The Hound of the Baskervilles* is among the "lost films": only sections are known to survive, and the sound track, the one element in those early-talkie days which made the film memorable, is completely lost.

The cast included a ruggedly handsome and favorite leading man, John Stuart, as young Sir Henry Baskerville, and Heather Angel as Beryl. (She was to have something of a later career in America as, among other roles, Bulldog Drummond's sweetheart in several films.) Watson was portrayed by a solidly dependable (but somewhat waspish) Frederick Lloyd. It was in the film's choice of Sherlock Holmes himself that the screen image was decidedly altered.

Since before the turn of the century the image of the detective had been synonymous with the tall, lean Holmesian look. But by the thirties the amateur criminologist—influenced perhaps by Alexander Woolcott—took on other shapes and sizes (although retaining a tendency towards pipe-smoking unabated). Sometimes the armchair detective, precisely because he lounged too much in armchairs, began to look solidly stocky; sometimes, in the films of this period, less careful studios permitted their Sherlock Holmes to be portly rather than lean, thinking perhaps that they surely should have the right to mold their Sherlocks as they saw fit. This was the case with Gainsborough's *Hound of the Baskervilles,* in which they cast character player Robert Rendel as Holmes. Rendel was tall, had a commanding presence, a rich voice, and clutched a pipe well. He had the visual credentials of an amateur criminologist: a piercing, investigative look and decisive manner. But he was too thick of beam ever to be mistaken for the famed illustrator Sidney Paget's definitive version—or any other—of the great detective.

Perhaps the most impressive member of the cast was the portrayer of the title role: the hound. Enormous in size, rather like a small pony, and quite animated, the animal looked somewhat too good-natured to effectively frighten the critics as it bounded over the moor (and over the cast members), but the mastiff was a registered canine aristocrat—Champion Egmund of Send—and looked every inch of it.

Another impressive contributor to the film was the great Edgar Wallace, who wrote the dialogue to the scenario sketched by the director, Gareth Gundrey. Soon after finishing this assignment, Wallace left for America, where he was to do several writing jobs for the RKO studios, including working on *King Kong.* It is fascinating to study the treatment which Wallace, surely the most prolific and popular mystery writer of the decade, was to give Conan Doyle, the greatest mystery author of all time. Let us pay special attention to the dialogue in this, the Wallace version of an epic Holmesian saga.

The Hound of the Baskervilles opens with the long-ago events on the moors as a prologue. Through the darkness a girl runs, with Sir Hugo and his men in pursuit on horseback. When she finally drops from exhaustion and dies, a spectral hound is superimposed over her body, and as the ghost-beast hurls itself on Sir Hugo, the paw-prints it leaves are glowing. We dissolve to the parchment on which the legend is written, being read by a crusty Dr. Mortimer at Baker Street: "And even as they looked the thing tore the throat out of Sir Hugo Baskerville, and as it turned its blazing eyes and dripping jaws upon them, the others rode, screaming, across the moor . . ." The camera pans down from Mortimer and across a table where a violin and a bound treatise on tobacco-ash have been carelessly placed. A man sits contemplatively puffing on a straight pipe; he is wearing a dressing gown. It is Sherlock Holmes, and as he gets up to pace we note that the Baker Street rooms are rather sparse and modernistic—there are, for instance, only a few bookshelves set into uncluttered white walls, and precious few books upon the shelves. Clearly a *new* Holmes, retooled for sound.

HOLMES: Surely you didn't travel from Dartmoor to read that to me?
MORTIMER: I hoped you'd advise me; you're regarded as the second highest problem expert in Europe.
HOLMES: The second highest—but who's the first?
MORTIMER: Well I've read of a Frenchman who—who—
HOLMES: Then why not consult him.

There is something of a Wallace flair to this exchange, but the words are more or less straight Doyle, as is the remainder of the conversation as Mortimer outlines Sir Charles's grisly death to the consulting detective. Rather speedily young Sir Henry enters the scene, and Wallace peppers the Canadian's lines with some Americanisms: talking of his uncle Henry says, "I never knew the poor old chap, but I bet it would have taken more than a spooky dog to scare him to death." He is very concerned over a stolen boot, and is to make frequent references jokingly that the ghost-dog has taken it, and is carrying it in its mouth. Later, when Holmes and Watson are alone and the detective is outlining the case, Watson remarks with a laugh: "Good Lord! You seem to suspect everybody—except the Hound of the Baskervilles!" To which Holmes replies drily that the ghostly hound doesn't interest him ... only the sort that leaves footprints and must be provided with a boot for a scent.

Events move rapidly to the moor. The business about the escaped convict is introduced, and we meet Laura Lyons of Coombe Tracey, the woman who had begun a romantic liaison with old Sir Charles Baskerville. (Despite being an interesting character, Laura was omitted from other major screen adaptations of the *Hound*.) Sherlock (supposedly left behind in London) once again surprises Watson at the sharecropper's hut on the moor—the detective has been keeping careful watch over the happenings at Baskerville Hall. Exploring the neighboring land, he has even discovered a cave which had been used as a kennel. ...

HOLMES: It was empty. The hound's moved frequently so that its hiding place could remain a secret to everyone except Henry Baskerville's cousin.

WATSON: His cousin?

HOLMES: Yes. Fifty years ago there was a black sheep in the family. He went abroad and started a new life under a new name. Later he died, leaving a son and that son is the only man on earth who could benefit by the death of Sir Charles and his nephew Henry.

WATSON: Cousin? What does it all mean, Holmes?

HOLMES: It means murder—cool, calculated, scientific murder.

Not only had Wallace revealed the vengeful cousin a good deal earlier than did the book, he also changed Holmes's "refined, cold-blooded, deliberate murder" line to add the thirties' interest in scientific criminology.

The remainder of the film is a swift approximation of the book. Henry, still muttering about his vanished boot, becomes attracted to John Stapleton's "sister," Beryl. Holmes quickly learns she is actually the man's wife—"He said there was a University post vacant, open only to single candidates"—but knew nothing of his real schemes. Holmes also persuades Laura Lyons to confess that Stapleton forced her into writing the note which brought Sir Charles onto the moor the night of his death. (Later, Laura was to snarl at Stapleton: "I told them all they wanted to know— *all* they wanted. Oh, yes, they learnt a lot—you'll find out how much when you're in the dock, you paltry rat!") There is the traditional misty rescue of Sir Henry from the hound, and Stapleton's end.

As the very first sound version of *The Hound of*

Holmes, with Watson peering over his shoulder, discusses a letter with Mrs. Laura Lyons.

The oppressive walls of Baskerville Manor are examined by Holmes and Sir Henry, as Mrs. Barrymore spies on them both.

the Baskervilles, this British film was certainly a landmark, but perhaps one had a right to expect more from a motion picture with a contribution by Edgar Wallace. The definitive *Hound* was yet to come to the screen, and much of this film—including the dialogue—smacked of very routine melodramatics. Take, for example the final wrap-up scene where the criminologist explains all and the lovers are united.

BERYL: Bit by bit I became suspicious—but I was never sure about anything.

HENRY: And you tried to warn me—and I was just a fat-headed chump who couldn't see an inch in front of him—

HOLMES: Only one thing remains to complete the case—the return to Sir Henry of the property which appeared to cause Sir Henry more concern than the whole of the Baskerville fortune—

Sherlock Holmes hands Sir Henry his missing boot.

Holmes and Stapleton engage in a climactic fight.

36

Sherlock Holmes

CLIVE BROOK

A thoughtful Holmes in dressing gown.

A Fox film, 1932. Script and dialogue by Bertram Milhauser "based on the play by William Gillette with the permission of the executors of the late Sir Arthur Conan Doyle." Directed by William K. Howard.

CAST

Sherlock Holmes, Clive Brook; *Alice Faulkner,* Miriam Jordan; *Moriarty,* Ernest Torrence; *Dr. Watson,* Reginald Owen; *Little Billy,* Howard Leeds; *Gore-King,* Alan Mowbray; *Pubkeeper,* Herbert Mundin; *Judge,* Montague Shaw; *Chaplain,* Arnold Lucy; *Hans, the Hun,* Lucien Prival; *Manuel Lopez,* Roy d'Arcy; *Tony Ardetti,* Stanley Fields; *Ardetti's Henchman,* Eddie Dillon; *Gaston Roux,* Robert Graves Jr.; *Erskine's Secretary,* Brandon Hurst; *Sir Albert Hastings,* Claude King.

For his second feature film impersonation of

Holmes, Clive Brook found himself at a new Hollywood studio, Fox, and a quite different interpretation of the role. The "perfect Englishman," reserved and domineering, had earlier that same year—1932—bested Marlene Dietrich in *Shanghai Express* over at Paramount; now he was to play a romantic Sherlock with sexy encounters just like the most sophisticated drawing-room dramas. After all, William Gillette had paved the way, having Holmes propose to Alice Faulkner as the curtain falls. This film (ostensibly drawn from the Gillette play, but actually melodrama specialist Bertram Milhauser demonstrating the same inventiveness he was to draw upon more than a decade later as scenarist for a score of Rathbone scripts) would go the play one better by having Holmes and his lady love plan wedded bliss at the very start.

An amorous Holmes demands a worthy object of his attentions; coolly alluring Fox actress Miriam Jordan fitted the bill perfectly as Alice Faulkner, the Gillette creation which the script converted into a banker's daughter. And certainly Holmes's love life would curtail his camaraderie with Dr. Watson; consequently, the good doctor's participation is minimized. (Reginald Owen, who played Watson with mustache, proper suits, and a foolish demeanor, made up for having little to do by grabbing the Holmes role in *A Study in Scarlet* the following year, the only man in screen history to portray both Sherlock Holmes and Watson.) Actually, the detective shared much more time in the film with Billy the page boy, his part inflated to such importance that he is kidnapped with Alice at the film's climax; the youngster is played by Howard Leeds as a Canadian emigrant to explain his accent.

There are other good players in the cast as well. The pompous British actor Alan Mowbray was to begin a cinematic association with Holmes (here as a Scotland Yard inspector at odds with the detective) that was to continue in roles such as Lestrade and Sebastian Moran. Scottish character player Ernest Torrence, then in his mid-fifties, who had enjoyed a long career in American silents most often as a heavy, riveted audiences as a leering Moriarty; one critic remarked, "You really wouldn't believe, unless you saw him, that Mr. Torrence could manage to look so menacing."

But the rich atmosphere of swirling menace which surrounded the film was in major part the work of unsung director William K. Howard, who—like Roy William Neill in similar directorial chores the following decade—had a special feeling for melodramatic darkness and tension, an almost Germanic gloom, and a sure movement of player and camera. While *Sherlock Holmes* the film was as a totality nothing too out of the ordinary, the product of a studio committed to a yearly output of "B" mysteries (its Chan series, for example), some of its individual scenes were truly memorable. The discovery of Erskine's body hanging in a secret recess in his study, the overwhelming montage of carnival grotesques, the shooting of Gore-King, and the climax in the bank tunnel were marks of a first-rate craftsman. Howard's sure hand, combined with Milhauser's script—inspired in part by Gillette's play and Doyle's "Red-Headed League"—made this cinematic Holmes a winner.

The Fox film begins with the credits superimposed over a very Sidney Paget–like silhouette of Holmes in dressing gown with pipe lounging against what appear to be French windows—a hint of the drawing-room drama to come. Then the film plunges at once into a doom-laden Germanic melodrama: Moriarty at the dock, sentenced to hang for murder, sarcastically thanking the judge and Scotland Yard Inspector Gore-King for the vigor of their prosecution, predicting that they all will be dead before he will, and as for his tormentor Sherlock Holmes (not present in court): "I shall be alive to see his disgrace and death."

The scene changes to the Baker Street rooms, where a dapper Holmes, in a well-cut dressing gown, ponders over sputtering electrical and scientific equipment so flashy they look left over from the sparklers used in Frankenstein's laboratory. Enter an elegant Alice Faulkner—and the dialogue here is such a lovers' exchange it is worthy of attention:

ALICE: Sherlock Holmes, *Esquire!*
HOLMES: What is it? Why, Alice, my dear! (*They kiss affectionately*)
ALICE: Wasn't I an optimist to think I could charm you away from all these jobs and bottles with a new frock!
HOLMES: Why, it's charming. I noticed it was new the moment you came into the room.
ALICE: Humbug, you didn't see me come into the room. Besides, I've worn it seven times already.
HOLMES: Is that the way to trip up a mastermind?
ALICE: Oh, I hate these rooms.
HOLMES: You mustn't, Alice, next to you it's the most important thing in my life.
ALICE: That's why. I'm jealous.

Enter Billy, the page boy—who obviously adores both Sherlock and Alice—with tea. The lad is in training as a criminologist, and is helping Holmes on a new invention (which they demonstrate on a model) that will stop automobiles in flight. "Motor transportation more than anything else is responsible for the frightful increase in crime." Dr. Watson bursts in; he has come from court where Moriarty has just been sentenced. Holmes regrets the elimination of an adversary worthy of him . . .

HOLMES: The only man to use scientific methods as I use them. . . . A marvelous man. And now he's gone.
ALICE: And we shall soon be going. You haven't forgotten your promise?

A romantic moment—or nearly one. Miriam Jordan looks searchingly into her lover's face, but his thoughts appear to be a thousand miles away.

HOLMES: Forgotten? Lock up the laboratory, Watson. Unload my pistols.

WATSON: Yes, my dear Holmes. But *where* are you going?

HOLMES: I'm ashamed of you, Watson, after all these years. Where are your powers of deduction. A beautiful girl . . .

ALICE: An impetuous lover . . .

HOLMES: A menace removed . . .

ALICE: What can follow but wedding bells!

HOLMES: We're off to apply for a special license!

ALICE: Sherlock Holmes and wife, farmers!

HOLMES: Sherlock Holmes—new laid eggs for sale!

WATSON: Incredible, my dear Holmes! Amazing!

HOLMES: Elementary.

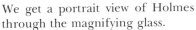

We get a portrait view of Holmes through the magnifying glass.

A glorious view of the Holmesian laboratory, with the detective busily at work, and Miriam Jordan distracting him.

Of course, in the very next sequence—fraught with horror—Moriarty escapes from prison, killing several guards and leaving a note scrawled on the wall: *Tell Sherlock Holmes I'm OUT.* Soon Prosecutor Erskine disappears (he had conducted the case against the Professor), and Holmes, in searching for his vanished friend, clashes with the official investigation conducted by Scotland Yard's Colonel Gore-King. This testy exchange reveals them to be enemies, and tells us something of Holmes's ways.

GORE-KING: Still muddling with the old-fashioned methods, eh, Holmes?

HOLMES: Scientific analysis may not be popular but it can hardly be called old-fashioned, Colonel. Here we are rather inclined to let a man's conscience betray him. Rather awkward when you're looking for a criminal without one. The French use espionage, but even that leaves something to be desired.

GORE-KING: Our American cousins rely on the strong arm . . .

HOLMES: I am told that is not altogether infallible. No, I am inclined to the German school myself. The laboratory is the hunting ground for criminals. . . .

Holmes theorizing to an attentive Watson.

GORE-KING: Rubbish!

The body of Erskine is found behind a secret wall of his study. He had managed to write the name of his killer—*Moriarty*—"the most notorious and revengeful criminal at large today," Holmes adds.

In an extraordinary scene done totally in mime, four of the world's leading gangsters—from Berlin, Paris, Madrid and Chicago—gather in the backroom of a waxworks at a Caligari-esque carnival where Moriarty, suddenly emerging from a tableau in which he has been posing as a wax figure, has summoned them. The criminal mastermind proposes to import American gangster methods to London. Holmes, learning of this influx, is fretful: "We're not used to American rackets; children machine-gunned in the streets . . . There's only one way to deal with these alien butchers: their own way. Shoot first. Investigate afterwards." Led to believe that the notorious Chicago assassin Homer Jones is breaking into Baker Street one night, Holmes *does* shoot first—and Gore-King falls to the ground.

All London is shocked at the death: BITTER RIVALRY ENDS IN TRAGEDY, the newspapers scream; PUBLIC'S IDOL DEGRADED. But actually Holmes has staged the shooting, with the grudging cooperation of the Scotland Yard man, to flush Moriarty into the open. Thinking their chief obstacle removed, Moriarty's new gang begins a reign of terror, bombing pubs and other small businesses to encourage "protection" payments.

At Alice Faulkner's aristocratic country home, the girl and Billy comfort one another, as Sherlock Holmes arrives in drag, disguised as maiden aunt Matilda, replete with petticoats, white hair, huge hat—looking, because of his gangling height, something like Edna May Oliver. He reveals himself to Alice's cranky banker father, and, as well, the surprising information that Moriarty's gangs are just a smokescreen to distract the police from the criminal's real purpose—to tunnel from a nearby shop into the vaults of the father's bank. (Presumably an informant has given him this news.) Suddenly Moriarty himself calls upon Mr. Faulkner. Very courteously he solicits the old man's aid in robbing his own bank—for he has kidnapped Alice Faulkner as hostage. Holmes must work fast.

The final portion of the film takes place in the tunnel under the bank; Moriarty's men are using acetylene torches to get at the vaults gorged with jewels and cash. But it is Sherlock Holmes rather than confederate Hans the Hun under the welder's helmet; there is a spectacular shootout, and Moriarty is killed.

We are back again at Baker Street, and once more the mood is happy. "A really remarkable man, Moriarty," Holmes eulogizes, startlingly. "Some people, without possessing genius themselves, have the amazing ability of stimulating it in others. I shall miss him." Wedding bells are yet to be heard, but Watson cannot stand as best man because—Billy reports—"his wife's mother has had an attack of talking sickness"; a genial Gore-King will substitute. The laboratory is to be locked up; Holmes and wife start life anew as genteel farmers.

Critics and audience alike were somewhat taken aback by this new, romantic Holmes exchanging marriage vows, and who, despite his ardor, seemed to lose none of his stiff, frosty superiority. Reviewers lauded the film's "rare old flavor," and self-confessed Sherlockophile Lucius Beebe declared himself eminently satisfied with Clive Brook. "His cast of countenance is happily adapted to the part,

his Britishisms are convincing, and sartorially and in manner sarcastic his is of the true Baker Street tradition. Among the burettes, pipettes and wash-bottles of his laboratory he is the scientific detective of fiction. His quilted dressing gown, stock ties and Ascots, plaid greatcoats and outrageously checked Norfolk suits follow the classic conceptions. . . ." (11/12/32). Even though the morphine injections have been discarded these are a minor oversight.

Clive Brook was never again to appear onscreen as Sherlock Holmes. Despite appearances in such films as Noël Coward's epic *Cavalcade* (released just after *Sherlock Holmes*), Brook left the American movie studios by 1935 for a career in films and theater in England. In 1963 John Huston persuaded him to accept an important character part opposite George C. Scott in the Philip MacDonald thriller, *The List of Adrian Messenger*. He died in 1974 at the age of 87, and obituaries noted his "power, authority and polish," qualities which stood him well for his turns as the world's greatest detective.

A tense scene between Clive Brook as Sherlock Holmes and Scotland Yard inspector Gore-King (Alan Mowbray), debating differences in crime detection. Holmes prefers scientific methods, as the test tubes certainly indicate.

A Study in Scarlet

REGINALD OWEN

Reginald Owen looks affable and unflatteringly portly in this pose as Holmes.

A World-Wide Picture, distributed by the Fox Film Corp., 1933. A screen drama by Robert Florey from the book by Sir Arthur Conan Doyle. Continuity and dialogue by Reginald Owen. Directed by Edwin L. Marin.

CAST

Sherlock Holmes, Reginald Owen; *Mrs. Pyke,* Anna May Wong; *Eileen Forrester,* June Clyde; *Thaddeus Merrydew,* Allan Dinehart; *John Stanford,* John Warburton; *Dr. Watson,* Warburton Gamble; *Jabez Wilson,* J. M. Kerrigan; *Inspector Lestrade,* Alan Mowbray; *Mrs. Murphy,* Doris Lloyd; *Will Swallow,* Billy Bevan; *Dolly,* Leila Bennett; *Baker,* Cecil Reynolds; *Captain Pyke,* Wyndham Standing; *Malcolm Dearing,* Halliwell Hobbes; *Ah Yet,* Tetsu Komai; *Mrs. Hudson,* Temple Pigott.

Spurred on by the Clive Brook success and a Depression interest in mystery melodrama, a small Hollywood studio, World-Wide Pictures—with Fox as American distributor—decided to tackle Holmes, a decidedly road-company version with last year's Watson elevated into the Holmesian spotlight and choosing one of Conan Doyle's best titles for filming. Only the title to *A Study in Scarlet* was used, however; the story dealt with members of a secret trust being killed according to the nursery rhyme about "little black boys" being decimated one by one. This has led several Sherlockian critics unfairly to accuse it of having been cribbed from Agatha Christie. Actually the film predates *Ten Little Indians* by several years, and more resembles, with its insurance ring and old dark house themes, the very best Edgar Wallace. It is minor Holmes, but nonetheless good.

Reginald Owen, formerly the buffoon to Clive Brook as Watson, makes up for it as Sherlock, completely in control, a commanding presence. Alas, he looked not at all like the Paget or any other version of Holmes (rather more like the general criminologist image contributed by Robert Rendel), but tried his very best to tailor his lines (he wrote both dialogue and continuity) to the Doyle mark; some of his terse and witty additions will be quoted as examples. His Watson (Warburton Gamble) is solid but unexciting, and the surrounding cast, headed by alluring Oriental menace Anna May Wong, is expertly chosen and, with eight of its principal players born in Britain, helps give an unusually authentic English flavor to a film made in Hollywood.

Plotting murder.

A Study in Scarlet begins with a body discovered in a railway carriage at Victoria Station. Then an advertisement in a newspaper agony column (the words "scarlet" and "Limehouse" surrounded by numbers) leads a young girl, Eileen Forrester, to a grim meeting of "The Scarlet Ring," held in an evil-looking waterfront dive. The Ring is a mysterious organization of seven men (Miss Forrester is there to represent her recently-deceased father) whose shares—an oily lawyer named Merrydew explains—are divided equally among the remaining members when any die. So far, two have.

The widow of the man found dead on the train, Mrs. Murphy, a barmaid infuriated that her hus-

The scheme is exposed in this final scene from the film—though Holmes is not in the picture. Lestrade holds Mrs. Pike, while Watson, in a dashing tweed cap, looks soberly on.

43

band left his earthly goods to "a trust" headed by lawyer Merrydew, brings her complaints to a worldly, affable Holmes at Baker Street—plus a poem her husband had just received: "Six little black boys/ playing with a hive/ A bumble-bee stung one/ And then there were five." (Interestingly, Agatha Christie's use of nursery rhyme murders in *Ten Little Indians* (in America, *And Then There Were None*) would not occur until 1939.)

MRS. MURPHY: Then you'll undertake me, Mr. Holmes?
HOLMES: I'll take your case.
MRS. MURPHY: Mind you, it'll have to be for love.
HOLMES: For *love*?
MRS.MURPHY: I've heard as how you like working for nothing.
HOLMES: My interest is to bring the criminal to justice.

Deep water, Holmes mutters later. Merrydew is "London's most dangerous crook, the king of blackmailers, a gliding, sliding, venomous snake."

Eileen Forrester is soon to be trapped in Merrydew's coils. She is witness as another member of the Ring, a Captain Pyke, is shot down and killed. He too received a similar nursery jingle. His widow—a mysterious Oriental played by Anna May Wong—identifies the body by a ring she had given him when they married in China six years before. A puzzled, overworked Lestrade (Alan Mowbray again with the Yard!) comes to Baker Street.

HOLMES: You came to see me professionally.
LESTRADE: Well—er—unofficially.
HOLMES: I see. Heads you win, tails I lose.

There have been other Ring deaths, and Inspector Lestrade is up to his ears. Holmes promises to help.

Disguised as an elderly gentleman, the detective makes a country visit to the ancestral home of the Pykes, the Grange—after first spending generously among the locals in an amusing village pub scene. The Grange is up for sale, and Holmes suspects that it has been and will be the scene of sinister activities. Over tea, the seductive Mrs. Pyke invites nervous Ring member Jabez Wilson (marvelously played by Irish character actor J. M. Kerrigan, with name borrowed from another Doyle story) to spend a weekend going over her affairs at her country estate. Eileen Forrester is also at the Grange, for the Chinese woman has brought her there, supposedly on Sherlock Holmes's instructions. And Merrydew comments to an unseen visitor: "Because of Holmes's interference, *everything must be finished at the Grange tonight.*"

The climax is straight Edgar Wallace. There are screams in the night, secret panels, sinister Chinese in Mrs. Pyke's employ, and Eileen is nearly killed by an unknown murderer dressed in black, as Lestrade's men grope through the night fog surrounding the old house. Fortunately, Holmes rescues the girl and unmasks the killer: Captain Pyke, not dead after all.

The lawyer Merrydew, arriving in the fog, is promptly arrested—and demonstrates his finesse as a villain by this exchange with Holmes as he loftily assists the police putting handcuffs on him:

MERRYDEW: What are the charges, Holmes?
HOLMES: The gravest possible. (*He outlines a long list.*) I've more than enough evidence to hang you.
MERRYDEW (*airily superior*): I think not. But then, who can tell? Who can tell?

The affable, equally smug criminologist then turns his attentions to Eileen Forrester and her lover, providing the film with these cheery closing lines:
HOLMES: You must invite me to the wedding.
EILEEN: Perhaps you'll give me away. (*She is, after all, now an orphan.*)
HOLMES: I appreciate the compliment, but I never give a lady away—except sometimes professionally. (*To Watson*) Come, Doctor, They'll send for you when they need you.

Reginald Owen received good notices for his role. The *New York Times* thought he gave "quite an effective performance. He is a good-looking Holmes and he speaks his lines with due reverence." (6/1/33) The *Herald Tribune* thought him "intelligent and amusing," the *Post* "human and likable." And yet he was not to play Holmes on the screen again. He would—like Basil Rathbone, who was to follow him into the Sherlockian spotlight— become a celebrated Scrooge and stage storyteller. But in the hundreds of screen parts he was still to play (he died in 1967, in his eighties) he was never again to be Sherlock Holmes. And the next great American screen Holmes was Basil Rathbone.

The Arthur Wontner Films

Arthur Wontner as Sherlock Holmes. Note the piercing eyes.

In the thirties a British player was to assume the mantle of the Holmesian cloth with such accuracy and flair he was thought by many critics and Sherlockian fans to have mastered *the* impersonation of the Great Detective. Shy-looking, unimperial, far from the dynamic figure Basil Rathbone was to cut a decade later, Arthur Wontner was to become an English favorite in the role—and portray Holmes in five films seen not only in his own country but imported to America (and elsewhere). The five were in economic terms only slightly above programmer level, but they had occasional flashes of greatness. Indeed, the quality of the five Wontner motion pictures, despite their limited budgets, had moments of unexpected richness generally not found in the mystery program pieces turned out by the British studios of the day.

Much of the high level of the films was due to Arthur Wontner himself. Not only was he an accomplished actor of some range and dignity, he *looked* like Sherlock Holmes—or actually exactly like the Sidney Paget illustrations of the Master. It was a resemblance upon which many people remarked, as he was to recall: even Sir Arthur Conan Doyle, whom the actor had met, noted it. It was destined for him to play the role, and for his part he relished it, lavishing love and attention to the part, even rewriting dialogue to conform to what he felt were more acceptable Sherlockian lines. It was an affection which showed.

Wontner was actually somewhat old to play the role. Born in 1875, he was well over fifty when he first portrayed Holmes in 1931, and sixty-two when last taking on the role. Before that he had been more remembered in stage rather than screen parts. Only the year before his first screen encounter with the most famous of all detectives, he had enjoyed a long stage run as *Sexton Blake*, the boy's adventure magazine carbon of Holmes, and critics at that time commented on his amazing similarity to the Paget drawings. It was that critical commentary which brought him to the attention of Twickenham Film Studios, and brought him the role. A new Holmes was born, a British interpretation which lasted a decade.

Wontner was not to possess Rathbone's quivering electricity; his performance is more studied, less barbed and rapierlike. He was also less overtaken by the role than Rathbone. Towards the end of his life (Wontner died in 1960), the actor was honored at a gathering of the Sherlock Holmes Society of London, and he still recalled his deerstalker days with warmth and amused affection.

The American Sherlockian scholar Vincent Starrett was among many to be won over by the portrayal. "No better Sherlock Holmes than Arthur Wontner is likely to be seen and heard in pictures in our time," he wrote in the thirties. "His detective is the veritable fathomer of Baker Street in person."

It is an interesting footnote to Arthur Wontner's career as Sherlock Holmes that, one year after beginning the role, he was to play a quite different part. In 1932 Wontner portrayed the revered judge Sir Charles Wallington in the Twickenham Studio film, *Condemned to Death,* horrified along with Scotland Yard that the enemies of a murderer he has sent to the gallows are being killed one by one at the hands of an avenger calling himself "Jack o' Lantern." For a time an Indian servant is suspected, but at the finish a psychiatrist reveals it is Wontner himself who is the killer, having been hypnotized by the condemned man to carry out his vengeance after his death. A curious psychological thriller, this, and a role which demonstrated that Wontner (as indeed the later Rathbone) was not above setting aside the deerstalker to play an occasional insane murderer.

SHERLOCK HOLMES' FATAL HOUR.

Twickenham Studios (British), 1931. Screenplay by Cyril Twyford and H. Fowler Mear based on "The Final Problem" and "The Empty House" by Sir Arthur Conan Doyle. Produced by Julius Hagan. Directed by Leslie S. Hiscott.

CAST

Sherlock Holmes, Arthur Wontner; *Dr. Watson,* Jan Fleming; *Mrs. Hudson,* Minnie Rayner; *Ronald Adair,* Leslie Perrins; *Kathleen Adair,* Jane Welsh; *Colonel Henslow,* Norman McKinnell; *Thomas Fisher,* William Frazer; *Tony Rutherford,* Sidney King; *Inspector Lestrade,* Phillip Hewland; *Marston,* Gordon Begg; *Colonel Moran,* Louis Goodrich; *No. 16,* Harry Terry; *J. J. Godfrey,* Charles Paton.

This first Arthur Wontner Sherlockian feature (released as *The Sleeping Cardinal* in England, but given its much more "commercial" title in the United States) shows both fidelity and care as to its source. Produced early in the sound era, it is somewhat primitive technically, and suffers as well from a limited budget, but it is an enjoyable film—enjoyable enough for the *New York Times* to say (July 13, 1931) with affection: "That brooding defender of Britain's lawful destinies—Sherlock Holmes, indeed—is back again. Once more he puffs his pipe and crawls around with magnifying glass and ultimately saves the revered Bank of England from an unsuspected, but still considerable embarrassment."

Actually, while the film is faithful to the *mood* of the stories, it rearranges and reworks the incidents therein, leading the *Times* to marvel at the scope of the film's villainy: "a potpourri of all known social and domestic crimes. There is a bit of card cheating, some counterfeiting, bank robbery, Foreign Office dalliance, murder, and simple assault with attempt to kill. Possibly this last isn't so simple, in view of Professor Moriarty's known predilections for the grimly and Oriental ornate. Anyhow, they are all there." Further, "there are secret doors leading into strange compartments and rooms, there are scufflings and caterwaulings in dark corridors. All the characters express their contempt for one another by that sinister laugh—the 'ha, ha!' which preceded the 'yeah' of modern gangsterdom. Detective Holmes barely escapes with his life, and dear Dr. Watson is drawn away by innumerable red herrings." The *Times* enjoyed the film hugely.

A robbery and murder at a bank open the film, done totally in silhouette and mime, with only scuffling and a moan heard on the soundtrack. Our attention is then drawn to a card game at the fashionable flat of young Ronald Adair of the Foreign Office—playing for high stakes and, suspiciously, always winning. His worried sister seeks out an old friend, Dr. Watson. (The good doctor, affable and dapper, is played here and throughout most of the series by Ian Fleming—*not* the creator of James Bond, though it is fascinating to imagine a famous writer portraying an even more world-famous writer! This Fleming cuts a Watson not without dash, but with steel-gray hair and slightly stocky. Watson's simple qualities are stressed, as well as his eye for the ladies, but he is a good and concerned companion to Holmes, and quite acceptable to us.)

Our first meeting with Holmes himself is impressive. Rising up from behind an armchair to stride confidently across the stage stressing that Sidney Paget profile, chatting amiably with Watson and even exchanging banter with an overweight, Cockney Mrs. Hudson (played by Minnie Rayner throughout most of the series as a warm but very earthy landlady clearly very dear to her tenants: "You are always a temptation to me," Holmes says humorously in *two* of the films, but we imagine he refers mainly to her culinary skills), Wontner is nigh perfect. The Baker Street rooms are well reproduced, too, providing fascinating nooks and corners for the eye. There is even a working fireplace from which Holmes extracts a hot coal with which to light his pipe. And the talk is good. "Have you ever heard of Professor Robert [*sic*] Moriarty? He is responsible for half the crimes the world over." For years now, Holmes has been aware of some "dark power"—the camera moves in on the detective as he broods the litany from "The Final Problem." Moriarty has hundreds of agents, but "none have ever seen him." Holmes is sure last night's murder of a bank guard was instigated by him. Both Watson and Lestrade chide Holmes for his belief; how could such a master criminal exist and Scotland Yard not know? "Oh, lots of people know Moriarty but they don't know that he *is* Moriarty. He has a hundred disguises and a hundred aliases."

Not only relying on his disguises, Moriarty speaks from behind a portrait—a painting on steel of a sleeping Cardinal Richelieu—in a secret room to Ronald Adair, who has been brought there blindfolded. The Professor uses his knowledge of Adair's cheating to force him to smuggle a suitcase to Paris in his diplomat's pouch, but Adair refuses. He is left a gun.

Soon Moriarty, wearing dark glasses and his face wrapped in a muffler, makes a personal appearance at Baker Street—after luring Watson and Mrs. Hudson away. The confrontation is along the classic lines of "The Final Problem," with a few alterations and additions: Holmes, for instance, is made to say that the only other time he saw the Professor his face "was completely covered with surgical bandages." This is of course a clue to the audience that the Moriarty of *this* film will be unmasked from another identity at the end in the manner of a whodunit!

But "Moriarty has made the worst slip since January, 1929" in giving in to the sudden impulse to warn off Holmes, the detective later crows to Watson, for during the interview he had the opportunity to study the Professor's boots and has recognized the bootmaker. A raid on the bootmaker's premises later reveals a printing press used to make counterfeit banknotes, and the secret room containing the "Sleeping Cardinal" painting. But this is only one of Moriarty's lairs—albeit an interesting one, with loudspeakers in every ceiling from which to anonymously address his minions—and the Professor has other surprises to deal out. That night Ronald Adair is found shot through the head.

Investigating Adair's rooms with Lestrade, Holmes chats about hunting tigers with an elderly friend of Ronald, retired Colonel Henslowe, who does not allow a missing arm—ripped off during a tiger hunt years before in India—interfere with a passion for cardplaying. Later Holmes says of tigers: "They interest me . . . a cold cruelty. There are human beings rather like tigers, you know." Adair's sister Kathleen is accused of his murder.

Events move quickly now, climaxing in an attempt on Holmes's life from the empty house across from 221-B. It is of course a bust figure which is shattered by the assassin's bullet, and we find Mrs. Hudson on the floor amid the pieces of the statue which she had been moving from time to time to animate the target ("Once more you've proven yourself far above ordinary women, Mrs. Hudson!"). We also find the captured marksman to be none other than Professor Moriarty himself, and when Holmes whips away his muffler we discover him to be the tiger-hunting Colonel, who perhaps unnecessarily still pretended to be missing an arm (it is under his jacket) even when firing an air rifle in his other identity as the Professor!

MORIARTY: You clever, cunning swine! You think you've won and that you're safe! But you're up against an organization—they'll get you and they'll destroy you! I might even do it myself!

HOLMES: Take him to the station, Lestrade. (*To Moriarty*) I think you'll find most of your organization waiting for you there.

Snarling and cursing, the Professor is pulled away, Inspector Lestrade cheerfully congratulating himself on *his* Moriarty theory! Of course, in later films in the Wontner series, when Moriarty reappears, both Watson and Lestrade revert back to their former disbelief in the Professor's villainy. This is made only slightly credible by having actor Norman McKinnel, the Moriarty of this film, replaced in the role by Lyn Harding, the flamboyant Dr. Rylott of Raymond Massey's *Speckled Band*. (Lestrade as well was to be played by a different actor.)

Our parting glimpse is of Holmes playing rapturously on his violin, with Mrs. Hudson beaming on. Scholarly and mild—even, indeed, kind and indulgent—Arthur Wontner made a stunning initial appearance as the great detective, a very positive image. He was to continue this skill through four more films.

THE MISSING REMBRANDT

Twickenham Studios, Ltd. (British), 1932. Screenplay by Cyril Twyford and H. Fowler Mear based on THE ADVENTURE OF CHARLES AUGUSTUS MILVERTON *by Sir Arthur Conan Doyle. Produced by Jules Hagan. Directed by Leslie S. Hiscott.*

CAST

Sherlock Holmes, Arthur Wontner; *Doctor Watson,* Ian Fleming; *Mrs. Hudson,* Minnie Raynor; *Baron von Guntermann,* Francis L. Sullivan; *Carlo Ravelli,* Dino Galvani; *Claude Holford,* Miles Mander; *Lady Violet,* Jane Welsh; *Inspector Lestrade,* Philip Hewland; *Marquis De Chaminade,* Anthony Hollis; *Manning,* Herbert Lomas; *An Agent,* Ben Welden; *Chang Wu,* Takase.

Charles Augustus Milverton, "the worst man in London," the despicable blackmailer of Hampstead Heath, was so solid a villain that his virtual neglect at the hands of the Holmesian filmmakers of the thirties and forties seems inexplicable. Happily, in this British Wontner production he is entrusted to the capable talents of one of the massively good character "baddies" of the British screen, Francis L. Sullivan—although in this screenplay he is masked under the name Baron von Guntermann. Here the unctuous scoundrel, his town house a treasure trove of stolen masterpieces, including of all things even a Rembrandt lifted from the Louvre, is not above using

a few compromising letters for blackmail in order to augment his income. It is this endeavor which brings about his doom, as Holmes comes to the rescue of the victimized letter-writer, Lady Violet.

Actually, not very much of the Conan Doyle case is retained in pure form, and the ending, in which the villain is—we are morally certain—justifiably eliminated by the fair victim, is considerably altered. There is, too, a secondary criminal for Holmes to bring to justice, the Baron's young secretary, Carlo Ravelli, whose smoldering Italian sexuality adds a touch of passion to the adventure the original adventure lacked completely.

The Missing Rembrandt starts with a police raid on a Limehouse opium den, a murky setting in which Holmes learns that a drug-ridden artist has been coerced by Guntermann into stealing a priceless Rembrandt from the Louvre—surely one of the most spectacular heists of all time. Guntermann—an American, interestingly—has the painting under wraps, as well he might, for an American detective from the Pinkerton agency (shades of the later *Valley of Fear* screen version) is on his trail. The Pinkerton man is naturally no match deductively with Sherlock Holmes, who during the course of his investigations and traps disguises himself as both an old woman and a hirsute clergyman, finally bringing the scheming Baron to ground—not so much for his art thefts as for his ungentlemanly ill-usage of Lady Violet.

Towards the middle of the film—after Holmes has been commissioned to recover the stolen Rembrandt, which the detective believes to be in England—there is a fascinating episode of cat-and-mouse. Holmes is disguised as a minister but that disguise is seen through by the Baron, who traps him in the vaults beneath an auction gallery. Is the clergyman unarmed? Guntermann thinks so, but Holmes opens the book he is carrying, *The Collected Sermons of the Reverend Erasmus Peabody*, and out pops an automatic. The detective makes his escape. Later, convinced that ordinary methods will never bring the Baron to justice, Holmes and Watson determine to recover Lady Violet's letters by burgling the Baron's safe, in Hampstead. While Watson waits anxiously in a two-seater getaway car, Holmes approaches the Baron's house—not quite in time to prevent Guntermann's murder of the Pinkerton agent. The detective, spotted by a constable, is nearly himself arrested for murder, and must make a wild scramble over a garden wall to escape pursuit.

There is yet one more death at the Baron's home

A Baker Street scene from *The Missing Rembrandt.* Mrs. Hudson is watching Holmes at his chemical experiments while Watson sits quietly off in a corner.

in Hampstead Heath—the pathetic, broken-down artist whom Guntermann has in his power, Claude Holford, is found slumped over a crude water-color he has just finished, victim of a fatal overdose of veronal. In a climactic denouement, Holmes exposes the Baron and reveals the Rembrandt's hiding place, by taking a sponge dipped in turpentine and scrubbing Holford's water-color, uncovering the missing masterpiece beneath.

The *New York Times* thought Wontner excellent, and perfectly at home as Sherlock, and the British *Picturegoer Weekly* felt the actor made Holmes live on the screen. It is interesting to footnote that Guntermann was a villain who along with Professor Moriarty shared an expensive taste for art treasures.

THE SIGN OF FOUR

Associated Radio Pictures (British), 1932. Screenplay by W. P. Lipscomb from the novel by Sir Arthur Conan Doyle. Produced by Rowland V. Lee. Directed by Graham Cutts.

CAST

Sherlock Holmes, Arthur Wontner; *Mary Morstan,* Isla Bevan; *Dr. Watson,* Ian Hunter; *Athelney Jones,* Gilbert Davis; *Jonathan Small,* Graham Soutten; *Captain Morstan,* Edgar Norfolk; *Sholto,* Herbert Lomas; *Mrs. Hudson,* Claire Greet; *Thaddeus Sholto,* Miles Malleson; *Bailey,* Roy Emerson; *Tonga,* Togo; *Tattoo Artist,* Mr. Burnhett; *Bartholomew,* Kynaston Reeves.

Curiously, neither Arthur Wontner nor the character Sherlock Holmes were under exclusive contract to Twickenham Studio. Therefore, this third Holmesian adventure of Wontner's was done for another British production company, Associated Radio Pictures. A mildly different Holmes resulted in 1932 in the screen adaptation of *The Sign of Four.* (A *very* different Watson was on hand, portrayed this time by Ian Hunter, a British actor who was later to come to Hollywood as a popular character player. Wontner's pace was somewhat speeded up, a tempo insisted upon by Associated's producer Rowland V. Lee, surely one of the most dynamic forces at work in cinema during that period.

Lee was one of the fascinating figures of melodrama, for much of his contribution was in that genre. An American who had begun a directorial career in the twenties—including a bravura version of Rohmer's *The Mysterious Dr. Fu Manchu,* with a murky waterfront setting presaging his visualization of *Sign,* in 1929—his organizing and executive

Holmes in disguise as a flirtatious old tar in *The Sign of Four*.

abilities moved him into production, and for a time to the British film studios. But by the end of the decade he was back in Hollywood, working on *big* productions for a studio noted for its devotion to melodrama, Universal (which was just then about to embark on its own Holmesian sagas, although not with Lee). For Universal in 1939 he was to mount two incredibly Gothic canvases, *Son of Frankenstein* (certainly the most darkly Germanic of all the Frankenstein films) and *Tower of London*, both starring Basil Rathbone. If Lee had one forte it was a feeling for the tapestry of melodrama, and *The Sign of Four* was certainly a literary tapestry from which he could well work.

The Conan Doyle story was closely followed in the film. It contained, after all, a made-to-order romance, the susceptibility of a smitten Watson for a frightened young client, Mary Morstan, who—alone in London, her father vanished—receives a lustrous pearl from a mysterious, unknown donor. Accepting the case, Holmes meets with the incredible Thaddeus Sholto in his strange abode, "an oasis of art in the howling desert of South London." (As it has been suggested that Oscar Wilde was in part Conan Doyle's model for Sholto, it is interesting to note that he was played here by the cherubic eccentric, Miles Malleson.) News of the fabulous Agra Treasure and a murder lead Holmes finally to one of the great villains of the Sherlockian saga, the one-legged Jonathan Small, and his pygmy accomplice, Tonga. There is an effectively cinematic finale—a chase by police boat down the Thames—and producer Lee made the most of it.

Lee also speeded up Wontner's Holmes interpretation, causing one reviewer in this country to complain, "The dialogue as spoken by the all-British cast is often unintelligible to American ears." But for the *New York Times*, the leading players all gave colorful and effective performances. Most effective, however, is the excellent interpretation by Arthur Wontner. He reads "biographies in a castoff end of rope and criminal histories in the formation of a shoe print in the dust." The reviewer also praises "the seamy atmosphere of the East End waterfront" out of which stalks the wooden-legged Small to terrorize his enemies, the Sholtos and the Morstans. And if those persons surrounding the Master seem rather too continuously overawed, the kindly critic places it all in proper perspective: "Dr. Watson stands wide-eyed at the great man's shoulder to murmur, 'Positively amazing,' at some unusually shrewd deduction of his friend. If Scotland Yard seems just a trifle too dull-witted even for the purposes of a murder mystery, it does have the advantage of throwing Sherlock's detective genius into bolder relief."

50

Rowland V. Lee was not called upon to do another Sherlock Holmes adventure, however, and soon thereafter returned to the larger studios and costlier productions of Hollywood. Interestingly, though, one of the most memorable characters of a later film triumph of his, the vengeful club-footed executioner of *Tower of London* (both produced and directed by Lee)—Mord, played by Boris Karloff—has faint echoes of Jonathan Small.

THE TRIUMPH OF SHERLOCK HOLMES

Gaumont-British Pictures Ltd. (British), 1935. Screenplay by H. Fowler Mear and Cyril Twyford based on THE VALLEY OF FEAR *by Sir Arthur Conan Doyle. Produced by Julius Hagan. Directed by Leslie S. Hiscott.*

CAST

Sherlock Holmes, Arthur Wontner; *Dr. Watson,* Ian Fleming; *Professor Moriarty,* Lyn Harding; *John Douglas,* Leslie Perrins; *Ettie Douglas,* Jane Carr; *Inspector Lestrade,* Charles Mortimer; *Mrs. Hudson,* Minnie Rayner; *Cecil Barker,* Michael Shepley; *Ted Balding,* Ben Welden; *Boss McGinty,* Roy Emerton; *Ames,* Conway Dixon; *Colonel Sebastian Moran,* Wilfrid Caithness; *Captain Marvin,* Edmund D'Alby.

The unquestioned best of all the five Arthur Wontner films in the Sherlockian saga, *Triumph,* was a close and reverential adaptation of the Conan Doyle novel which that Grand Master of the mystery, John Dickson Carr, considered among the five best detective novels of all time: *The Valley of Fear. The Triumph of Sherlock Holmes* reproduces all the major incidents of the book so lovingly and so closely, it rivals even the Basil Rathbone *Hound of the Baskervilles* as the most faithful Holmesian derivation from the Conan Doyle source. Only in one particular does it grievously improvise: instead of allowing Professor Moriarty to remain in a shadowy background as the instigator of the evil—as he was in the book—he is brought for a few scenes into center stage. And this is almost forgivable for that outrageously dramatic actor Lyn Harding—the menacing Dr. Rylott in Raymond Massey's *The Speckled Band*—was for this film (and the next) cast as the wicked Professor, purloining every bit of dialogue in which he shares.

Holmes and Watson discuss the "thick walls" of Birlstone Manor in *The Triumph of Sherlock Holmes.*

Wontner in the traditional deerstalker.

We are treated to Moriarty's presence almost from the very start of the film. Holmes has announced his retirement, and—almost to personally assure himself of this blessing—the Napoleon of Crime makes a surprise visit to Baker Street. The lines are reworkings of the confrontation in "The Final Problem" (used extensively as well in Wontner's *The Sleeping Cardinal*), but the drama crackles.

MORIARTY: Mr. Holmes, it has been an intellectual treat to cross swords with you, and I say unaffectedly it would have been a great grief to me to have been forced to take any extreme measures.

HOLMES: Danger happens to be part of my trade, Professor.

MORIARTY: Danger? It isn't a question of danger but of inevitable destruction! Therefore I say again you are wise to retire! When you once get to the country take my advice and *stay* there!

HOLMES: And suppose I should reconsider my decision?

MORIARTY: You have my warning. I wish you a pleasant and *permanent* retirement.

In the very next scene an American gangster, Balding, comes to Moriarty's headquarters to enlist his aid, and discovers it a veritable house of tricks, with doors locking themselves and the Professor vanishing practically before his eyes. Balding seeks help to eliminate an American who has recently arrived in England.

We next find Holmes at his bee farm in Sussex, with Watson visiting him, and from thenceforth the adaptation follows closely the sequence of events in *Valley*. Holmes's informant Porlock sends him a coded message, and it is to the film's credit that the detective's complex reasoning in deciphering the missive is leisurely carried over into the dialogue. Some deviltry is afoot at Birlstone Castle, says the message, and Inspector Lestrade, who has just arrived, announces that John Douglas, the owner of Birlstone, was just found murdered, his head blown away by a sawed-off shotgun. Holmes bets a disbelieving Lestrade a beehive against the Inspector's bowler hat that Moriarty is behind it all.

Inside the massive structure of Birlstone (a local at one point calls its walls "a mile thick") Holmes continues his careful investigation, surmising that Douglas had been a member of an American secret society called the Scowlers, in the strike-ridden, lawless Pennsylvania mining community called Vermissa Valley. (Conan Doyle had based this fiction on the real-life Molly Maguires.) This triggers

from a not too distraught Mrs. Douglas a lengthy narrative about the Valley, how she had met her husband there, and how he—masquerading as a wanted gangster—had actually been the notorious strike-breaking Pinkerton agent called Birdy Edwards. This entire sequence is told in flashback, occupying a generous part of the film (as it does the novel), and while the accents are as much Pecos as Pennsylvania, the entire sequence is so rich in charm it is a high point in the drama—especially as the rest of the film is practically nonstop deductioning on Holmes's part. We learn how Douglas (called Murdock) worms his way into the gang, reveals himself as the Pinkerton man ("I am Birdy Edwards!"), and is forced to flee with his new wife, first to Switzerland and then to England.

As night falls back at Birlstone, Holmes makes the astonishing revelation that Douglas is still alive: it was not his faceless body found, but that of his would-be assassin. (While this "surprise" solution may seem overly familiar today, it was actually used for the very first time by the inventive Doyle.) Douglas has been hiding in a secret room, from which Holmes now frees him, but with a caution: the detective is sure Birlstone will have a dangerous midnight visitor. And we are sure, too; we are witness to a cackling, snarling Moriarty, throwing an endless scarf over his shoulder with wild abandon, ready to depart for the castle, his mission to rescue the assassin he does not realize is dead, and little knowing he is actually motoring to a climactic showdown.

Holmes, Watson and Lestrade are lurking in the bushes as the evil Professor drives onto the castle grounds. (Watson has just muttered: "Capturing Moriarty will be the triumph of Sherlock Holmes," giving the film its title but forgetting that at the beginning of this adventure and throughout all the other films in the Wontner series he virtually denied the Professor existed.) There is an attempted arrest, but a maniacal Professor dashes up the castle's ruined tower and—much as George Zucco's Moriarty was to do half a decade later—topples (screaming "Curse you, Holmes!") from its top into the moat below.

WATSON: Good heavens, Holmes! It's a long drop.

HOLMES: Yes—rather more than is required by law, my dear Watson, but equally effective.

The *New York Times* (May 28, 1935) thought the film a good one, especially praising its star. "Mr.

Holmes in the center, with an attentive Watson to his immediate left, discusses the case of the missing race horse (and its murdered trainer) in *Silver Blaze*.

Wontner decorates a calabash pipe with commendable skill, contributing a splendid portrait of fiction's first detective. Lyn Harding is capital as Moriarty." It is also a true and loving filming of a landmark mystery novel, despite the fact it not only gratuitously adds the physical presence of Moriarty, it manages to destroy him in the end as well. (Naturally, in the very next film in the series, the Professor is hale and hearty, with no mention whatsoever of how he escaped the moat.)

Nevertheless, as the New York *Herald Tribune* commented (May 28), "It is delightful to meet again our old friend Holmes, his deep-bowled pipe hanging out of the side of his mouth, his silk dressing gown tied about him so carelessly and yet elegantly. Pacing his laboratory with abstract gaze, he tosses quips at the obtuse Dr. Watson, ever faithful, but still always guessing wrong, and there is also present old Professor Moriarty, spinning his web of evil design which the great detective must shatter." It *is* delightful.

SILVER BLAZE

Twickenham Studios (British), 1937. Adaptation by H. Fowler Mear from the story by Sir Arthur Conan Doyle. Produced by Julius Hagan. Directed by Thomas Bentley.

CAST

Sherlock Holmes, Arthur Wontner; *Dr. Watson,* Ian Fleming; *Professor Moriarty,* Lyn Harding; *Inspector Lestrade,* John Turnbull; *Colonel Ross,* Robert Horton; *Sir Henry Baskerville,* Lawrence Grossmith; *Diana Baskerville,* Judy Gunn; *Jack Trevor,* Arthur Macrae; *Moran,* Arthur Goullet; *Straker,* Martin Walker; *Mrs. Straker,* Eve Gray; *Miles Stamford,* Gilbert Davis; *Mrs. Hudson,* Minnie Rayner; *Silas Brown,* D. J. Williams; *Bert Prince,* Ralph Truman.

Like most last entries in screen series, *Silver Blaze* is not top drawer. But it is still a workmanlike adaptation of the classic Conan Doyle horse-kidnapping story, with many fine touches. It faces, however, the recurring problem of fitting a spare short story into a feature-film format, and therefore embellishes with zeal. Just as in *Triumph,* it adds the physical presence of Moriarty and henchmen—not to be found in the source.

In another fleshing-out effort, it even returns Sir Henry Baskerville to the Sherlockian saga, merely in a sort of cameo appearance, and goes so far as to give him a grown, marriage-age daughter for the film's romantic interest. Indeed, this British film was not released in the United States until 1941, well after the success of the Basil Rathbone *Hound*; the American distributor attempted to capitalize on its popularity by—with devious cunning—retitling the import *Murder at the Baskervilles*. (There is actually mild justification for this, as there *are* Baskerville family members in the cast.)

The film opens with Professor Moriarty and Colonel Moran plotting some unknown deviltry in a loft they have just rented above an abandoned subway station. (The film tried for a "thirties modern" air.) Meanwhile, Inspector Lestrade—as he does in other films in the series—manages to scoff at Holmes's views on Moriarty: "You see him behind every other crime in the calendar. The Yard doesn't share your views, I'm afraid. They think it all moonshine."

But Holmes has received a summons from his old friend Sir Henry Baskerville—it is twenty years after the events of the Hound—and soon he and Watson are off to the West Country. There the familiar story unfolds: Silver Blaze, a favorite for the Barchester Cup, disappears from the stables of a neighbor, Colonel Ross, the horse's groom is found murdered, and Jack Trevor, the young horseman in love with Sir Henry's daughter Diana, is chief suspect. The mystery is told at a leisurely pace, and some exterior location shooting at actual horse farms and moorland add much to the enjoyment of the film.

The picture is little more than half over when Holmes discovers the stolen horse disguised with paint on a neighboring farm (called, interestingly, Stapleton) on the moor. He says nothing of this at the Baskervilles'; answerable only to himself, he confides to Watson, "I can say as little or as much as I choose." The dialogue involving "the curious incident of the dog in the nighttime" is used exactly, but later Holmes deviates from Conan Doyle by exclaiming, "The Professor is behind all this!"

On a midnight drive back to London, Holmes and Watson are fired upon by Moran, who is using a powerful airgun "made especially for the Professor by a well-known foreign gunsmith." The assassination attempt is happily unsuccessful. The next day the Cup Race is scheduled, and the missing Silver Blaze makes a surprise appearance in the lineup.

ROSS: *That's* my horse!
HOLMES: Yes, and *that's* the murderer of James Straker!

It was a kick from the horse which had killed the trainer, who had attempted to steal the horse for Moriarty. But Colonel Ross is still to be cheated of his race, for Moran—his deadly airgun concealed in a newsreel camera—shoots the jockey before the horse can win.

We return to Baker Street, and another of those charming innuendo-filled exchanges between Holmes and his landlady which are a special touch of the series:

MRS. HUDSON: Mr. Holmes, it's nearly midnight! You must eat something. Can I tempt you with a nice piece of haddock?
HOLMES: My dear Mrs. Hudson, you've always been a temptation to me, but haddock at this moment is *not*.

The climax comes that night; Watson is captured by the enemy and taken to Moriarty's new London hideout above an abandoned tube station. Holmes, of course, is quickly to the rescue. A chortling Professor tries to force a brave Watson down an eighty-foot elevator shaft, but Holmes and Lestrade, with guns drawn, appear in the nick of time.

HOLMES: I think our "quiet rest in the country" has been a great success.
MORIARTY: Damn you, Holmes! Blast you!
WATSON: Well, it's the most amazing case we've ever solved.
HOLMES: Elementary, Watson—elementary.

And on that warm yet unspectacular note—the shackled, fuming Moriarty does not after all in any way leap to his death or make any sort of breathtaking escape—the Wontner film portrayals of the Great Detective come to their end.

"SHADOWED" by Sherlock Holmes

How an actor who plays on the screen the part of a famous detective of fiction finds private life difficult in consequence is described in this entertaining article

by ARTHUR WONTNER
The Sherlock Holmes of British Films

I HAVE been shadowed by Sherlock Holmes. I can even claim, with truth, to have been dogged by that laconic and pipe-smoking sleuth for many years of my life.

It has been my fate—perhaps my misfortune—to have been mistaken for fiction's greatest crime-tracker, or for one of his detective-disciples, long before I ever portrayed him on the screen.

Many people may be surprised to learn that there are parts of the world to-day where Conan Doyle's fictitious rival to Scotland Yard is not only believed to be an authentic personality, but is actually held to be alive. I may add that I have these spots marked on my holiday maps with a large red star, as a warning not to venture within their radius!

Constantinople Barred

One of the places I feel bound to bar myself visiting is Constantinople. Young Turkey, it seems, devours the surprising adventures of the Wizard of Baker Street with great eagerness and also with touching credulity. There are Turks who regard him as a flesh-and-blood person who combines in some miraculous fashion the most striking attributes of Mustapha Kemal and Haroun-al-Raschid.

In 1920, when it was decided to complete the occupation of Constantinople in a military sense, certain elements which might have organised resistance were, as a result of information received, rounded up in the early hours of the morning. Later in the day the occupation of the Turkish War Office and Admiralty was effected without incident.

The Turkish populace was much mystified as to how this had come about. Presently the rumour arose, and spread like wildfire, that the great English detective, Sherlock Holmes, was present in person behind the scenes directing operations. His keen intellect and faultless tracking-sense were held responsible for the spiriting away of the recalcitrants, and the consequent peaceful completion of the military manœuvre.

Compliments or Brickbats

A great compliment to Holmes's creator, Conan Doyle! But should I receive compliments—or brickbats—were I to make a personal appearance in Constantinople?

It has been confided to me on more than one occasion that I have been mistaken for a detective when I have been in some public place, such as an hotel lounge. I have certainly noticed people looking at me with considerable interest, and sometimes nudging each other and whispering. But I did not at first suspect the reason. Actors and actresses are accustomed to being stared at, either because they are recognised as stage personalities, or because their features are vaguely familiar through photographs in the Press. It came as a great shock to me not very long ago when I learned that I had routed a little party of crooks from a snug corner in a smoke-room! I had hardly noticed them—but they had spotted me. They cannot have known my real identity, or they would not have worried about me. What harm could a screen Sherlock Holmes do to the most daring desperado?

In some way, I suppose, my appearance suggested a detective—or a "busy," to use the crooks' vernacular—and they were taking no chances!

Although each part an actor is called on to play is absorbing to him as an artist, I must confess that I would find it a relief to shake off this detective-personality sometimes. I have played detective parts of different types. I have also played non-detective characters. Now I feel I should like to play, say, Hamlet—my boyhood's ambition—for a complete change.

I recall very vividly the part of Anderson in "The Bat," one of those "tough guys" of American creation. This character was immense fun to act, especially as the arch-criminal of the piece was really the detective himself. This play ran for nearly a year at the St. James's in 1922, and was the first of the great wave of mystery plays which has deluged the theatres.

Shortly afterwards Sax Rohmer asked me to portray a detective of his creation, Paul Harley, in "The Eye of Siva," which was produced with great success at the New Theatre. Harley was a totally different kind of detective from Anderson. Rohmer had drawn him as a man of quiet charm, with no officiousness of manner. Rough habits, wisecracks, and chewing-gum were no use for him.

In those days my thoughts often wandered to the doyen of fictitious detectives, Sherlock Holmes. People had remarked so frequently: "You really ought to play Sherlock Holmes. I've never seen anyone so like Sidney Paget's drawings." I had met Conan Doyle a year or so previously, and we had talked about his stories, discussing whether he would dramatise one for me. We did not think of films which, in those days, and in England, at any rate, were nothing like what they are now. I was overjoyed when the famous author said he would like me to play his celebrated sleuth. But the stage production did not mature.

Rumour in 1928

It was not until 1928, when I was acting in New York, that a rumour reached me that one of the big Hollywood companies was thinking of filming a Conan Doyle story. Oddly enough, at that very moment a request came to me to make a film test. This, as I discovered later, had nothing to do with the Holmes' picture. I had booked my passage home, and thought no more about it.

A year or so later one more detective part came my way. Imagine my surprise when I learned that it was none other than Sexton Blake, Holmes's great rival in Baker Street!

We produced the play at the Prince Edward Theatre in 1930, but it was not a great success. How long would it be before I became Sherlock Holmes? I wondered.

As it turned out it was not long. Within almost a month Mr. Julius Hagen invited me down to the Twickenham studios and imparted the news that he was going to make a talkie of Conan Doyle's great character, and thought of me for the part. "The Sleeping Cardinal," as the picture was called, was started at once, and with its screening in London last February my bow as Sherlock Holmes at last was made.

Two More Adventures

This one picture brought me offers from Hollywood, and two more adventures of Sherlock Holmes, to be made shortly in British studios. I start one at Twickenham almost immediately, and later will make "The Sign of Four."

I am often asked whether any special mental effort is necessary to achieve the aura of a detective, and the atmosphere of a detective story. I think not, for an experienced actor. One thinks and lives the part, whatever it is, from the moment one steps on the boards or before the camera.

But I am beginning to get some qualms regarding my reception in circles where I am not personally well known as my appearance becomes more and more familiar to a wider and wider public as the master-detector of crime and mystery. I have only too good grounds for my fears that it may be my lot, when at a wedding-reception, say, or a dinner-party, to be regarded with disfavour by some of my fellow-guests as a sleuth hired by the hostess to see that they do not make away with the wedding-presents or the family silver plate!

Arthur Wontner, the famous British stage actor, as the screen Sherlock Holmes.

Der Mann, der Sherlock Holmes War

THE MAN WHO WAS SHERLOCK HOLMES

UFA (German), 1937. Written by R. A. Stemmle and Karl Hartl. Directed by Karl Hartl.

CAST

Sherlock Holmes, Hans Albers; *Dr. Watson,* Heinz Rühmann; *Mary Berry,* Marieluise Claudius; *Jane Berry,* Hansi Knoteck; *Madame Ganymar,* Hilde Weissner; *Monsieur Lepin,* Siegfried Schürenberg; *The man who laughed,* Paul Bildt.

The film industry in Germany in the thirties was undergoing—as was the nation—dramatic change. Many of its great directors had already left for the financial lures of Hollywood or because of the internal political climate. But what remained unchanged was the Teutonic love for melodrama and enduring affection for Herr Sherlock Holmes.

Within a decade there had already been two adaptations of *Hund von der Baskervilles:* in 1929 German director Richard Oswald used American matinee idol Carlyle Blackwell for a very Gothic silent version; then in 1937 there was an even more fog-swirling, dark dramatization with an up-to-date Holmes (Bruno Güttner) sporting mod clothes and packing a gun. Strong-meat mystery was always popular in Germany, peculiarly always set in England—seemingly the right atmosphere for German acceptance. Also in 1937—as reported by Holmesian screen scholar Michael Pointer—gangster Jimmy Ward (Herman Speelmans) in *Sherlock Holmes: Die Graue Dame (The Gray Lady)* is

involved in an Edgar Wallace–style jewel heist gang, and unmasks as the great English detective at the finish. Such a tacked-on ending, an obvious grab for audiences, could be possible only for a nation no longer cooperating with the Conan Doyle estate! But that same year, Conan Doyle would be involved in a Holmesian screen contribution which starred one of the greatest players of the German cinema, Hans Albers.

Big, masculine Albers, a romantic hero who died in 1960 at the age of 67, appeared in a wide variety of roles in a long screen career, and could certainly be considered the German Gable of the thirties. He was Mack the Knife in UFA's *The Threepenny Opera,* the tragic hero of Molnar's *Liliom,* the adventurer at the *White Hell of Pitz Palu,* and appeared with Marlene Dietrich and Emil Jannings in *The Blue Angel.* Siegfried Kracauer in his psychological study of the German film, *From Caligari to Hitler,* refers to Albers as personifying the underlying theme of the German cinema of the thirties: that everyday life itself is a fairy tale. Albers became the nation's number one screen favorite, invariably a glorious victor; he "quivered with radiant vitality, was extremely aggressive and like a born buccaneer seized any opportunity within his reach . . . This human dynamo with the heart of gold embodied on the screen what everybody wished to be in life . . ." This was the man who, stocky-jawed and very stern, clenching a straight pipe between his teeth and wearing a flat cap, in 1937 portrayed an acceptably Teutonic Holmes.

But actually, despite its title, *The Man Who Was Sherlock Holmes* deals not with the detective but with an impostor, Albers, along with comedy star Heinz Rühmann—playing a baby-faced, apprehensive Watson-like assistant—are two happy-go-lucky private eyes who are mistaken for the Conan Doyle creations and decide to play out the roles. (Albers is taken for Holmes because of his clothing: an official, looking at his plaid outfit and pipe, says, "I recognized Sherlock Holmes right away"—and this plot surely owes much to *The Captain from Köpenick,* a German classic about uniforms which turns on much the same device.) The setting is the elegant Hotel Palace in Paris during the 1936 World Exposition, rife with thieves, where sisters Jane and Mary Berry, daughters of the recently deceased Professor Berry, have just learned that their priceless Mauritius stamp might be counterfeit, and that indeed their father might have been a master swindler. A chance encounter with the supposed Sherlock Holmes (actually the opening scene, as Albers stops the crack North Express at night by waving a lantern on the tracks) wins the two pretty girls a fierce, dauntless ally.

Albers finds himself just one short step ahead of the Paris police chief, who first resents the intrusion of the English detective and then starts suspecting his identity. There are scenes in a gloomy castle (a stock German mystery-film setting) and in the dark cellar headquarters of the Paris underworld, ruled by a sinister Monsieur Lapin. Throughout Albers is unflappably cheerful; he and Rühmann even have a song they sing, which became for a time quite popular. Roughly translated, the title is "Yes, Sirs" (*"Jawohl, meine Herren!"),* and the words bubble with some of the adolescent exuberance of the film itself: "Yes, friends, that's how we like it, from today onward the world belongs to us! Sad times are far away, we're going to do what we please! On that you can bet!!" (The only other time a Holmes figure breaks into song is three years later, when Basil Rathbone masquerades as a music hall entertainer.)

In his quest for the real Mauritius stamp, Albers is finally arrested, and is the defendant in a trial that is the sensation of Paris. The charge: impersonating Sherlock Holmes! It is this climactic trial which earns the film a special place in the Holmesian screen chronicles.

The trade newspaper *Variety* sent a correspondent in Berlin to review the film at UFA's Palast-am-Zoo Theater. The critic was pleased with what he saw, and with Albers: "It would be hard to find a face anywhere so suited to the role of the suave Sherlock Holmes." (August 20, 1937) He also tips the film's very curious ending:

... The film is chock-full of thrills and complications. Always in the background is another man also dressed in a huge checked coat similar to Holmes who does nothing but laugh in lusty, ripping guffaws whenever Holmes gets into a tough spot. Is he the *real* Holmes?

After many misadventures Holmes and Watson get pulled in, and the Man Who Laughs is at their trial. Our heroes are unmasked as the unsuccessful owners of a dinky detective agency. But the mysterious one reveals himself as none other than Conan Doyle and declares that Sherlock Holmes never existed, except in his brain.

He gives the impersonator permission to call himself "the man who was Sherlock Holmes."

An extraordinary revelation ... and an interesting plot twist.

Of course, the *real* Sir Arthur Conan Doyle had died some seven years before (the role is played by Paul Bildt), and there is no statement of permission from the Doyle estate—nor any mention of Conan Doyle—in the credits. Even though the Holmes figure in this case was ersatz, imitation is the sincerest form of flattery, and only served to demonstrate (as did the news that the 1937 *Hound* was included in Hitler's private film collection) how popular Sherlock Holmes was to German audiences.

HANS ALBERS

Enter Basil Rathbone

From 1933 until very near the end of the thirties, Hollywood steered curiously clear of the Canon. Then, one extraordinary interpretation was to dominate the following decade. In 1939, at a Hollywood cocktail party—so legend has it—Twentieth Century-Fox studio head Darryl Zanuck suddenly turned to a fellow guest, British actor Basil Rathbone, and declared he would make a perfect Sherlock Holmes.

Tall, lean, with aristocratic bearing and Shakespearean training, Rathbone was born in Johannesburg, South Africa, in 1892. As a young man he traveled with British repertory companies, and after service in World War I he became a regular player on the London and then the New York stage. An early performer in films in both England and America, by the thirties Rathbone was a dapper leading man and seasoned character per-

former. No stranger to whodunits, in 1930 he portrayed detective Philo Vance in *The Bishop Murder Case*. He was nasty Mr. Murdstone in Hollywood's 1935 version of *David Copperfield*. *The Last Days of Pompeii* (1935) saw him as Pontius Pilate. That same year he dueled with Errol Flynn in *Captain Blood* and in 1936 crossed swords with John Barrymore in *Romeo and Juliet*. Although his role as the tormented flight commander in *The Dawn Patrol* (1938) was sympathetic as well as memorable, most of the parts he played were villains—as in *Love from a Stranger* (1937, from an Agatha Christie short story), *The Adventures of Marco Polo*, *The Adventures of Robin Hood* (both 1938), and as the driven scientist who was the *Son of Frankenstein* (1939). Extraordinarily, no one before had thought of him in the Holmesian image.

Perhaps, after all, the cocktail party inspiration

was apocryphal. Michael Pointer, in his admirable British study, *The Public Life of Sherlock Holmes,* tells another version of the casting. He quotes Rathbone that at a dinner party—at which the actor was not present—writer Gene Markey, who often advised Darryl Zanuck and was a man to whom Zanuck listened, abruptly suggested to the studio head that he consider filming the Conan Doyle "classics." But who would be Holmes? As quickly, Markey proferred Rathbone's name, and corpulent British character player Nigel Bruce as Watson. Zanuck thought it a capital idea, and it was settled immediately. The property—the cinematic *Hound*—and actors were signed "within a matter of days."

"Hi there, Sherlock, how's Watson?" Variants of the chant were to haunt Rathbone the rest of his career. In his autobiography, *In and Out of Character,* Rathbone laments at "being 'typed,' more completely 'typed' than any other classic actor has ever been or ever will be again. My fifty-two roles in twenty-three plays of Shakespeare, my years in the London and New York theater, my scores of motion pictures, including my two Academy Award nominations, were slowly but surely sinking into oblivion. . . ." All too true, for since that year no one could think of the actor in any other part. When, ultimately, he declined to associate himself further with the role, it was more or less the end of his career as a film star in Hollywood.

And all because his impact as the Great Detective was so great.

Even though several times removed from the very first dramatization of perhaps the world's most beloved novel of mystery, this version of *The Hound of the Baskervilles* honed truest to its Conan Doyle source, and was, besides, a landmark adaptation in that it was the first Sherlock Holmes film to be set deliberately *in period.* As we have seen, Holmes on the screen has very much been a product of his time, moving into the twentieth century and adjusting handily to motor cars, telephones, the scientific apparatus of the thirties, even the motion picture itself. Here, quite innovatively, Holmes was sent back some fifty years and more to the original time in which the stories were set, accentuating the rich Victorian details separating that more peaceful epoch with a disordered 1939, where war-clouds were already gathering. It has been said that converting *Hound* into a "costume classic" was less a daring than a commercial move, very right for audiences thirsting for escapist entertainment; nonetheless, the idea of a gaslit

Holmes was strikingly original, quite set apart from the many modern-dress Sherlocks familiar to thirties moviegoers, and one of the most important decisions arising from that first inspired Zanuck gathering.

No better American studio had ever turned itself to the Sherlockian task. Twentieth Century-Fox had an enormous, well-designed back lot with winding European streets ideally suited for London and the British villages detailed in the story. As for the moor itself, bleak, desolate expanses of rock and fen were constructed on an indoor soundstage in such a manner that, by filming from a variety of different sides and angles, the moor country appeared to stretch on *forever.* Perhaps a bit overenthusiastically, a studio press release reported that $93,000 alone was spent on the artificial ground-fog rolling across the enormous reconstructed moor reaching to the "horizons" of Fox's largest soundstage.

The cast, too, was carefully assembled with an eye to quality. For Rathbone, there could hardly have been a more comfortable choice for Watson than Nigel Bruce; they had long been warm, affectionate friends. "There is no question in my mind that Nigel Bruce was the ideal Dr. Watson, not only of his time but of all time," Rathbone wrote. "There was an endearing quality to his performance that to a very large extent, I believe, humanized the relationship between Dr. Watson and Mr. Holmes. . . ." Would, indeed, he wondered, the films of them both been as successful had there been a "less lovable companion to Holmes than was Nigel's Dr. Watson." No doubt Rathbone's appraisal was influenced by the closeness of their friendship and his delight in the man's Falstaffian characteristics. Others were more critical. Bruce had made a career of comedy, generally portraying buffons. (This is something of an oversimplification, as in years immediately before 1939 he had appeared on the New York stage as W. S. Gilbert in *Knights of Song,* and played important roles in such films as *Treasure Island, Becky Sharp* and *She.*) Portly and blustering, and perhaps a shade too old-appearing to be a true Watson— actually he was only 44 in *Hound,* three years younger than Rathbone, surprisingly—Nigel's approach to the role was essentially comedic. Made increasingly bumbling and silly by later films, Bruce has not found favor with Sherlockian film students. Withal, despite his sputtering, broad caricature, Bruce's Watson is a warm-hearted and kindly fellow, and it must be noted that in many of the tight corners our heroes find themselves he proves his true mettle, sets his jaw and turns tiger. Establishment and British to the core, Nigel Bruce as Dr. Watson tried his best to be that fixed point in the Victorian age.

The studio surrounded its new team with such menacing supporting players as Lionel Atwill and John Carradine. For romantic interest—needless to say, not to interest Holmes but the young Baskerville heir—they chose British actress Wendy Barrie, who had attracted Hollywood notice first in *The Private Life of Henry VIII* seven years before. (She was later to be attentive to the American adventures of such detectives as the Falcon and the Saint.) Contract player Richard Greene, an Englishman who had entered films with John Ford's *Four Men and a Prayer* (1938), was cast as Sir Henry Baskerville. Young and dashing, the handsome Greene had played opposite such Fox heroines as Loretta Young and Shirley Temple; it was typical of studio practice, Rathbone noted with some chagrin, that Greene was given top billing—even before Sherlock Holmes! It was perhaps understandable insurance—but it was not to happen to Rathbone again.

Writer Ernest Pascal constructed a script which followed closely the Conan Doyle book, making few changes other than purifying the relationship between the Stapletons (they are brother and sister in the screenplay, rather than secretly husband and wife) and adding spiritualism as an interest for Mrs. Mortimer so that a seance could be included in the film for atmosphere. Pascal's feelings were obviously that one shouldn't tamper too much with a masterpiece, and as a result the film comes across as slightly heavy. The choice of director mars the film as well: Sidney Lanfield was definitely out of his forte. Previously a jazz musician, and known for directing such light, frothy efforts as *Hat Check Girl* (1932) and *Sing Baby Sing* (1936), he could not evoke quite the full melodramatic potential the story offered. So—very much like a mastiff—the movie itself might be described as plodding and faithful.

And yet it is a landmark. Spectacularly produced by a major studio, *The Hound of the Baskervilles* serves Conan Doyle well and presents us for the very first time with a dynamic Holmes that was to electrify the world. For those reasons it is often considered the best individual Sherlock Holmes film. We will give it close attention.

A variety of studio poses of Basil Rathbone in Sherlockian garb, identifying him closely with the dress of the
character and establishing period—a radical screen departure. Note the comparison with the Sidney Paget illustration.

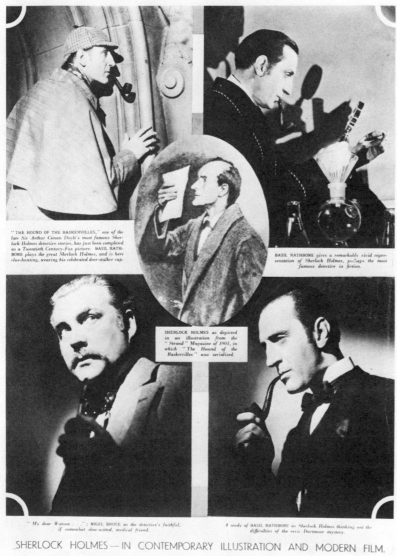

"THE HOUND OF THE BASKERVILLES," one of the
late Sir Arthur Conan Doyle's most famous Sherlock Holmes detective stories, has just been completed
as a Twentieth Century-Fox picture. BASIL RATH-
BONE plays the great Sherlock Holmes, and is here
clue-hunting, wearing his celebrated deer-stalker cap.

BASIL RATHBONE gives a remarkably vivid representation of Sherlock Holmes, perhaps the most
famous detective in fiction.

SHERLOCK HOLMES as depicted
in an illustration from the
"Strand" Magazine of 1901, in
which "The Hound of the
Baskervilles" was serialised.

"My dear Watson . . . ": NIGEL BRUCE as the detective's faithful,
if somewhat slow-witted, medical friend.

A study of BASIL RATHBONE as Sherlock Holmes thinking out the
difficulties of the eerie Dartmoor mystery.

SHERLOCK HOLMES—IN CONTEMPORARY ILLUSTRATION AND MODERN FILM.

Basil Rathbone and his wife Ouida.

A characteristic pose of Rathbone and Nigel Bruce.

Rathbone and
The Hound of the Baskervilles

The ferocious hound. Many animals were tested: the dog had to have a menacing appearance yet respond instantly to command, and most importantly his howl had to have an eerie, spine-tingling quality to strike terror in the hearts of listeners. The winner was Chief, a towering, 140-pound Great Dane, from a kennel in the San Fernando Valley.

20th Century-Fox Film Corporation, 1939. Produced by Darryl F. Zanuck. Associate Producer, Gene Markey. Screenplay by Ernest Pascal ("adapted from THE HOUND OF THE BASKERVILLES by Sir Arthur Conan Doyle"). Directed by Sidney Lanfield.

CAST

Sir Henry Baskerville, Richard Greene; *Sherlock Holmes*, Basil Rathbone; *Beryl Stapleton*, Wendy Barrie; *Dr. Watson*, Nigel Bruce; *James Mortimer*, Lionel Atwill; *Barryman**, John Carradine; *Mr. Frankland*, Barlowe Borland; *Mrs. Mortimer*, Beryl Mercer; *John Stapleton*, Morton Lowry; *Sir Hugo Baskerville*, Ralph Forbes; *Mrs. Hudson*, Mary Gordon; *Mrs. Mortimer*, Eily Malyon; *Cab Driver*, E. E. Clive.

*The butler at Baskerville Hall is in the book of course called Barrymore, and the name change is obviously not to confuse him with the famed acting family.

It is the year 1889. *"In all England there is no district more dismal than that vast expanse of primitive wasteland, the moors of Dartmoor in Devonshire."* It is night, and we see a man running across those moors, breathless, frightened. Behind him we hear the baying of a hound, a sound so fearful it chills the soul. The man falls. From the desolate rocky nightscape another man peers: he is bearded and rough-looking, perhaps a convict from the nearby prison. At the great house which looms in the darkness, Baskerville Hall, a servant woman opens the door, lantern in hand—and finds her master dead.

At the local coroner's court, sinister-looking Dr. James Mortimer (Lionel Atwill, with great thick glasses accentuating a demonic appearance) testifies that Sir Charles Baskerville has died of heart failure. "For some time Sir Charles was in a highly nervous state. Worried. Something was preying on

In an interesting Gothic poster, one has to look hard to spot the silhouette of Sherlock Holmes behind the lovers' faces. This is the result of the same uncertainty on the part of 20th Century-Fox Studios that made them give Richard Greene billing ahead of Rathbone.

his mind." He had been running up the yew alley by the Hall when he died. Irascible Mr. Frankland (Barlowe Borland), also at the inquest, jumps up to insist that his neighbor Sir Charles was *murdered*. "There's more than one person in this room knows I speak the truth."

Big Ben chimes. We are in London, at Baker Street. Dr. Watson, dressed in a smoking jacket we will seldom see again, grumbles as he cuts newspaper clippings for Sherlock Holmes. (The *Times* headline reads: "Sir Henry Baskerville Arriving from Canada. Young Heir Will Assume Title and Estates.") But the clippings are vital; Holmes conjectures, purely as an intellectual exercise, that the heir will soon be murdered. Crisply arrogant in his speculation, this fresh new cinematic Holmes is as sharply honed as a razor; like Watson, he wears a dressing gown covering a stiffly starched shirt. Mrs. Hudson enters; a visitor, a Doctor Mortimer, has come and gone while they were out, but left his walking stick. Again for mental stimulation, Holmes amusedly asks Watson to describe the unknown caller. "Let me hear you reconstruct him, from his walking stick, by our usual method of elementary observation."

It is the classic exercise in deduction carried over from the book. Watson makes a few observations; "Has anything escaped me?" "Almost everything, my dear fellow," Holmes retorts drily, and draws the full picture of Mortimer, a doctor "with a small practice in the country and the owner of a dog . . . ." There is a knock on the door, and the country doctor is announced.

Mortimer is relieved to recover his stick, and gets quickly to his major concern. "Mr. Holmes, you're the one man in all England who can help me." His friend, Sir Henry Baskerville—here Holmes and Watson exchange significant glances—is in grave danger. "I am in mortal fear Sir Henry's life will be snuffed out." For centuries past every Baskerville who has inherited the estates has met a sudden, violent death. Even though Henry's uncle, Sir Charles, died—according to the coroner's verdict—a natural death, Mortimer had noticed footprints close to where the body was found. "Mr. Holmes, they were the footprints of a gigantic hound!" Later, rummaging, as executor of the estate, through Sir Charles's papers, the doctor comes across an ancient family document telling of the curse of the Hound of the Baskervilles.

Mortimer begins to read the ancient paper: "It won't bore you, Mr. Holmes, I promise." It is a wild, terrible story, and we see it in flashback.

At home on Baker Street, Holmes saws at his violin. Note Watson's opulent smoking jacket.

About 1650 Baskerville Manor was held by Sir Hugo, "a profane and godless man." One dark night he stole the daughter of a neighboring farmer and locked her upstairs in the Manor. As Hugo and his friends caroused drunkenly below, the girl escaped, but not without being discovered; Hugo pursued her across the moor on horseback. "I'd give my soul to the devil for that wench!" Hugo's drinking companions, concerned when he didn't return, went searching for him. They found the body of the girl, and from just over a rise, heard a sound which froze the blood in their veins. Looking up, they saw a huge spectral hound tearing Sir Hugo to shreds—and vanish. "Such is the history of the Hound that has cursed the Baskerville family ever since, many having been unhappy in their deaths—sudden, violent and mysterious!"

Holmes sucks on his pipe. "Interesting. Very interesting." He suggests that when the young heir arrives the next day from Canada, Mortimer should bring him to Baker Street.

The journey on the following day to Holmes's rooms is not without incident to Dr. Mortimer and Sir Henry; a rock is hurled into their cab bearing a warning to stay away from the moors. The letters of the message, Holmes observes, were clipped from the London *Times*. "You must admit, Dr. Mortimer, there is nothing supernatural about *this*." Has anything else unusual happened? Sir

Henry relates with some bewilderment that one of his brand new boots had been stolen from outside his hotel room door.

Night has fallen before Henry and Mortimer return to their hotel, but they decide to walk. As they stroll down Baker Street—an angular, winding Baker Street, quite unlike the straight thoroughfare it is in actuality—they are covertly followed by Holmes, who notices a cab keeping pace with them. A gun protrudes from its window. Holmes manages to rout the vehicle as his charges walk on unnoticing: he has foiled an assassination.

The next day Holmes dispatches Watson to find the driver of the cab, but the latter can tell them nothing. His fare identified himself as "a detective—Sherlock Holmes." The real Holmes is amused. Henry is eager to see Baskerville Hall. "This story of the Hound—it's nonsense, a silly legend." He will leave in the morning, but urgent business in town prevents Holmes from accompanying him. But he asks Dr. Watson to go with Henry in his place.

The terrain of Dartmoor is evil and foreboding. The travelers in their dogcart pass the rocks of Stonehenge, and then the dark patches of the Great Grimpen Mire, "as treacherous a morass as exists anywhere," Mortimer explains. "Thousands of lives have been sucked down to its bottomless depths." At last they come upon the immense, brooding stone Manor, and are welcomed by the dour butler Barryman (John Carradine) and his wife.

That night an alert Watson comes upon Barryman apparently signaling someone from an upper window. Flustered, the butler explains he was checking the fastenings. But is there a dim answering light out in the dark of the moor? Watson and Henry rush out among the rocks, just in time to see a wild-eyed, bearded creature hurl a large stone at them and disappear. "Who the devil can that be?" A terrible howling cuts the night.

The next day is somewhat more cheerful, and Henry decides to explore the moor alone, much against Watson's orders. Anxious to catch up with him, the doctor runs across another resident of the region, a young naturalist named Stapleton (Morton Lowry), who warns him that the place is mysterious as well as beautiful, and has its share of dangers. Further on ahead, Henry is stopped in his ramblings by a girl on horseback, Stapleton's stepsister, Beryl (Wendy Barrie). A few more steps and he would have blundered into the Grimpen Mire. Only yesterday a wild moor pony was caught in the innocent-looking green patch of soft ground and nothing could save it. The young heir is quite taken with the pretty girl, and consents to dine with the Stapletons.

Among the guests at the Stapletons' welcoming dinner party is Dr. Mortimer, whose small, timid wife (Beryl Mercer) shares his interest in the occult and herself has strong mediumistic abilities. She agrees, at first reluctantly, to conduct a seance—to try to contact the spirit of Sir Charles. The lights are dimmed, and Mrs. Mortimer slips into a trance. "Speak to us, Sir Charles, if you are here. There are things that only you can explain. Tell us of all the weird, horrible things that have happened on the moor." A frightful howl is heard outside, and Beryl cries out; the seance is over. A shivering girl holds Henry's hand: "I wish you wouldn't have come here."

The next day Beryl and Henry ride to High Tor, where prehistoric man lived fifty thousand years ago. Primitive savages, "but still laughing and dreaming just as we do," muses Henry. "Do you suppose when one of those fellows met a girl that he liked, he had to wait a respectably long time before he dared tell her?" Henry takes Beryl in his arms and proposes.

Watson reports this and all the other occurrences on the moor in daily written reports to Holmes in London. The desolate terrain has its surprises. A faint howling is often heard; is it, as Stapleton explains, the cry of a bittern or actually the wail of the phantom hound? An old peddler is seen limping across the moor, bearded and half-mad; for a moment Watson thinks he has switched his limp from one foot to the other. Watson receives a crude note: "If you want to learn something to your advantage come at once to the stone hut at the edge of the Grimpen Mire."

Characteristically without hesitation or fear, Watson hikes across the rock paths to the prehistoric remains. (Unknown to him, from an upper window of his moorside cottage, Stapleton watches through a spyglass the doctor making his journey, and there is more than just curiosity in his eye—there is villainy.) Inside the dark hut, Watson hears the sound of a cane and dragging foot: the peddler shuffles into view. The doctor is astonished; what is it that the peddler wanted him to hear? "Only this zither, Sar," raves the old man, playing madly. Nonsense, retorts Watson, demanding to learn the peddler's real mission: "I am Sherlock Holmes. I can't be hoodwinked." The old fellow whips away his beard with a laugh. "Then my name must be

Doctor Watson." It has been Holmes all along.

Watson feels betrayed; Holmes's presence on the moors meant he did not fully trust his friend with the case. The detective calms him; through this subterfuge he has been free to work unwatched. Now he will reveal himself to Baskerville Hall. As the two cross back over the moor in the swiftly gathering dusk, the doctor confesses himself puzzled. Days of watching, and what have they gotten? "Murder, my dear Watson. Refined, cold-blooded murder. There's no doubt about it in my mind—or perhaps I should say in my imagination. For that's where crimes are conceived and where they're solved." A few more days and Holmes will have all the answers. "My one fear is that the murderer will strike before we're ready." He is interrupted by a blood-curdling, savage growl. On a rise above them, on a rock edge, a huge, terrifying animal is tearing at the figure of a man. Is it Sir Henry? The man falls, the dog vanishes into the twilight.

Holmes and Watson with some difficulty clamber to the bottom of the ridge where the body lies, its skull crushed. The figure is wearing Henry's clothes—but it is not the heir. Holmes turns him over. "The Notting Hill Murderer—a convict escaped from prison last month. Hiding on the moor ever since." It was he whom Barryman was signaling, and no doubt the butler had also given him Sir Henry's garments. "These clothes were the cause of that poor devil's death!" The hound was after Sir Henry, but mistook the convict for him because of the scent. The reason, too, why the heir's boot was stolen in London.

The good-natured young Canadian is heartily pleased to see Holmes on his arrival at the Hall. The detective asks to see Mrs. Barryman, to tell her that her convict brother is dead. "He is beyond the law now. He is in more merciful hands." The butler's wife breaks into sobs; she could not turn him over to the police, he was her kin. Sir Henry assures her that he understands.

"That about clears up everything, I think," says Holmes to the heir, after the two servants have gone to their quarters. The heir is jubilant; the poor demented convict was the cause of it all, even the dreadful noises on the moor. Now he is really free to marry Beryl Stapleton as he has just planned; a farewell party hosted by her brother the following night, then marriage in London, and off to Canada for a honeymoon. Holmes and Watson must stay. But Holmes declines; he and Watson must rush back to Baker Street tomorrow afternoon. As he talks, Holmes's eye wanders to

Holmes and Watson discover the body of the convict dressed in Sir Henry's clothes.

Although actually a publicity pose, this portrait of Rathbone holding a revolver is dramatic and effective.

an old portrait of the villainous Sir Hugo Baskerville on the wall. There is something familiar about it. Not a very valuable painting, Henry scoffs. "On the contrary: one day it may prove to be of the greatest value."

On the train chugging across the moorlands towards London, Watson confesses himself perplexed still on "one or two little points." Surely the convict wasn't in London? Did not send the threatening letter or steal the boot? "Of course not," snaps Holmes. The murderer is still at large, and will strike again tonight. The two friends will switch trains at the next station and return, hopefully to catch the killer red-handed, for otherwise there would be no shred of evidence against him and no case. That means gambling to save Sir Henry's life.

After a festive dinner at the Stapleton cottage, Henry decides to walk home alone across the moor; after all, he has had Sherlock Holmes's assurance that there is nothing more to fear. Jack Stapleton darts out the back way, his gloved hand holding a boot. The young naturalist heads for an abandoned country churchyard; from a covered pit he releases a savage, snarling great dog, letting it sniff at the shoe. The animal bounds away into the darkness.

Delayed in the swirling night mists, Holmes and Watson arrive at the moorpaths just in time to see Sir Henry running for his life, pursued by the hound. The man falls—and the beast is at his throat! Holmes fires twice; the dog yelps and streaks off. The detective and the doctor rush to the wounded Henry; he is bloody but not too badly hurt. Holmes asks Watson if he can manage to help the heir back to Baskerville Hall alone: "I've got things to do." Holding a lantern, Sherlock follows the animal's tracks back across the path while, unknown to him, Stapleton follows.

Moments later, the detective reaches the ruined country cemetery shrouded in darkness. He comes upon the pit and climbs down into it, as Stapleton swiftly closes and bolts the hinged cover, making Holmes a prisoner below. There is silence. No sign of panic can be read on the sleuth's face as takes stock of his situation. Removing a small pocket knife from his coat, he begins to hack away at the trapdoor above.

At Baskerville Hall Watson is treating Henry's wounds. Stapleton enters: "I've just heard the dreadful news. Now we know for certain this is no legend, no myth. There really is a hound!" He tells Watson that he has run across Holmes on the

moor, that the detective needs Watson urgently. The faithful doctor hurries away. Stapleton sends Mrs. Barryman into the kitchen for more boiling water, then—alone with the weakened heir—secretively pours a dark potion into a glass. "Drink this, Sir Henry, you'll feel much stronger. It may taste a little bitter, but don't mind that." Henry raises the tonic to his lips.

"Sir Henry!" It is Sherlock Holmes who has entered the room. "Feeling better?" he asks, examining the young man's lacerations, carelessly knocking the drink from his hand. Beryl and the Mortimers rush into the room, having heard of the nocturnal events. Holmes continues: "I owe you an apology for jeopardizing your life—and for deceiving you last night, for when I told you that your troubles were over I knew that they weren't." The person who wanted to snuff out the heir's life wanted to lay claim to the whole Baskerville estate, for in tracing back his lineage he learned both that he was next of kin and the family legend. "So he brought the Hound to life." Holmes moves to the portrait of Sir Hugo. "The most amazing instance of a throwback I've ever seen." The eyes of the painting are familiar. They are the eyes of Stapleton.

The final little dinner at Stapleton's. Dr. Mortimer (Lionel Atwill) proposes a toast, while listening are Stapleton, Beryl, Sir Henry, Mrs. Mortimer (Beryl Mercer), and Mr. Frankland (Barlowe Borland).

Romance blooms on the moor. The incredible set stretched 300 feet long by 200 feet across, and the horizon one sees here is painted. The moor set was so big, Richard Greene once got lost in it!

In a marvelously atmospheric portrait shot, Richard Greene evokes a mood of mystery by lowering the gas flame.

The naturalist draws a gun. "One move from any of you and I'll blast you to kingdom come!" He dashes out into the night, knocking over in his flight the returning Watson. Holmes follows, blowing a police whistle. "He won't get very far. I've posted constables on both the roads, and the only other way is *across the Grimpen Mire.*"

(There is no further mention of Stapleton and his fate, so no doubt Holmes's ominous conjecture came to pass. One wonders where those two constables were earlier in the evening, when they were really needed!)

That officially finishes the case, leaving only the most extraordinary closing dialogue in the history of Sherlockian cinema. Sir Henry has just finished telling Holmes how he owes the master detective an enormous debt of gratitude, when a gushing Dr. Mortimer enjoins: "Why, we all do! Mr. Holmes, we've admired you in the past as does every Englishman. Your record as our greatest detective is known throughout the world. But this—seeing how you work—knowing that there is in England such a man as you gives us all a sense of safety and security. God bless you, Mr. Holmes."

The speech touches a weary Holmes, and after saying thanks and good night, he starts to leave the room. "If you don't mind, I've had rather a strenuous day, I think I'll turn in." The warm serenity of the parting is suddenly, startlingly broken as the detective calls out to his companion: "Oh, Watson, the needle!"

An extraordinary request. No screen hero up until that time had made such a daring and unpunished offhand confession to a serious, mainlining addiction. Only the stature of the Holmesian character could have permitted this without a national hue and cry, an outrage that would have surely been stirred by a similar request from any other motion picture figure. And Holmes himself, cured or no, would not indulge onscreen again for thirty-seven years—until the debilitating, far less frivolous indulgences of *The Seven-Per-Cent Solution.*

Twentieth Century-Fox's version of *The Hound of the Baskervilles* was an immediate and rousing success, one of the studio's biggest releases for the year. Critical commentary was also mostly favorable. Frank Nugent, writing in *The New York Times* (March 25, 1939) felt "the film succeeds rather well in reproducing Sir Arthur's macabre detective story along forthright cinema lines. The technicians have whipped up a moor at least twice as desolate as any ghost-story moor has need to be, the mist swirls steadily, the savage howl of the Bas-

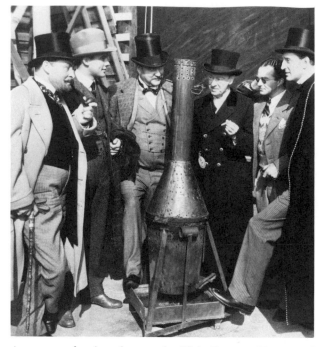

A rare production shot on the 20th Century-Fox sound stage. Lionel Atwill (Dr. Mortimer), Richard Greene, Nigel Bruce, character player E. E. Clive (dressed for his role as a cabman), director Sidney Lanfield and Rathbone gather about an ornate fog-making machine—which saw plenty of use on the bleak, treacherous moor set.

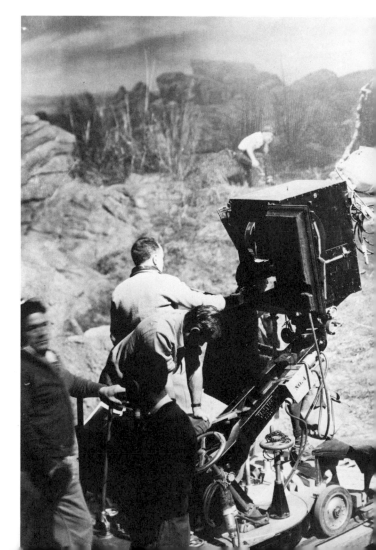

Dr. Mortimer, looking sinister.

Barryman the butler signalling from the upstairs window of Baskerville Hall.

A fascinating production still of the studio moor, with camera.

Sharing a repast of sardines. Note the revolver with which Watson has girded himself.

kerville hound is heard at all the melodramatically appropriate intervals . . . It's fairly good fun and like old times to be seeing Sherlock again. . . ." The New York *Herald Tribune*'s Howard Barnes was not quite so enthusiastic that same day, but had—surprisingly—some warm, admiring words for Nigel Bruce as Watson: "Mr. Bruce contributes a rounded and credible portrayal which keeps you interested in the action." But the lion's share of most critical praise was for Basil Rathbone. Graham Greene was among those completely won over by "that dark knife-blade face and snapping mouth," an eager face wearing an "expression of intense and high-strung energy." *Variety* led the trade press in enthusiasm, declaring "Rathbone gives a most effective characterization of Sherlock Holmes, which will be relished by mystery lovers." Even Rathbone derived great satisfaction from his portrayal. Reflecting some two decades later, he was to say wryly, "Had I made but the one Holmes picture, my first, *The Hound of the Baskervilles*, I should probably not be as well known as I am to-day. But within myself, as an artist, I should have been well content. Of all the 'adventures' *The Hound* is my favorite story, and it was in this picture that I had the stimulating experience of creating, within my own limited framework, a character that has intrigued me as much as any I have ever played."

And audiences across America agreed with Hearst newspapers critic Rose Pelswick's assessment of the new *Hound* Holmes. "Smoking the traditional pipe and playing the violin, but otherwise making the character credible rather than eccentric, Mr. Rathbone is vastly superior to the previous screen impersonators of the Baker Street genius." He had won the role—for life.

(It is interesting to footnote, in a final comment on the 1939 *Hound of the Baskervilles*, that the film underwent a rebirth in the mid-seventies. Twentieth Century-Fox had allowed its literary rights to the property to expire by the early 1960s, and rather than bothering to renew them just let the film gather dust in its vaults. Then, fired by the growing interest in all things Holmesian that swept through 1975, a small but selective distribution company called Film Specialities Inc. picked up the rights to the now-classic thriller and released it—crisp, mint-new 35 mm prints—to theaters in Seattle, Portland, San Francisco and New York City, combined with the Fox-Movietone newsreel interview with Sir Arthur Conan Doyle and the Buster Keaton *Sherlock Jr.* into a complete program. Despite the irreverence of the seventies, young people took to the revival, treating it as treasure rather than just camp. Most critics did too. The distinguished Judith Crist chose the bill as the centerpiece of her farewell review for *New York* magazine on July 28, 1975. She called *Hound* "a feast for movie-lovers, the pure pleasure of the work enriched by social and historical perspectives . . . both a satisfying Holmesian adventure and a delectable Hollywood period piece." As for Rathbone, his detective, "perhaps a bit more human and a touch more brisk than the Master, is still true to the image." The landmark film's power to entice had still not dimmed after nearly four decades.)

Stimulated with the success of its first pairing of Rathbone and Bruce, Twentieth Century-Fox without hesitation projected a second vehicle. Feeling that they were helped by choosing a heavy "class" literary source, and deciding against moving on to other, perhaps lesser-impact stories from the Canon, the studio instead elected to dramatize the old William Gillette stage play for their film, to be called *The Adventures of Sherlock Holmes.*

All the official credits for the subsequent film carried due acknowledgement of the Gillette source, yet hardly anything was actually used. Holmes *did* cross the evil genius Moriarty's path, and Billy the page boy *was* in several scenes, but only with faint resemblance to the play. Slavishly faithful to *The Hound*, the studio decided instead with its second venture—because of the play's familiarity, old-fashionedness, and the fact it had been used twice before for movies—to all but abandon the classic it purchased on which to base a scenario.

Rathbone did not disagree at all with this judgement. He was never to be fond of the Gillette work, dismissing it perhaps with unconscious jealousy, for the author was also a fellow thespian. "In the early years of the present century theater audiences were chilled to the marrow by William Gillette's famous portrayal of Sherlock Holmes, in a play I have read and been invited to revive. This play, believe me, is so ludicrously funny today that the only possible way to present it in the sixties would be to play it like *The Drunkard*, with Groucho Marx as Sherlock Holmes . . . Modern audiences would laugh this play off the stage." He could not guess that nearly a decade after his own death London's Royal Shakespeare Company would make of the Gillette antique theatrical dynamite on both sides of the Atlantic.

In his second film Rathbone settled very com-

The attack on Sir Henry, circumvented by the arrival of Holmes and Watson.

fortably into the role of the master detective. We sense his content, and the playing is sheer perfection—as the critics would later also note. In addition, he was allowed to do something quite unusual for him professionally—sing, if only a music-hall ditty. But he manages his scene as a song-and-dance man (Holmes in disguise) with ease, having been coached by the studio's dance director, Nick Castle. And happily enough, Rathbone had the satisfaction of being given top billing in this Holmes film.

The studio was to provide other support for Rathbone, too. Assigned to the film was director Alfred Werker, far less plodding a craftsman than Lanfield in *Hound*; in films like *House of Rothschild* and *Kidnapped* Werker proved he could handle period drama and adventure. A first-rate cast was assembled as well. For the troubled heronie they selected young Ida Lupino, daughter of a British theatrical family who—then in her early twenties—had already spanned a successful five-year career in Hollywood. Australian Alan Marshal was cast as the romantic lead, doubling as red herring suspect; he had already appeared with Basil Rathbone in a film, *The Garden of Allah*, three years before, and—unlike Richard Greene—was a comfortable fourth in the billing lineup. (In 1961 he was to die while on stage acting with Mae West.)

But by far the most vital addition to the cast was George Zucco as the demonic Professor Moriarty, exuding calculated evil and grinning treachery. The British actor, then over fifty, had made a career on English stage and screen, and had shortly before come over to Hollywood to begin a new career which was ultimately to bring him into close, superb association with the American horror film genre. His first U.S. film, which he accepted while on a vacation in California, was *After the Thin Man* (1936); just prior to the Sherlockian venture he was the adversary to John Howard in *Arrest Bulldog Drummond*. The distinguished film histo-rian William K. Everson in his *The Detective in Film* classed Zucco as one of the screen's best Moriartys—and best villains, but of course it's the same thing. "Zucco's face not only had the ability to suggest intellectual superiority, but also had the happy facility of being able to light itself up with satanic glee at his own perfidy." Everson also notes that Zucco's unctuous diction and suave manners were on a level with Rathbone's, and therefore the two were perfectly matched. Zucco went on in the immediate years following to portray maniacs and evil scientists in such terrors as *The Mummy's Hand*, *The Mad Monster*, *The Mad Ghoul*, and was even to clash with Holmes again, this time as a modern Nazi spy, but his hissable best was undoubtedly the Napoleon of crime. After some years in retirement, he died in 1960.

Twentieth Century-Fox also invested two good melodrama screenwriters to the project, Edwin Blum and William Drake, who completely scuttled the William Gillette play from which they supposedly were to draw their scenario.

The advertising copy devised by the studio made full use of the unfettered plots and, more importantly, the major confrontation: *"The master detective against his arch-enemy, Moriarty, fiction's most famous criminal genius . . ."* And even more frenziedly, *"the strange case of the chinchilla fetish—the Traitor's Gate—the fiendish instrument that strangles, crushes, vanishes—the albatross of doom! A woman in love, the victim! The British crown jewels, the loot!"* With such a pitch, and a film laced with such production values as Twentieth Century-Fox's vast backlot European areas—perfectly usable for Victoria's London—and such expert character players as eleven-year-old Terry Kilburn (as page-boy Billy), Henry Stephenson and E. E. Clive, and most vitally, a fantastically good new Holmes in his second go-round, *The Adventures of Sherlock Holmes* could hardly miss. And it didn't.

The Adventures
of Sherlock Holmes

Basil Rathbone and Ida Lupino in a publicity shot for
the film, Miss Lupino looking tasteful and fetching in
mourning clothes.

20th Century-Fox Film Corporation, 1939. Darryl F. Zanuck in Charge of Production. Associate Producer, Gene Markey. Screenplay by Edwin Blum and William Drake ("Based on the play SHERLOCK HOLMES *by William Gillette with the permission of the executors of the late Sir Arthur Conan Doyle"). Directed by Albert Werker.*

CAST

Sherlock Holmes, Basil Rathbone; *Dr. Watson,* Nigel Bruce; *Ann Brandon,* Ida Lupino; *Jerrold Hunter,* Alan Marshal; *Billy,* Terry Kilburn; *Professor Moriarty,* George Zucco; *Sir Ronald Ramsgate,* Henry Stephenson; *Inspector Bristol,* E. E. Clive; *Bassick,* Arthur Hohl; *Mrs. Jameson,* May Beatty; *Lloyd Brandon,* Peter Willes; *Mrs. Hudson,* Mary Gordon.

We know we are to concentrate on a struggle between titans; we are made aware of it from the first as the camera seeks out an open book, upon which is written: *"In all my life I have encountered only one man whom I can truthfully call the very genius of evil—Professor Moriarty. For eleven years he has eluded me. All the rest who have opposed him are dead. He is the most dangerous criminal England has ever known."* The signature reads: *Sherlock Holmes, May 1894.*

Moriarty is on the dock, being tried for murder. He is owlish-looking, bearded. The jury can only find him not guilty—for insufficient evidence. As the judge, with some reluctance, discharges the prisoner, Sherlock Holmes rushes into the court with important new evidence that can destroy Moriarty's alibi. But he is too late.

Outside, the weather is grim. Finding themselves sharing the same doorway, Holmes and Moriarty exchange wary glances, and the Professor suggests with oily charm: "May I give you a lift? Cabs are scarce in this rain." Holmes accepts.

Once inside the hansom, the two engage in a Gillette-like confrontation that reminds one of the

Poster art for *The Adventures.* Note the eloquent copy-line (all too true): "The struggle of the super-minds in the crime of the century!" Note as well that for this second film Rathbone gets official top billing.

Opening day at New York City's Roxy Theater, with throngs eager to get in.

spirit of the play's barbed dialogue. Holmes says somewhat snidely: "You've a magnificent brain, Moriarty. I admire it. I'd like to present it pickled in alcohol to the London medical society." With equal affability Moriarty counters: "Holmes, you only now barely missed sending me to the gallows. You're the only man in England clever enough to defeat me. I'm going to break you. I'm going to bring off right under your nose the most incredible crime of the century, and you'll never suspect it until it's too late. It'll be the end of you, Sherlock Holmes. Then I can retire in peace. I'd like to retire; crime no longer amuses me. I'd like to devote my remaining years to abstract science." They arrive at Baker Street—the same crooked Baker Street we observed in *Hound*—and Holmes wishes his host good-night, and alights into the rain.

Later, we find Moriarty in his opulent mansion, puttering among the ferns in his greenhouse. Strange, mournful music as if from a flute issues from another room. To a lieutenant, Bassick (Arthur Hohl), who is curious about a letter he has been asked to mail, Moriarty reflects on the fate of the vanished Higgins, of whom all that could be found was a boot. "He had your unfortunate habit of asking too many questions." Then abruptly the Professor begins to talk about his plan. It depends upon a peculiarity of Holmes's brain: the man's perpetual restlessness. He's like a spoiled boy losing interest in one toy when given another. So the professor will ready two toys. The first is a letter addressed to the Tower of London. The second, a crude drawing of a man with an albatross hung around his neck, to distract him from the letter and a crime, "a truly great crime, that will stir the empire, that children will read of in their history books!" Is Holmes the enemy?, Bassick asks. *"Always Holmes . . . until the end."*

It is a sunny morning in Baker Street. Watson watches in some astonishment as Holmes plucks at his violin over a wine glass full of flies. "I am observing the reaction of the chromatic scale on the common housefly." He has received a note from an Ann Brandon, heiress to a mining fortune, whose father died ten years ago somewhat mysteriously; the girl wants his advice—about a garden party—and will stop by that morning. "How can you trifle with such inconsequentialities when Moriarty is loose upon London?" Watson admonishes, but it is the very trifles of the appeal which intrigue Holmes, and about the professor he'll do nothing. "Moriarty is as curious about my movements as I am about his, so I sit here and wait for him to come to me." There is a knock on the door.

George Zucco as the evil Professor Moriarty—*before* he has removed his beard.

Inside Baker Street, where Miss Lupino has come for aid. We see a busy corner of the famed consultation rooms.

It is not the girl, but elderly Sir Ronald Ramsgate, Constable of the Tower of London (Henry Stephenson), who has come to Holmes with an anonymous note he has received: "The Star of Delhi will never reach the Tower." The stone, "possibly the largest emerald in the world," is a gift to Her Majesty from India, to be delivered on the weekend from the cruiser *Invincible*. Holmes dismisses the threat, but agrees to be on hand, for Sir Ronald is an old friend.

An agitated Ann Brandon (Ida Lupino) arrives. She has a strange story to tell: her brother has received a drawing of an albatross hung about a man's neck—dated that very day, May 11. Ten years ago on May 11 Ann's father received just such a note, and was murdered. "I saw him, lying there on the pavement, with the back of his head off. . . ." There is a knock on the door, and young solicitor Jerrold Hunter (Alan Marshal) enters; he

has followed Ann, and is angry with her. Surely the drawing is a prank. They quarrel—Jerrold is her fiance—and he storms out. Holmes comforts the girl, telling her he will take the case, and sends her down to Mrs. Hudson for a cup of tea. Once she is out the door, Watson admonishes Holmes; surely his duty is to guard the Star of Delhi, and no other case should distract. "Oh, bother the Star of Delhi! A man's *life* may be involved here! There is something grotesque about this business!" Holmes retorts, enunciating briefly but clearly his two greatest priorities.

Later, Holmes asks Ann whether the name Moriarty has meaning for her family, but she denies it. Why does he ask? "Somehow I have the feeling of renewing an old acquaintance." But what can the albatross signify to the Brandons? Ann can think of nothing—only the poem. "You've hit on it," Holmes exclaims. " 'And instead of the cross, the albatross about my neck was hung!' This is no childish prank, but a cryptic warning of avenging death. We must go to your brother at once!" Watson bursts in on the pair; keeping Hunter's law office under surveillance, he has seen the young man in conversation with Professor Moriarty. Our friends hasten for a cab in the foggy dusk.

A very nervous Lloyd Brandon, Ann's brother (Peter Willes), has also just left Hunter, who has assured him: "The safest place for you in all London right now is your own home." He is walking cautiously through the quick-falling night, unaware that an armed Hunter follows at a distance. Lloyd takes a short-cut through the park square near his home, and something else stalks him in the rolling fog. There is a scream. As Holmes's cab draws up, a small crowd has already gathered around Lloyd's body—his head bashed in.

Not an hour later Holmes has seen to it that a distraught Ann is resting in the palatial Brandon town house, while a peppery Inspector Bristol (E. E. Clive) is ready to arrest Jerrold Hunter, claiming he used the blunt end of his pistol as the weapon of murder. Not so, intercedes Holmes: the blows were administered after death; Lloyd was actually strangled. Despite the brutality, however, this is an intellectual crime. Jerrold moans mysteriously: "I did my best to guard him day and night, but they

found him all the same, there on an empty street. I couldn't have been far behind." He will explain no further. Holmes takes Inspector Bristol to one side, and suggests Hunter should for the moment be left at liberty. Bristol, who has often benefitted from Holmes's behind-the-scenes help, whispers: "You'll work on the case—in the usual way?" The detective agrees, and Hunter is not detained.

Holmes and Watson hurry out into the park square to seek out clues. A distance from the scene of the crime they find footprints—of a club-footed man. From the depression of the toe "the club-footedness must have some other compensating deformity to sustain these footprints—just one more unnatural element in this rather puzzling case." Close by they find a chinchilla-foot charm. The footprints stop. Did the clubfoot stop here and project some weapon? But no weapon's been found, and what could both strangle a man and crush his skull in?

Inside the Brandon house, Ann hears the notes of a strange, mournful flute—and screams. Holmes hurries to her. She has seen from her window, down on the foggy street, a peddler play the flute, then scurry off. She had heard the music once before, the night her father was killed.

Back at Baker Street Holmes spends some time strumming the atonal melody on his violin, and

Outside Baker Street, where two troubled clients chance to meet (the man is Sir Ronald Ramsgate of the Tower of London). With the cab in front and the messenger at the door, it is an interesting view of the world-famous address.

finally identifies it: "an ancient Inca funeral dirge, used by the Indians in the remote Chilean Andes as a chant for the dead." Sir Ramsgate stops by, but the detective is too preoccupied to worry about the Star of Delhi. The gem arrives tomorrow night at ten o'clock, and—most inconveniently, Sir Ronald fusses—must be put in the Tower vaults at once. Holmes promises to be at the Tower of London when the jewel is delivered, and bring some extra policemen as an added precaution. But the Star of Delhi is far from his mind when Ann Brandon rushes in; an albatross drawing has now been sent *her,* and the date on it is May 13—tomorrow!

It is the night Ann has been invited to Lady Conynham's garden party, an event she already has faced with some reluctance, although Jerrold Hunter has been strangely insistent that she go. Holmes, too, urges her to attend, just to make an appearance, "perhaps take a walk around the grounds . . ." There will be considerable risk, but Ann is a brave girl, and agrees. Once she has left, however, Watson reminds Holmes that he had promised Sir Ramsgate to be at the Tower of London tomorrow night. No fear, "I am going to delegate the most dependable man I know to guard the Star of Delhi in my place—you, my dear fellow." Watson beams.

Professor Moriarty has also been busy. He has shaved his van dyke beard, and—practically unrecognizable—boards a hansom cab driven by his man Bassick and heads for the Tower.

There is music and laughter and outdoor lanterns at Lady Conynham's garden fete, and Ann tries to forget the recent horrors. But she is on her guard; no one, however, has asked for her, nor has any stranger singled her out. A music-hall entertainer begins a sprightly song-and-dance. *"I do like to see beside the seaside—I do like to be beside the sea. . . ."* Ann finds herself unamused. The music-hall singer comes to her as she sits lonely in a dark corner of the garden; behind the coal-black handlebar mustache and striped jacket we see he is Holmes. He whispers to her not to worry, that he is watching her, but not to stray from the lights and the crowds. Then the disguised detective disappears. A South American gaucho orchestra begins to play. To Ann, the flutist seems to stir a memory. She feels a chill, and goes inside the house.

At the Tower Sir Ramsgate is annoyed that Holmes himself is not at hand, but Watson assures him that "I've been with Holmes on a good many cases, and you could do considerably worse." Anyway, the detective is sending along six hand-picked policemen to help guard the delivery of the gem. The police arrive, led by a seasoned-looking officer. "Sergeant Bullfinch, at your service," he salutes smartly. We perceive—but Watson does not—it is the clean-shaven Moriarty.

At ten the Royal Navy delegation delivers the Star of Delhi, and Sir Ramsgate carries the stone triumphantly to the Jewel Room, where it will be deposited with the other Crown jewels on display under heavy lock and key. "The accumulated wealth of ten centuries of Egnlish kings. It's not often this door is unlocked." Suddenly, the light goes out, there is a scuffle, the policemen vanish. Watson and Ramsgate give pursuit, and luckily enough find the Star of Delhi dropped in the Tower's corridor. They are jubilant, for they have saved the day; "no thanks to your brilliant friend Holmes," reminds Ramsgate as they place the gem among the other riches and depart from the vault room. From out of the shadows inside steps Moriarty, still in his sergeant's uniform. He moves towards the Crown jewels.

In a marvel of intercutting sequences to build suspense, the film returns again to Lady Conynham's home; the party is over, and servants are gathering the lanterns from the garden. In her room, where she is to stay the night, Ann once more hears the mournful flute. A gentleman asks to see her on the terrace; she thinks it is Holmes, but it is Jerrold Hunter. Overwrought, she flares up at the young man and runs from him hysterically, into the dark garden. We watch her plunge headlong down a path while, behind, a clubbed foot stalks.

Ann is lost in the night; pushing through the brush she comes upon a clearing, a garden statue looming before her—and the figure of a gaucho. He swings a rope with balls attached to it. Before he can hurtle it towards her, Holmes appears out of the mists and deflects his aim; the statue is suddenly headless as Ann faints. The assassin moves towards the girl and Holmes shoots him. Watson and police appear; and Holmes picks up the rope. "This is a South American *bolas,* the instrument which killed Lloyd Brandon!" He turns his attention to the wounded murderer, removing his shoe to reveal the supposed deformity as just another diversion. "Yes, it's just as I suspected. This clubfooted shoe was a very clever device. Who put you up to this?" *"The Professor,"* the gaucho gasps. So that clears up our case, Watson says smugly, but Holmes, a whirlwind of energy, shouts that it has only just begun.

The detective uses a pocket tape measure to investigate a footprint.

The murder weapon—having just beheaded a statue.

They break into Moriarty's home, find it empty, see the shaving remnants and guess he has shaved his beard. They find a guidebook—"Why? Moriarty knows London like a cabdriver"—opened to the Tower entry, and guess the aborted Star of Delhi theft was planned by the Napoleon of crime, alias Bullfinch. "Moriarty concocted that Brandon case with all its fantastic convolutions just to distract me from stealing the emerald." And yet he *didn't* steal it. "The real crime has not yet come to light. Somewhere in London at this very moment something tremendous is happening." The crowning act of his career. Crowning? Light dawns on Holmes. "Watson, we're wasting time!"

Holmes commandeers a cab and they race through the city streets, cutting the fog. At the gates of the Tower, the cab overturns; while the royal guards rescue a sputtering Watson, Holmes sneaks inside and makes his way cautiously up to the vault room. The shadowy figure of a police sergeant spies him on the stair, and a cat and mouse game begins. The detective and Moriarty come to grips finally on the murky battlements of the structure. There is a struggle, and a shot, and the Professor falls from the tower top.

The Adventures of Sherlock Holmes is in so many ways a superior film that to criticize it seems carping. Yet Moriarty's grand scheme is so complicated and unwieldy that it is embarrassing to see it almost work. Indeed, when Holmes allows himself to be wildly distracted it is the more responsible Watson who at several points sternly reminds the detective not to neglect his initial case.

In every other respect, however, Watson does not measure up. It has often been repeated that the doctor's character deteriorated only in the later Universal features, but he has clearly begun to bumble even here. Nigel Bruce was not restrained in his silly-ass mannerisms, and Rathbone is encouraged by the script to (affectionately, of course) tweak and indulge him. Shockingly, Watson is permitted to show jealousy against a mere child—the house-page Billy, who is studying Holmes's techniques and wishes to grow up to be just like him. Every time he sees the lad he darts him a black glance; once he complains to Holmes, "I don't know why you allow that insufferable little brat to come in here!" He glowers at every word of praise Holmes gives the boy, a situation certainly not in keeping with the Gillette play version of harmonious relationships at Baker Street. (Child actor Terry Kilburn, who played Billy, was to put the lessons learned from Holmes to good use when, in his late

teens, he became assistant onscreen to Bulldog Drummond.)

Despite the film's inconsistencies and illogical bypaths—Jerrold Hunter's suspicious behavior, for instance, is airily dismissed at the end, and the chinchilla-foot charm serves no function except to allow Billy to surmise its owner may be a South American for that is where the animal is to be found—its winning pace and good lead performances enchanted critics. "One can't help liking the new Holmes film," crowed Frank S. Nugent in *The New York Times* for September 2, 1939. "Delightful the way the fog follows Moriarty around; delightful, too, the equally synthetic melodramatics of the entire production... Would you wonder why Moriarty, with the 'jools' in his grasp, should prefer to go chasing Holmes over the embrasures of the Tower of London? If you would, alas, then Mr. Holmes's new adventures will leave you lukewarm; but as for me I haven't stopped quaking yet."

While the Nugent review was friendly but tongue-in-cheek in its appraisal, the commentary by Howard Barnes in the New York *Herald Tribune* (also 9/2) was unrestrainedly enthusiastic. "Extraordinary good sense and skill have gone into the making of *The Adventures of Sherlock Holmes*... at once an exciting thriller and a faithful re-creation of a famous literary figure." The film "is packed full of intriguing incidents and has been given a first-class treatment... Far from seeming old-fashioned, the mystery melodrama takes on heightened effectiveness and rivals any contemporary murder mystery that you are likely to find in the picture playhouses." He heaps praise on the performances of Rathbone and Bruce, and notes that George Zucco "takes the part of Professor Moriarty and makes it as vivid a criminal portrait as I have seen in a long time."

It came as some surprise, then, that Twentieth Century-Fox abruptly decided after this second film to discontinue their Sherlock Holmes series. Although *Adventures* was a commercial success, the studio was less than keenly enthusiastic about its distribution: in double-bill situations the film was slotted in the secondary position, most often under a Tyrone Power romance. The holocaust in the Europe of 1940 made the gaslit doings of Victorian villains seem entirely too pale. So the studio exiled Holmes and his deerstalker from the cobbled streets of the legendary Fox backlot.

To Basil Rathbone, it was not a total disappointment. Earlier that year, in a publicity interview, he

Watson and Holmes at the Tower of London.

declared he would rather be Holmes than Hamlet. (He had, in fact, never played *Hamlet*.) "Ever since I was a boy and first got acquainted with the great detective I wanted to be like him . . . To play such a character means as much to me as ten 'Hamlets'!" But now he had the role under his belt twice over. It was time, perhaps, to go on to other ventures.

Other ventures were in the offing. Already in 1939 he had starred with Douglas Fairbanks, Jr. in *The Sun Never Sets,* a wildly flamboyant drama of British colonialism, and was superb as the evil Richard III in the historical settings of *Tower of London.* Ahead of him the following year was a plum role in *The Mark of Zorro,* once again—this time with Tyrone Power—demonstrating his extraordinary fencing skills.

A career in radio had opened up as well. By the late thirties radio had become an important new medium for drama, and dramatic productions broadcast on a national scale. "Ellery Queen" (the writing team of cousins Fred Dannay and Manfred Lee) had pioneered an experimental weekly detective series, proving to a skeptical network that the form would be popular to audiences listening at their home sets. In the autumn of 1939 Basil Rathbone and Nigel Bruce were hired to reprise their Holmes and Watson roles in a series of half-hour radio productions, initially for twenty-four weeks. Rathbone's crisp, clean voice and dramatic range ideally suited him to the microphone. With the variety of projects ahead of him, Basil Rathbone's professional future seemed very bright.

Very dramatic posed portrait shot of Sherlock Holmes at the Tower. Note he is holding a .44 revolver. Graham Greene was to say "Basil Rathbone is physically made for the part of Holmes; one feels he was really drawn by Paget," almost too good: "one can't imagine this Holmes indolent, mystical, or untidy." In the years to come, with the radio and film series, Rathbone was to become the *compleat* Holmes.

84

MORE TYPED THAN ANY ACTOR...

A little more than two years later found Basil Rathbone in a comfortable, but not much further advanced, position. Most of his film roles comprised the same sort of part he had been familiar with in the mid-thirties: heavies, maniacs, the hero's older brother. But that was to be expected; as a maturing actor, at age fifty—in 1942—he could best hope for good character roles billed immediately beneath the hero and heroine. He could reflect, however, that with the exception of two very "B" mystery film quickies he did "for the money," the last time he had been absolutely *top* billed in a movie (and, actually one of the few times he was billed first in an important motion picture) was as Sherlock Holmes.

And certainly no one was forgetting him as Holmes. His weekly radio series had been tremendously successful, and he—with Nigel Bruce—had actually signed a seven-year contract, an obvious checkbook indication of its wide popularity. Week after week, radio audiences were stepping back into the Victorian mists with Rathbone—for the scripts were straightforward adaptations of the Conan Doyle Canon in period.

Then Mr. Jules Stein of the Music Corporation of America talent agency, the giant group which represented Rathbone, came to him with a novel idea: a series of Sherlock Holmes films to be done for Universal Studios in which the detective—a radical change—was to be brought right up to the present, tackling the problems of the day. The very conditions in Europe (war, bombings, modern espionage) which had made the turn-of-the-century Holmes of the misty Fox films seem so hopelessly dated and out of place were to provide the cases for the new, 1940s Holmes! It seemed to Rathbone—who had never played the detective except against a hansom-cab-and-gaslight backdrop—a refreshing concept indeed.

(Of course, no Holmes film had been deliberately put back into the Victorian era before Twentieth Century-Fox studios did it in 1939. However, in a rapidly changing America where a Holmes film other than at Fox had not been produced for nearly a decade, the fact that before Rathbone *all* Sherlocks were contemporary had been forgotten.)

Basil Rathbone and Nigel Bruce signed with Universal Pictures. Quick to exploit crises torn out of wartime headlines, the studio was to call the first film *Sherlock Holmes Saves London.*

Universal was not the towering giant Twentieth Century-Fox was in those pre-*Jaws* days, and was not able to afford the budgets which had previously been given the characters. Indeed, the studio rarely rose above the "B" film level—their chief star and money-earner was at that time Deanna Durbin; but their programmers were characteristically slick and competently made. Happily, also, Universal had an expansive back lot with wondrous European streets and vistas, thanks in part to the studio's being one of the earliest operating in California, already very active in silent film days. This back lot was to serve the series well, rivaling in scope even the Fox "England." (Indeed, one notes that in *Adventures* over at Twentieth Century-Fox, both the cab rushing to save Lloyd Brandon and the cab hurrying to the Tower pass through the same "British street." This might not have happened so obviously at Universal.)

The studio's attempt to modernize Sherlock was underscored by this carefully worded, almost apologetic explanation after the opening credits of the first few films: "Sherlock Holmes is ageless, invincible and unchanging. In solving significant problems of the present day he remains—as ever—the supreme master of detective reasoning." To ease the shock of transition, however, the London against which Holmes moves is made as Victorian as possible. Rathbone himself, though, is allowed to shuck his encumbering Victorian clothes for looser, more modern apparel, a windswept, almost bohemian hair style that grew more startling with each film (suspiciously curling across a receding brow), a soft-brimmed, comfortable slouch hat instead of the deerstalker so prominent both in *Hound* and *Adventures.* "Holmes, you *promised!*" admonishes Watson when once during the first film Holmes inadvertently reaches for the deerstalker, and the detective abandons the cap. What can we infer from this? That Watson—the source of all our information on the detective's dress—was his fashion arbiter as well? More likely Holmes just promised to wear things more up-to-date. And Watson is given the line to explain away the absence of a hat clearly identified with the Master.

There has been a certain move to sneer at the twelve Holmesian contributions from Universal, but they all have their points. Uncertain as to the direction the modern-dress concept was to take them, the first three films are spy-heavy with espionage themes, but this is then abandoned for more generally mysterioso motifs—certainly for the betterment of the series, for it is the middle films which are the most inventive. It is in the middle films, too, that we perceive more of the Conan Doyle source: bits and pieces and touches from the Sacred Writings. For instance, the code of the Dancing Men, but nothing else is utilized in *Secret Weapon*, and the premise of the Dying Detective is a sort of prologue to *Spider Woman*. Somewhat changed, The Musgrave Ritual is the basis for *Faces Death* and The Five Orange Pips for *House of Fear*—and in both cases the adaptations manage to convey the spirit of the source without sticking to the letter. But the final films in the series abandoned the stories altogether, becoming merely "based on the characters created by Sir Arthur Conan Doyle." The best film of the lot, *The Scarlet Claw,* is completely original, not set in England at all but in Canada, and first introduces Holmes at an international occult convention. And yet it violates nothing, and is an excellent show.

But many of the stories are a disappointment, and even though quite a few of them stick to fiendish sensations ("finger murders," "creeper murders," "pajama suicides") most are ordinary and pedestrian. Even the least of them, however, are saved by the vigorous and electric playing of Basil Rathbone, who at times seemed to invest far more into the role than the script demanded, and often treaded so close to the raw edge of dramatic hysteria that we riveted our attention on him and away from the paucity of the script. Most of the films, too, are saved by the masterful direction of Roy William Neill ("dear Mousie," Basil often called him, and relates that while the films had nominal producers and writers Mousie was the final word in all these departments as well, and in general control). Neill, an unsung genius of the camera, brilliantly plumbed every shadow and created the atmosphere that often was the series' primary asset. It's not easy to forget the dread, shrouded moors of *The Scarlet Claw*—far more cloaked in mystery than the Fox Dartmoor of *Hound*—or when Holmes (and, simultaneously, the camera) first realizes in *Faces Death* that the Main Hall floor of Musgrave Manor is a gigantic chessboard. It is Neill's stunning camera in its sure movement through light and shadow which dresses an otherwise empty film in the group.

(The Irish-born Neill, who really was the Renaissance Man of the Hollywood "B" thriller, serving as the producer, co-writer and creative spirit behind even those films in which he did not receive such official billing, died in 1946 shortly after directing the final Rathbone Holmes screen adventure. Universal, with typical studio hype, claimed that it had imported Neill from Europe especially for the series. Actually, even though he had immediately before directed some films in England, he had long labored in Hollywood; among his many credits was Columbia's *The Black Room* of 1934, in which Boris Karloff played a double role in an elaborate Gothic melodrama.)

The Universal series was also felicitous in its casting. Dennis Hoey, one of the most competent British character players in Hollywood, made the most of Inspector Lestrade in more than half the films. Motherly Mary Gordon, a Scottish actress then in her sixties, was to return as Mrs. Hudson: she had appeared as the cheerful and industrious Baker Street landlady already in both the Fox films, and it was a role she was born to play. The villains, too, were impressive. Professor Moriarty is presented twice, each time portrayed by a different actor—Lionel Atwill in *Secret Weapon*, Henry Daniell in *Woman in Green*—and dies irrefutably at the climax of each film. George Zucco, who *had* been Moriarty, plunging off the Tower of London in the Fox *Adventures,* is a German spy in *In Washington.* In the title role of *Spider Woman* Gale Sondergaard was interesting enough to merit a sequel—*The Spider Woman Strikes Back* (1946)—which had nothing to do either with Holmes or the original film. Other players who formed a sort of stock company of familiar faces for the series included the very underrated Gerald Hamer, Miles Mander, Paul Cavanaugh and Hillary Brooke. Hamer's contributions especially will be discussed within the context of his particular films.

Actually, Neill's control of Nigel Bruce's performance as Doctor Watson improved and enlarged the actor's contribution. Contrary to popular legend, the Watson of the Universal films is a much more positive individual than the Watson of the two prior Fox dramas. Of course, nothing could alter Bruce's basically comic characterization, but under Neill it is considerably refined. Interestingly, bringing the role up to modern times helped tone down the period country-squire mannerisms Bruce brought to his costume parts. He was given solo responsibilities in several of the films as well, making him less primarily a foil for Rathbone. He is also a more active partner to Holmes. He is allowed to make some really cogent observations, is a good man (and a good shot) to have about in a tight scrape, and indeed in the climax in at least two of the films (*In Washington* and *Spider Woman*) it is he who saves Holmes after the latter has stupidly allowed himself to be trapped by the enemy. Despite his bad luck with friendships other than Holmes's—in two of the adventures his "old school chums" turn out villains, one of them Colonel Sebastian Moran—he is a loyal companion, worthy of (as Holmes puts it in *House of Fear*) "our long and happy association together."

The first of the twelve Rathbone films for Universal was released in September of 1942. The Universal producer assigned to the series, Howard Benedict, expressed concern over public acceptance of a Holmes transplanted into the present, the hunting cap gone, the cuffed trousers gone, all the Sherlockian props cast away except for the pipe, the first time "this has ever been done with a major character in fiction." Of course the rooms at Baker Street seem somewhat unchanged, still friendly and cozy and cluttered (indeed, the set Universal constructed seemed far more happily crowded with bric-a-brac and delights than the larger, barer Baker Street digs previously occupied at Twentieth Century-Fox), but once the detective leaves his quarters he steps into the 1940s. Audiences will go along with this time travel, Benedict insisted, because the Sherlockian method was free of gadgetry: "Holmes did all his work with his brain. Brain work is the same today as it was fifty years ago."

But the final imprimatur to the change was to come from the son of Sherlock Holmes's creator, Denis P. S. Conan Doyle, in a widely publicized, extraordinarily enthusiastic letter: "My sincere congratulations! This is incomparably the best Sherlock Holmes film ever made. Mr. Basil Rathbone is extremely good as Sherlock Holmes. Mr. Nigel Bruce is perfect as Dr. Watson. The modern setting was a daring experiment which has succeeded admirably. Truly, genius has no age."

(Of course, the Conan Doyle estate stood to gain much from the success of the films. The royalties from the network radio programs and the Universal screen series, coupled with the new editions of the writings the renewed interest in Holmes inspired, were bringing the estate into its most flourishing period.)

The uncertain war news out of Europe made calling the first film *Sherlock Holmes Saves London* unwise and a trifle presumptuous. It was retitled *Sherlock Holmes and the Voice of Terror*. For Americans in the 1940s this film and the eleven that followed comprised a lengthy and detailed cinematic introduction to the master detective attacking the "significant problems of the present day."

Sherlock Holmes
and the Voice of Terror

Our introduction to Holmes and Watson at home in
the 1940s; despite the modernization of backgrounds
the master has not lost his enthusiasm for the violin.

*Universal Pictures, September 1942. Associate Producer,
Howard Benedict. Screenplay by Lynn Riggs and John Bright
("based on the story, "His Last Bow," by Sir Arthur Conan
Doyle. Adopted by Robert D. Andrews.") Directed by John Rawlins.*

CAST

Sherlock Holmes, Basil Rathbone; *Dr. Watson,* Nigel Bruce;
Kitty, Evelyn Ankers; *Sir Alfred Lloyd,* Henry Daniell;
Meade, Thomas Gomez; *Sir Evan Barham,* Reginald Denny; *General Lawford,* Montagu Love; *Jill,* Hillary Brooke;
Mrs. Hudson, Mary Gordon; *Crosbie,* Arthur Blake; *Captain Shore,* Leyland Hodgson; *Admiral Prentice,* Olaf Hytten.

From the very first film and throughout the
series, our first image is of the camera moving up

to a portrait of Rathbone and Bruce, with their
credits superimposed over their stern visages, *before* the title of the film. Under the rest of the credits the camera follows the shadows of the pair as
they move through darkness and ground-fog, accompanied by a wondrously *agitato* musical signature by Frank Skinner.

From transmission towers in Germany come
taunting broadcasts: *"People of Britain, greetings from
the Third Reich. This is the voice you have learned to
fear—this is the Voice of Terror."* Sabotage and destruction is promised, and each specific act—a
munitions factory blown up, a train derailed—
happens minutes after it is gloatingly predicted.
The entire nation is close to panic, and in London
the "Intelligence Inner Council", under attack by
the press, resolves somehow to stop or jam the
broadcasts. Suave Sir Evan Barham (Reginald

Denny) announces he has enlisted the services of Sherlock Holmes: "He is the most extraordinary private investigator of our time." (Also, Holmes's friend Watson was an old schoolmate.) Some of the other members of the Council object to this unorthodox move, especially Sir Alfred Lloyd (Henry Daniell), who calls the detective "theatrical." But Holmes is ushered in, and further criticism is forestalled by another Voice of Terror transmission, and the explosion of a troop train is accurately detailed. The Council is shaken; no one was to have known the exact route of the train. Can Holmes silence the Voice? No, the detective replies, we must keep listening. "I'm convinced the disasters are a mere prelude, a smoke screen, to cover a more diabolical plan." Sir Alfred haughtily demands that Holmes keep the Council informed at all times as to his activities and progress, but this the detective refuses to do.

Holmes and Watson return to Baker Street—it is a concession to the times that the route is sand-bagged because of the bombings, and their driver is a girl, Jill (Hillary Brooke), in the uniform of the British Army Women's Corps, assigned by Sir Evan. Holmes is moodily listening to a BBC transcription broadcast of Beethoven's Fifth—an oscillograph is registering nearby—when a man staggers through the door, a knife in his back. Before he dies he manages to say: "Christopher." It is an agent Holmes had sent "to the dark and sinister alleys of Limehouse." His death is a warning. The two head for that evil section of London.

Prowling through the docks of Limehouse, a knife is thrown at Holmes—a German knife. He and Watson make their way to a cellar club, whose owner, having crossed paths with the detective before, warns "there's an especially ugly lot here tonight," and indeed there is. Finding a table, Holmes ask to see the agent's girl, a waterfront entertainer named Kitty (Evelyn Ankers), who takes the news of his death very hard. Holmes becomes hypnotically persuasive when he asks the girl what "Christopher" can mean. *Our country—England—is at stake. The cutthroats of the world menace us all. You can help stop this savagery. Yes, you, Kitty. You know every nook and corner of London. Your friends can become an army—secret, invisible and mighty.* Stirred by patriotic instincts, Kitty calls the motley underworld group in the cellar to the colors: "England's at stake! Your England as much as anyone else's! No time to think about what side we're on—there's only *one* side, *England,* no matter how high or how low we are! Spread out all over London; find out what 'Christopher' means!"

A posed dramatic trio: Holmes holding the spy Meade at bay.

The world's greatest detective is quite at his ease as he whips up the patriotic zeal of waterfront girl Kitty (Evelyn Ankers).

The Inner Council listens to the snarling, vicious broadcasts of the Voice of Terror. Sir Evan Barham (Reginald Denny) stands soberly to the left, while Sir Alfred Lloyd (Henry Daniell) glowers between Holmes and Watson.

Smartly uniformed, army driver Jill (Hillary Brooke) introduces herself to Holmes and Watson, both dressed for Whitehall. The sandbags behind them—grim protection against the bombings—are another modern reminder. (This was to begin for Miss Brooke a long association with the Universal series.)

The following night the Council listens ashen as the Voice chortles over the destruction of the East India Docks, and the flames can be seen outside the Council windows. Holmes, startling the members, points out that the dock fires were started a few minutes *before* the Voice broadcast; this was no cause and effect, but split-second planning weeks in advance. Holmes further theorizes that the Voice of Terror is actually a recording, and that while the transcription is broadcast from Germany the man himself is in England. At irregular intervals a Nazi plane under cover of a raid lands on an English meadow to pick up. . . .

An excited Kitty interrupts the conference; she and the detective hold a whispered conversation. Holmes must leave at once for a destination he cannot reveal—even to the Council. "Until we meet again, and I sincerely hope we will, take no unnecessary risks. We are all in grave danger!"

(It is pertinent to note here that the smirking, snarling voice used for the Voice of Terror was that of the well-known Universal contract player Edgar Barrier. He is seen nowhere in the film; the broadcasts are his only function.)

Holmes and Watson head again for the Limehouse docks—the old, abandoned *Christopher* dock. They discover Sir Alfred following them, and suddenly realize that they have been trapped by a sinister, gun-carrying leader of a gang of foreign agents. The heavy man (Thomas Gomez) sneers: "I'd hoped the entire Council would have come." But at a signal from Holmes, a crew of waterfront rats springs from nowhere and overpowers the enemy. Only the leader manages to escape—through a trapdoor and away in a launch—and Holmes blames himself. Sir Alfred agrees, angrily: "If you hadn't been so stupidly mysterious and asked Scotland Yard for adequate protection the man would never have got away."

Of course the spy leader, Meade, has only been *allowed* by Holmes to escape; later he shelters in his London flat a girl pickpocket seemingly running from the police: it is Kitty. It is an alliance planned by the detective, and through the girl he learns that something evil is scheduled to happen at Sir Evan's remote country estate, Seven Oaks. Evan is spending some time there, and he is the local air raid warden. As Holmes joins him walking down a dark country lane, sirens are heard; an enemy plane lands on a meadow close by. Evan fires at it, but the plane manages to take off. And is that Meade Holmes sees darting behind some bushes?

Meade returns to his flat, where Kitty—clearly

The oratorical Kitty (standing, left) argues with the wharf types that *our* England's at stake, "no matter how high or how low we are!"

but unstated—serves as his mistress; he exposes to the girl his more startling private fantasies: "When I was a boy, I dreamed a dream. I was dressed in armor, shining armor. I rode over the bodies of underlings; their blood ran out along the gutters like a river. What if this was no dream. What if it was prophecy?"

That night the Council hears the Voice brag of an air invasion the following day on England's "defenseless coast," in the north. Holmes is puzzled; always previously the broadcasts talked of *now,* instead of *tomorrow.* Could this be a ruse to deploy our armies? Then an ancient cabman brings Holmes the news that Meade has been trailed to a small south coast village. The south it is—and a phone call presumably from Downing Street commands the Council to accompany the detective.

In a ruined church on the southern coast—very reminiscent of the bombed cathedral at Coventry—Meade and a handful of followers, all now in black uniforms, await the invasion forces as a welcoming committee. A small squadron of British soldiers led by Holmes easily takes them by surprise. His hands held in the air, Meade sees Kitty run to Holmes, and knows he has been betrayed.

Holmes steps easily into the center stage. The Voice had wanted us to shift our defenses north, to leave the Channel unguarded; the Voice is here in this church, and a member of the Council, for too many secrets have been leaked. The Voice is Sir Evan Barham, who last night fired on a spy plane to warn it away. The Council is aghast: "There's been treason before, but this is beyond belief!" No treason is involved, Holmes explains, for Sir Evan is *not* Sir Evan. "In March 1918 Lieutenant Evan Barham was a prisoner in a German prison camp. There his amazing resemblance to a certain Heinrich von Bork, a brilliant young member of the German Secret Service, sealed young Barham's fate." Von Bork returned to England as Barham in a twenty-year masquerade, a testament to long-range planning. The first giveaway to Holmes was the scar on Evan's face: "The real Barham carried a scar from childhood. This one is only about twenty years old. A detail, but significant." But Barham brought the detective into the case! "A colossal bit of egocentric conceit."

Barham/von Bork smilingly admits all. "Even now our Messerschmitts are roaring overhead. Where are your antiaircraft guns? Preserve your vaunted British vanity as best you may, in this your hour of most humiliating defeat!" But the planes are Spitfires and Hurricanes, returning victorious from dispersing the invasion forces. "Do you really think us so blind," Holmes snarls, "that we would

91

Holmes and Watson are led to a sinister den.

A rather odd-looking brawl, but actually it is our plucky British dock rats who are overpowering foreign agents. (The foreign agents are the ones wearing suits.) Notice that the evil Meade (Thomas Gomez, right) is about to make his getaway.

strip this coast of its defenses because of a voice on a phonograph record?" In the excitement, Meade manages to reach for a concealed gun; when Kitty shouts a warning he shoots the girl before he himself is riddled with bullets. Kitty is dead, and Holmes eulogizes over her fallen body: "This girl merits our deepest gratitude. Our country is honored in having had such loyalty and devotion." (Of course, in the prevailing movie code of the day, good-bad girl Kitty could scarcely be allowed to live at the fade-out. And her sacrifice underscored the nobility of the "little" people caught in the war, a romantic notion of then current propaganda.)

We last see Holmes and Watson in this film at cliffside looking over the Channel, and quoting more or less verbatim the closing lines of Conan Doyle's *His Last Bow,* written some twenty-five years before, yet relevant with a throat-catching charm.

HOLMES: There's an east wind coming, Watson.
WATSON: No, I don't think so. Looks like another warm day.
HOLMES: Good old Watson—the one fixed point in a changing age. There's an east wind coming all the same, such a wind as never blew on England yet. It will be cold and bitter, Watson, and a good many of us may wither before its blast. But it's God's own wind, nonetheless, and a greener, better, stronger land will lie in the sunshine when the storm has cleared.
(Music swells to finish.)

Most of the critics received *Sherlock Holmes and the Voice of Terror* with the same ho-hum attitude Mrs. Hudson granted Watson's revelation in the film that Holmes was on the greatest case "of his, er, *our* career." (Replied the good woman: "Oh, mercy, he *always* is!") But Bosley Crowther in *The New York Times* (September 19, 1942) was enraged

at the time change and the cliché-riddled, routine plot. "It is surprising that Universal should take such cheap advantage of the current crisis to exploit an old, respected fiction character, and that it should do so in a manner which throws suspicion on Britain's administrators. The late Conan Doyle, who obviously never wrote this story, as Universal claims, must be speculating sadly in his spirit world on this betrayal of trust."

(Of course, nothing of *His Last Bow* was used with the exception of the closing passage, and the fact that the World War I spy whom Holmes pursues is also named von Bork. It was a stipulation of the Conan Doyle estate at first that the scenarios be based at least in part on the original stories. Universal's compliance was far from total.)

Howard Barnes in the New York *Herald Tribune* was concerned that youngsters might not realize Holmes was prowling around in the gaslit era, and questioned the taste of the transposition. "Whatever Sherlock did against appropriate backgrounds and with appropriate crimes to solve, such as catching a marauding hound, constituted first-rate, old-fashioned melodrama. As a sort of intelligence officer in the present conflict, the detective is bizarre and ineffective." He considered Nigel Bruce "highly unsatisfactory" as a latter-day Watson, and concluded: "My advice to Universal is to leave Sherlock Holmes in the period to which he so peculiarly belonged."

It was not advice Universal was interested in taking. The studio was committed to a twentieth-century Holmes, and at any rate box-office returns indicated that audiences responded to the film—at least to its novelty—and not to the critics. So, prepared for release a scant three months later, Universal began a second Sherlock Holmes adventure, again dealing with espionage and current headlines, but with one important addition the studio hoped would make all the difference: Professor Moriarty.

Sherlock Holmes and the Secret Weapon

Universal Pictures, January 1943. Associate Producer, Howard Benedict. Screenplay by Edward T. Lowe, W. Scott Darling and Edmund L. Hartman, based on "The Dancing Men" by Sir Arthur Conan Doyle. Directed by Roy William Neill.

CAST

Sherlock Holmes, Basil Rathbone; *Watson,* Nigel Bruce; *Charlotte,* Kaaren Verne; *Moriarty,* Lionel Atwill; *Lestrade,* Dennis Hoey; *Peg Leg,* Harold DeBecker; *Dr. Tobel,* William Post Jr.; *Mrs. Hudson,* Mary Gordon; *Mueller,* Paul Fix; *Braun,* Robert O. Davis; *Sir Reginald,* Holmes Herbert; *Brady,* Harry Cording; *Kurt,* Phillip Van Zandt.

Not only did this film begin Dennis Hoey's career as Inspector Lestrade, it gave directorial reins to Roy William Neill for a significant upgrading of the series. As critic Andrew Sarris was to comment in *The Village Voice* years later (August 18, 1975), "the Holmes series with Basil Rathbone and Nigel Bruce got better as it went along, particularly when Roy William Neill was at the helm."

But any comparison with "The Dancing Men" (the story adapted for this film by Darling and Lowe, two journeyman programmer writers) stretches credulity. Holmes's decoding of the crudely sketched pattern of dancing figures which in the Doyle tale frightened a housewife has been abandoned, with only the code itself surviving, patched into a tale of wartime espionage. The original story, dealing long-range with Chicago gangsterdom, might have been as interesting.

For a time the film was to be titled *Sherlock Holmes Fights Back,* somewhat oblique in meaning today but in 1943 a clear reference to the war effort and Holmes's contribution to a beleaguered Britain. Ultimately however it was decided to give the film somewhat more range with the title suggestion that not only was Sherlock returning fire, but with incredible, fantastic new weaponry.

The film opens at an inn nestled in the mountains of neutral Switzerland, where a crafty old gray-haired bookseller *seems* to be organizing "for Berlin" the kidnapping of the young inventor of a new bombsight, while warning his two cohorts that "amateur English detective" Sherlock Holmes, is out to save their intended victim. We next see the bookseller—and of course, it is Holmes himself in disguise—at the door of the young Swiss, Dr. Franz Tobel (William Post Jr.) plotting his escape aboard a Royal Air Force plane and packing the four parts of the invention in a hollow thick volume of William Shakespeare.

We are next at 221-B Baker Street, where Holmes places the book on an open shelf, assuring Tobel that the American writer Poe was right about the most obvious hiding place being best. Holmes must rush off to meet a cabinet minister, leaving Tobel in Watson's care, and both doctors settle down to sleep till dawn.

But young Tobel has a secret assignation in London, a girl named Charlotte (Kaaren Verne), and stealthily hurries off to meet her, unaware he is being shadowed. He gives Charlotte an envelope; "if anything happens to me," the envelope is to go to Sherlock Holmes. Leaving his girlfriend, Tobel is attacked in the street below, but an alert air raid warden manages to frighten away the assailant. There is a scent of opium in the night.

The next morning's demonstration of the bombsight is a complete success: "It will revolutionize aerial bombardment." Back at Sir Reginald's office at Whitehall, however, Tobel refuses to turn over the plans, intending to supervise the manufacture of the mechanical parts from a small office. "I have devised a plan to guard my invention—a plan as intricate as the bombsight itself." Sir Reginald (Holmes Herbert) is aghast at the young scientist's stubborn independence, but as he is a citizen of Switzerland, Scotland Yard—in the person of Inspector Lestrade (Dennis Hoey)—cannot officially be put on the case. Holmes, however, is not a governmental employee, and will stay. "Glad to have you hanging about," sneers Lestrade.

Events move quickly. Tobel distributes the four parts of his bombing device to four different Swiss craftsmen living in London, with instructions to reproduce in quantity. Then he disappears. Holmes traces down the girl Charlotte, but the message she has for him reads simply: *"We meet again, Mr. Holmes."* This was not the paper Tobel put in the envelope; that had been a drawing of figures. Had any stranger been in her apartment? Only a workman, to fix lights that had suddenly gone out. A big man, with heavy lids, and a slight film over his pupils, eyes like a snake. "Dr. Tobel is being held by one of the most brilliant men in the history of crime," Holmes shouts. "Come along, Watson, there isn't a moment to lose!" England is at stake, and the antagonist is Professor Moriarty.

Disguised as a "murderous Lascar," Ram Singh, Holmes prowls Soho. In a vile den he comes face to face with Professor Moriarty, who recognizes him—but this is Holmes's intent, to bring them together. The detective pleads with Moriarty and his sense of country, but the avarice of the master criminal is overriding. Besides, he welcomes the opportunity to triumph over his old enemy. At gunpoint he forces Holmes to lie in the false bottom of an old sea chest (a faint hearkening to the Conan Doyle *Disappearance of Lady Frances Carfax*), intending to drop the chest from a ship at sea. Interestingly, it is clever Watson—he has followed his friend into Soho, accompanied by Lestrade—who observes two seamen struggling with a far too heavy box, and effects a rescue.

"Moriarty is *dead*," sputters Lestrade (and indeed, although no reference is made to that adventure at another studio, he *had* fallen from the Tower scant years before). Holmes rushes to Charlotte's flat, and, tracing the impressions made by Tobel on the message pad, brings forth the pattern of dancing men. He handily breaks most of the code—three names Holmes divines as the craftsmen to whom Tobel had secretly entrusted bombsight parts. Moriarty has the cipher too, and of course the men are dead. A few hours later, the Professor kidnaps the fourth Swiss, elderly and bearded, and brings him to his waterfront hideaway. But is there something familiar about the old man? Holmes unveils himself.

The Professor's stronghold is opulent, and Moriarty himself—a successful man of his profession—is comfortable in smoking jacket as he playfully asks his captive: "What shall it be, Holmes? The gas chamber, the cup of hemlock, or a simple bullet through the brain?" Holmes chides the Professor. Is he after all a simple cutthroat? *He* would have something more imaginative to offer.

Professor Moriarty (Lionel Atwill), who certainly believes in formal dress, struggles with Holmes, above an artist's visualization of a gun battle at the Limehouse docks.

Holmes in disguise, struggling with wharf rats. An unshaven Harry Cording, playing his usual waterfront thug role, is on the left.

More disguises! As Moriarty's German thugs kidnap another Swiss craftsman, they do not realize it is Holmes behind the beard.

An apprehensive scene not in the film—Kaaren Verne shudders between Holmes and Watson at the terrors unleashed by war and Moriarty.

The bombsight in operation. Observing along with the detective is Inspector Lestrade (Dennis Hoey, in his first appearance in the series), as Holmes—in his "This fortress England" speech—quotes Churchill for the first time, and uncredited.

Moriarty cannot even content himself with being the winner, for after all the detective allowed himself to be captured. Then Holmes makes a most bizarre suggestion. "Do you know that a man dies when he loses five pints of blood?" The life is drawn slowly and exquisitely, while the victim is in full possession of his faculties until the end. Speedily Moriarty straps Holmes on a handy downstairs operating table. "Drop by drop, Holmes. In a way I'm almost sorry; you were a stimulating influence for me." Moans the dying detective: "I shall be conscious long after you're dead, Moriarty."

Of course it's all a play for time, for Scotland Yard, rather clumsily, is following a trail of paint droppings. Both Tobel and Holmes are rescued, and the spies are rounded up as they dash into the night. The Professor, however, has hidden himself for later escape through a secret passage in his laboratory. But behind the panel is Holmes with a revolver, waiting for him, looking little the worse

for his ordeal. The sound of whirling mechanism he had heard earlier made him suspect a door, Holmes remarks drily, and Moriarty counters he guessed Holmes had known. It would not have mattered much, as the passage is outfitted with a trap—triggered "behind me, of course"—so that any pursuer would fall sixty feet into the sewers below. Watson makes an unexpected entrance, and Moriarty pushes Holmes to one side and rushes into the passage. There is a scream. "Poor Moriarty. I neglected to warn him. It seems some careless person came across his trap door and left it open. Come along, Watson."

In an epilogue, as the detective and his friend watch British planes outfitted with Tobel bombsights in formation overhead, Holmes is allowed a bravura curtain.

WATSON: Things are looking up, Holmes. This little island's still on the map.

98

HOLMES: Yes. This fortress—built by Nature for herself. This blessed plot, this Earth, this realm, this England.

No one in Hollywood could read those lines with the perfection of Basil Rathbone.

A baffling bit of casting in *Sherlock Holmes and the Secret Weapon* was the use of splendidly saturnine Henry Daniell, featured as a red-herring Cabinet minister in the first Universal film, here in the brief role of a Scotland Yard man in the final car pursuit of the Professor. He hardly says two words, and it is a waste—but Universal makes it up to him towards the end of the series when he is given the opportunity to portray Moriarty. He does as well with the role as his two predecessors, with even perhaps a trace more deviltry. Note, too, that this is the second recent American film in which Moriarty supposedly dies in a plunge—although sixty feet down a waterfront sewer the corpus delecti may be less recoverable. As Joseph Pihodna points out in the New York *Herald Tribune* (January 5, 1943) in a mildly favorable review: "There is, however, considerable doubt as to Moriarty's death. The chances are that Universal will see fit to bring him back."

The New York *Journal-American* also thought well of the film: "It is all interesting enough, smoothly played and quite up to par." (1/5/43) Happy at the respectable success of their new prestige series, Universal plunged immediately into the third film in the lineup. Espionage was once more the keynote, but the gimmick this time was to bring Sherlock Holmes to modern-day America.

A disguised Holmes and the young inventor arrange an ingenious hiding place for the bombsight.

Sherlock Holmes in Washington

Holmes is concealing the microfilm in the match cover. We have the opportunity to study his curious coiffure in full frontal view.

Universal Pictures, April 1943. Associate Producer, Howard Benedict. Screenplay by Bertram Millhauser and Lynn Riggs. Original story by Millhauser from characters created by Sir Arthur Conan Doyle. Directed by Roy William Neill.

CAST

Sherlock Holmes, Basil Rathbone; *Watson,* Nigel Bruce; *Nancy Partridge,* Majorie Lord; *William Easter,* Henry Daniell; *Heinrich Hinkle,* George Zucco; *Howe,* Don Terry; *Mr. Ahrens,* Holmes Herbert; *Senator Babcock,* Thurston Holmes; *Detective Grogan,* Edmund MacDonald; *Cady,* Bradley Page; *Bart Lang,* Gavin Muir.

Abruptly about-facing the policy of heavy Victorian atmospheres of the first two films, *Sherlock Holmes in Washington* provided Universal's master detective with his first American adventure. The settings were no longer crooked Limehouse streets or English manor houses, but the United States capital in wartime. It was the ultimate step in modernizing the Canon.

The film was hardly an unqualified success; Holmes seemed slightly a transplant, saved only by Rathbone's still brilliant impersonation—though even his studiedly modish hairstyle and wide-brimmed modern tweedy hat seemed somehow at odds. Another performance helped the film along as well—the ressurrection of a crackling good turn-of-the-century monster into World War II affairs: George Zucco, so memorable as Moriarty in *The Adventures,* was cast as a devious German agent in wartime Washington. Whether masquerading as a prim antiques dealer, or gloating as he prepares to dispatch Holmes in the finale, he is a superb villain. (Henry Daniell, also among the players, was later—in *The Woman in Green*—to be given a chance at Moriarity, as well.)

Though robbed of his supportive English-fog surroundings, Basil Rathbone nonetheless made the most of his sea change, and won the plaudits of most of the critics. "This picture is a pleasure," crooned the New York *Post* for May 29, and proceeded to detail the reason why: "What a public thinker that man Rathbone is! You can practically see the mightly muscles of his mind tense, grab, and get to the heart of the toughest mystery!" In *Sherlock Holmes in Washington,* the tensing, throbbing Rathbone may well have been overacting, for the mystery at the core of the film was hardly all that demanding. (Indeed, the problem confronting Holmes, as we shall see, is nothing more than a Hitchcock-style MacGuffin, a bit of nothing passed along from player to player, jerking Holmes along behind in pursuit.) But it is a pleasing enough story, however slight, and the change in backdrops adds to the interest—although we fervently hope it is a one-time-only Holmesian defection, and that he soon will be back where he belongs.

Sherlock Holmes in Washington starts out familiarly enough in Baker Street, after a curious transatlantic prologue in which we follow wispy senior clerk John Grayson (played by an unbilled Gerald Hamer, who was to contribute several superb characterizations to the Universal Holmes films), crossing by plane from London to New York, and boarding the Washington Express. His movements are being closely watched by spy William Easter (a sinister Daniell) and his gang, who rightly suspect that it is the clerk who is transporting secret plans, and not the ace British diplomat making the same journey—a diversion "so old it's new!" Before they can get at him, Grayson mingles in the train's club car, having a drink and exchanging addresses with an American senator ("have a grape juice—from my home state"), admiring the pet mice carried in a cage by an eccentric old lady, lighting the cigarette of a pretty girl and cavalierly dropping his book of matches into her purse. But then the train is plunged into darkness and Grayson disappears.

We are then transported to the comfortable Holmesian digs in London, where a Home Office official details Grayson's abduction to the detective and implores him to retrieve the secret document the agent was carrying "before it can be used against us." (The plans were on two large sheets of legal paper; "too bulky to swallow," Watson muses, and *dry,* Holmes retorts with only a trace of a twinkle, fearfully dry.) The pair must hurry at once to America—"a bomber is waiting for you at Croyden"—and Watson, though forced to miss a cricket match, is eager to acquaint himself with the game of baseball.

Before leaving England, however, Holmes visits the quiet London sidestreet where Grayson shared a home with his unsuspecting mother. In a cluttered study the detective finds evidence—ashes in the fireplaces of the ragpaper used in official documents, cameras, special lenses, bits of microfilm, a collection of American matchbooks—which lead his agile mind to the conclusion that the agent had disposed of the bulky secrets by microfilming them, concealing the tiny celluloid inside the cover of a book of matches, "unknown in London but common in America," similar to the ones with "V" for war victory printed on them scattered all over the room. It is a breathless exercise in mental gymnastics, made less suspect when an attempt is made on Holmes's life as he leaves the house: a cement block crashes down from the roof. The pair is off to America to seek out a matchbook.

In Washington, Holmes and Watson are taken on the usual tourist route past the national monuments; soon the body of Grayson, packed in a trunk, is delivered to their hotel. Holmes instructs the American federal men who have accompanied him to make a minute examination of the corpse, then apologizes for implying anything might escape their investigations: "I'm so accustomed to working quite alone at my lodgings in Baker Street that I sometimes forget the more modern scientific methods so particularly effective here in America."

The club car in which Grayson disappeared has been ransacked, and Holmes quickly guesses—to the amazement of the American police, who have yet to be exposed to his methods—that all the occupants, including the mice-cage woman and the senator, have recently been assaulted. His interest quickens when a train steward tells him of the girl whose cigarette Grayson lighted. Could he have passed her the match folder? The girl's identity is unknown, but she was met at Washington station by a Navy lieutenant, and the steward observed the young flier placing a ring on the girl's finger. Holmes is pleased with the man.

Much of the remainder of the film concerns itself with the passing of the V-for-victory match folder from one unsuspecting smoker to another, each igniting more of the matches inside. ("I'd give anything to get my hands on that document," says one of the Washington diplomatic corps grimly lighting a cigarette, not knowing that very briefly

The villainous foreign agent Hinkle (George Zucco) menaces Nancy Partridge (Marjorie Lord) and Sherlock Holmes.

the microfilmed document, glued inside the matchbook, is *in* his hands.) Holmes manages to trace the girl, debutante Nancy Partridge, but she has already been kidnapped. He deduces from scientific traces that the old blanket in which Grayson's body had been wrapped had perhaps seen service in an antique shop, so he and Watson make the rounds of such establishments. Noticing an antique store selling imitation Chippendale at prices the authentic furniture might bring, Holmes feels he has found his lair—a place capable of far greater villainy than price-inflation.

Holmes is correct. The shop's proprietor, suave Richard Stanley, is actually Herr Heinrich Hinkle, "in 1914 secret agent of the German Kaiser; since then, head of the most insidious spy ring that ever existed." The master spy, wonderfully played by Zucco, carries on a cat-and-mouse encounter with Holmes, who skillfully avoids being sliced in half by a Moorish death-trap:

HOLMES: The Moors were an incredibly inventive people, weren't they?

HINKLE: Yes. The piece was in shocking condition when I got hold of it, but I had it restored.

HOLMES: Very lively, *now*.

Lowering his guard, the detective allows himself to be captured, but he and the girl are rescued by a brave Watson and the FBI, while Hinkle escapes behind an Egyptian sarcophagus through one of the antique store's many secret passages, of course carrying the vital matchbook with which throughout the scene he had abstractedly been lighting his pipe. Holmes rightly guesses that the spy's next move would be against the senator with whom Grayson had last talked on the train, and hurries to the Senate chambers to warn the man. The politician's surprised retort to his danger has distinct overtones of a Moriarty-style parallel: "Why, Richard Stanley's one of the most respectable citizens in Washington! Has been for years!" (Like Sir Evan in *Voice of Terror,* this German agent has burrowed himself into an enemy land—with remarkable foresight—a long time ago.) Again Holmes allows Hinkle to draw a gun on him, and feigns nervousness. "Do you mind if I smoke? Have you a match?" The obliging German hands the detective the MacGuffin—there is but one match left—just before the police swarm over him.

Our last look at Holmes and Watson in this film is driving down Pennsylvania Avenue, the Capitol building in the distance. They are heading back to

Holmes goes through the effects of the mysteriously disappeared Grayson.

The American detective, Grogan (Edmund MacDonald), joins Holmes in questioning Nancy's aunt; the girl has disappeared.

The body of Grayson tumbles out of the trunk. Gavin Muir—in several of the films in the Universal series—is among the onlookers, second from left.

Holmes discovers a secret door in the rear of a Washington antique shop—a rather opulent shop, from the look of the Egyptian artifacts!

wartime London, and their conversation is worth the attention of patriots:

HOLMES: This is a great country, Watson.

WATSON: It certainly is, my dear fellow.

HOLMES: Look. Up there ahead. The Capitol—the very heart of this democracy.

WATSON: Democracy—the only hope for the future, eh, Holmes?

HOLMES: It is not given for us to peer into the mysteries of the future. But in the days to come, the British and American people for their own safety and the good of all will walk together in majesty and justice and in peace.

WATSON: That's magnificent. I quite agree with you.

HOLMES: Not with me. With Mr. Winston Churchill. I was quoting from the speech he made not long ago in that very building.

There had been speculation at Universal about building further adventures for Sherlock Holmes laid in America, quite logical speculation, for certainly, having once modernized the Canon, one could go the full distance and reset the stories in the New World. But the wrenching of Holmes from his familiar surroundings was felt too disturbing, and the mix did not quite work. Despite mild amusement at Watson's coping with such cultural deviations as Sunday newspaper comics, chewing gum and the Brooklyn Dodgers, *Sherlock Holmes in Washington* lacked a strong story, and as a mystery offered little more than a climactic gunfight. The studio's next Holmesian episode, released less than a half year later, returned the detective to old haunts, not only bringing him back to England but an England of swirling fogs and murder mansions; in short, a return to an old, recognizable school of mystery. And while the war does intrude in the events—in the England of 1943, it could scarcely be ignored—it does not motivate the drama of sinister rituals and a cursed family.

The final encounter. Hinkle thinks he has the draw on Holmes and garrulous Senator Babcock (Thurston Hall).

Sherlock Holmes Faces Death

A marvelously atmospheric studio shot with Nigel Bruce happily in the foreground.

Universal Pictures, September 1943. Screenplay by Bertram Millhauser. Based on a story by Sir Arthur Conan Doyle. Produced and Directed by Roy William Neill.

CAST

Sherlock Holmes, Basil Rathbone; *Watson,* Nigel Bruce; *Inspector Lestrade,* Dennis Hoey; *Dr. Sexton,* Arthur Maretson; *Sally Musgrave,* Hillary Brooke; *Brunton,* Halliwell Hobbes; *Hrs. Howells,* Minna Phillips; *Captain Vickery,* Milburn Stone; *Philip Musgrave,* Gavin Muir; *Major Langford,* Gerald Hamer; *Lieutenant Clavering,* Vernon Downing; *Captain MacIntosh,* Olaf Hytten; *Geoffrey Musgrave,* Frederic Worlock.

The next film in the Universal series was the first in the studio's updating concept not to entrap Holmes in the problems of World War II, its spies, bombsights or secret plans. The film *does* give passing reference to the global struggle, but as the New York *Herald Tribune* reviewer noted with a sigh of relief, "at least this one has practically nothing to do with the Nazis." (10/8/43) Instead, *Sherlock Holmes Faces Death* is the first Universal Holmesian saga to make full use of a Sir Arthur Conan Doyle story. Despite acknowledgments in the credits, previous entries had not bothered with very much of "His Last Bow" or "The Dancing Men." Here, however, the treatment is richer, and while only "a story" by Doyle is identified as source, it is very familiarly "The Musgrave Ritual."

What all the critics took pains to admire ("it is strictly a matter of clutching your courage and trying to whisper without a quaver," advises the *New*

York Times), and what *is* admirable about the film is the wonderful sense of atmosphere, of mystery, of sepulchral gloom that oozes like a fog throughout the melodrama. No government spy work for Sherlock this time; despite his being contemporized by the studio right up to the minute, this adventure was, paradoxically, a return to all of the shadowy Victorian trappings of a richly old-fashioned mystery. That the mood is so well sustained is due in no small measure to the talents of Roy Neill, and we note this is the first film in the series he produces as well as directs.

Interestingly, just as the Doyle tale on which it is based is *sans* Watson (and told first-person by Holmes himself), *Sherlock Holmes Faces Death* begins without the great detective. Watson is discovered as the doctor in charge of a retreat for convalescent officers, Hulstone Towers in Northumberland, ancestral home of the Musgraves, haunted by ghosts and the wailing of lost souls heard on the limewalks. The Musgraves have "opened their home" to these patients, but it is a grim, cheerless place. The officers, all suffering from shattered nerves, are brooding and eccentric; Sexton, the doctor assisting Watson, is stabbled—though not seriously—by an unknown person; and the clock in the tower strikes thirteen, an event local legends say precedes the death of a Musgrave. Watson decides to hurry back to London and consult with his old Baker Street friend.

Holmes returns with Watson to Musgrave Manor, and his immediate impression is one of foreboding: "Houses, like people, have definite personalities and this place is positively ghoulish!" Why should a pile of leaves be raked in a pile before a greenhouse ("No gardener in the world would do that")? At the bottom of the pile they find the body of Geoffrey Musgrave, the oldest of two Musgrave brothers. Soon Inspector Lestrade is on the scene, interrogating younger brother Philip, his sister Sally, and a sparse staff headed by the enigmatic butler Brunton, who listens at keyholes, and the strong-willed housekeeper Mrs. Howells, who reminds Holmes of a trunk-murderess he has known. An extraordinary house.

The next evening a curious ritual takes place: amid thunder and lightning raging outside, Sally Musgrave—as next in line after Philip—must recite a series of ancient, seemingly meaningless heraldic verses handed down from generation to generation of Musgraves, a family tradition. As she haltingly repeats the ritual, helped over the rough passages by Brunton, a stab of lightning shatters a stained-glass window and topples a suit of armor standing beside her with a crash. The girl is too unnerved to continue.

Is that Watson's footstep on the stair? Holmes at home at Baker Street, being served breakfast by Mrs. Hudson (played through the series by Mary Gordon, inspiredly cast).

Murder at Musgrave Hall, and Inspector Lestrade (Dennis Hoey) resents Holmes's presence. The rake has been used to pile leaves over the body of Geoffrey Musgrave. Captain Vickery (Milburn Stone) is between them.

Weird happenings continue to occur. The ancient Brunton, drinking heavily, proposes a toast to the Musgraves: "Some were murderers and some worse, but they all knew how to keep a secret and so do I"—and then disappears. The next day Holmes and Watson stroll to the village (Universal's familiar backlot European village streets) and stop inside a pub curiously titled The Rat and the Raven (a very young Peter Lawford playing a sailor can be seen at the bar during an earlier scene). As Sally drives up in her roadster to find Holmes, for her brother Philip has also vanished, the pub's tame raven—a scavenger bird, the detective notes, "they can smell a carcass a mile off"—flies outside and begins pecking at the trunk of the car. Inside they discover Philip's body.

Lestrade suspects the missing butler as killer, but Holmes is not so sure. Lestrade also suspects a convalescing American pilot with whom Sally had fallen in love and Philip had quarreled, a Captain Vickery (played by studio contract player Milburn Stone years before he was to achieve fame on television's *Gunsmoke*). Holmes feels certain the answer is somewhere in the ritual. The heraldic terms used in the rhymes—king, queen, knave—may, the detective muses, be chess terms. Then, in one of the series' most stunningly effective scenes, Holmes, while descending the stairs to the Main Hall,

realizes that the Main Hall floor of Musgrave Manor is indeed a gigantic chessboard!

The residents of the house then become human pieces in the chess puzzle outlined by the rituals. Directed by the lines, Holmes begins to explore secret passageways leading to a burial crypt in unused cellars bellow the Hall. (The sets are from *Dracula*.) Here they find Brunton's murdered body. Beside the corpse Holmes spies an old document and some scratches near the butler's hand—a dying attempt to identify the killer. He covers the marks with a handkerchief, and we naturally guess it is all a ruse. Much later, in the dark, Dr. Sexton creeps down into the crypt. As he reaches for the cloth, a hand grasps his arm in a viselike grip. Holmes has his man.

There follows some explanatory dialogue about Sexton's hopes to marry Sally, about the document making Sally of the supposedly land-poor Musgraves "the richest woman in England"; Holmes for a few moments allows Sexton to wrestle his gun away from him (it's loaded with blanks) so as to trick the fellow into a confession: "These egomaniacs are always so much more chatty when they feel they have the upper hand."

Sally is disturbed when Holmes informs her that the newly-found Musgrave Crown Grant is worth millions. "The people on this land . . . it's their

In the nearby village, our friends visit the local pub, The Rat and Raven. A good view of Universal's fabled backlot.

In a quiet corner of the pub, Sally Musgrave worriedly consults the detective, while Watson enjoys a stein of lager. Note the bottom of the propaganda sign: " . . . can cost lives!")

Why is that bloodthirsty raven so interested in the trunk of Sally's roadster? Might there be a body inside? Indeed there might.

Mrs. Howells (Minna Phillips) warns butler Brunton (Halliwell Hobbes) to keep silent.

A drunken Brunton speaks to Holmes in rhyme, reciting the cryptic Musgrave ritual.

As Holmes and Watson peer down the stairs, they perceive the Hall floor is—a giant chessboard!

homes I'll be taking. Do you think I'm going to kick these people out?" She tosses the old parchment into the fireplace.

Later, we eavesdrop on Holmes and Watson passing through a Northumberland village on their drive home.

WATSON: It's a grand gesture—one that she might regret.

HOLMES: I don't think so, Watson. There's a new spirit abroad in the land. The old days of grab and greed are on their way out. We're beginning to think of what we *owe* the other fellow, not just what we're compelled to give him. The time is coming, Watson, when we cannot fill our bellies in comfort while the other fellow goes hungry, or sleep in warm beds while others shiver in the cold. And we shan't be able to kneel and thank God for blessings before our shining altars while men anywhere are kneeling in either physical or spiritual subjection.

WATSON: You may be right, Holmes . . . I hope you are.

HOLMES: And, God willing, we'll live to see that day, Watson.

It's a splendid, stirring wartime speech, and for once not a quote from either Churchill or Roosevelt; in both length and fervor scriptwriter

As Holmes, Watson, and Captain Vickery look on, Sally decides to toss the land grant into the fireplace.

Millhauser outdid himself, and interestingly allowed Holmes to prophecy the more democratic climate of what would be the postwar British government. (Would the real Holmes have spoken this way? At least the critic for the *New York Times* seemed to think it in character, or at least to his liking: "The days of grab and greed are over, remarks that remarkable man, Mr. Holmes. It gives one new confidence that he should think so.")

At any rate, Rathbone, with, as the *Times* pointed out, his "absolutely mathematical precision and clipped peremptory tones," was becoming more and more set in the role, comfortably able to project the spirit of the great detective in every conceivable mood. It remained only for producer Neill and scriptwriter Millhauser to come up with more challenges, more interesting puzzles, enveloping atmospheres. So, at the start of the following year, Sherlock Holmes was given a novel new villain against which to test his mettle: the female of the species.

Note: The Musgrave ritual in the film differed significantly from the litany and responses invented by Doyle for the parent story. Scriptwriter Millhauser buried a number of chesspiece terms and royalty within the recitation in order to direct Holmes to the Hall's subterranean secrets.

In the crypt Holmes is confronted by the murderer, Dr. Sexton (Arthur Margetson). (The set was also used for *Dracula*.)

Between *Faces Death* and *Spider Woman*, however, Basil Rathbone and Nigel Bruce made a brief cameo appearance in a film entirely unrelated to the Universal series. They portrayed Holmes and Watson, however, quite unmistakably.

All the principals clutter a melodramatic group pose.

Crazy House

A non-Sherlockian look at *Crazy House*, but more representative of the film as a whole, as Cass Daley adopts a threatening stance between Ole Olsen and Chic Johnson.

Universal Pictures, October 1943. Screenplay by Robert Lees and Frederic I. Rinaldo. Associate Producer, Earle C. Kenton. Directed by Edward F. Cline. Starring Ole Olsen, Chic Johnson, Cass Daley, Patric Knowles, Martha O'Driscoll, Thomas Gomez.

While the titles to *Crazy House* list Rathbone and Bruce among a large list of guest performers, there is a curious reversal of importance: all the names are shown on screen in a credit column arranged (to please the eye) according to their width, so because "Nigel Bruce" is much shorter than "Basil Rathbone," the doctor is billed a good many names above the detective—who gets *last* listing!

The film is a showcase for the peculiar humor of comics Olsen and Johnson, who had scored nearly two years before at Universal with a screen version of their stage success, *Hellzapoppin*—a rapid-fire succession of insane humor resembling a prototype of "Laugh-In." The current film begins with this same format, supposedly documenting the Hollywood hysteria at the comedians' return after finishing a Broadway revue, *Tons O' Fun*. Every Universal contract player (Andy Devine, Allan Jones, Leo Carrillo and many others) was pressed into service to show panic at the coming of Olsen and Johnson: even armed guards were lined up behind sandbags at the studio gates. Rathbone and Bruce were filmed while shooting *Spider Woman;* the dangling pygmy skeleton used in the upcoming film is clearly seen in the sequence. (Because it is not so dramatically lit and photographed as it would be later we realize it is actually a realistic cardboard cutout. The set used—although the minutiae suggested the Baker Street rooms—was in fact the room in which spider specialist Dr. Ordway was to die.) Watson bursts in to find Holmes holding curved pipe and magnifying glass. Here is the complete exchange.

WATSON: I say, Holmes, there's a lot of excitement in the studio. Everyone's running for the air raid shelter. Do you know what's happening?

HOLMES: Olsen and Johnson have arrived.

WATSON: What!? How do you know?

HOLMES: *I am Sherlock Holmes. I know everything.*

Spider Woman

Standard mood shot of Holmes and Watson, dressed in greatcoats because of the January release of the film.

Universal Pictures, January 1944. Screenplay by Bertram Millhauser. Based on a story by Sir Arthur Conan Doyle. Produced and directed by Roy William Neill.

CAST

Sherlock Holmes, Basil Rathbone; *Watson,* Nigel Bruce; *Adrea Spedding,* Gale Sondegaard; *Lestrade,* Denis Hoey; *Norman Locke,* Vernon Downing; *Radlik,* Alec Craig; *Mrs. Hudson,* Mary Gordon; *Gilflower,* Arthur Hohl; *Larry,* Teddy Infuhr.

Universal studios began its new year 1944 with a Sherlock Holmes release and a choice for theater owners: the potent subject matter could carry the film instead of the Holmesian name. While in various outlets the picture was known as *Sherlock Holmes and the Spider Woman,* the title unreeling on the screen reduced this just to *Spider Woman*—in the interests of marquee efficiency, no doubt, but indicating that, with a new adventure every few months, the impact of the Sherlockian name had lessened. From this film onwards, in the Universal series, the detective's name was optional—such as *Sherlock Holmes in Pursuit to Algiers*—but never officially within the registered title.

Spider Woman, however, was an interesting initial choice for Holmesian anonymity. It offered the punch of a fascinating villain, hopefully strong enough to pull audiences on its own. And the novelty of a woman nemesis for Sherlock added an enticing sexual touch. The film played up the battle of the sexes; Holmes's philosophic comments regarding the perfidy of female evil and the

Trapped in the Deadly
Web of a Silken Killer!

BASIL RATHBONE as Sherlock Holmes
and NIGEL BRUCE as Dr. Watson in

SPIDER WOMAN

with
DENNIS HOEY   VERNON DOWNING
MARY GORDON and
GALE SONDERGAARD
as the Spider Woman

The first Sherlock Holmes film from Universal with the detective's name out of the title.

Lestrade (Dennis Hoey) and Holmes view a murder attempt on the detective: it is a dummy head, with prominent nose, on the pillow.

danger of female wiles are enough to send any feminist to arms. However, his judgments regarding the aptly-named "Spider Woman" are no less than accurate: she is evil. Adrea Spedding is a distaff Moriarty—the comparison is Holmes's own—and she manages to outwit the detective uncomfortably often. She is well played by Gale Sondergaard. The tall, feline actress—indeed, she played a humanized cat in the 1940 version of *The Bluebird*—had appeared in such prestigious motion pictures as *Anthony Adverse* (for which she became the first person to win the Best Supporting Actress Academy Award, in 1936) and *The Life of Emile Zola* (1937), but she is best remembered for her sinister roles. In *Spider Woman* her portrayal is so superb, that she manages at times even to overshadow Rathbone's electrified Sherlock.

It is actually an uneven script, with Millhauser pasting together scenes and suggestions from a variety of Doyle sources. The opening, with its

murders-as-suicides and borrowed premise from "The Dying Detective," is interesting, and there are a number of memorable moments, dark and chilling, throughout. But the film's ending is somewhat unsatisfying—as Holmes stupidly allows himself to be target for Watson's bullets, tied up behind a life-size cutout of Hitler (the only concession to the war this time) at a shooting gallery. The weakness of this finish is disappointing, especially as much of what has gone before evokes the same sort of shuddery terror as might a crawling spider. To quote Ms. Wanda Hale's summation in the New York *Daily News* (1/15/44): "Gale Sondergaard is so good you almost wish she would get the best of the great detective."

Actually, most of the critical notices were favorable. G. E. Blackford in the New York *Journal-American* felt "the current installment of the master-sleuth serial is above the average in plausibility, suspense and interest and has been really

The Spider Woman (Gale Sondergaard) replaces the lid on her sinister pygmy.

quite well presented." Astonishingly, John T. McManus in *P.M. New York* concluded: "I honestly believe this current episode is better plotted in many ways than 'The Speckled Band,' the Conan Doyle story it resembles most." Very little of the film compares to the snake-death tale; Adrea Spedding of the title most resembles the femme fatale of the old-fashioned gothic romance, the classic vamp sending male adversaries to their doom. The nearly outclassed detective finds himself, in the words of the movie's poster copy, "trapped in the deadly web of a silken killer."

Spider Woman starts with all London nervous at a series of "pajama suicides"—a rash of self-inflicted deaths of prominent people occuring in the dark hours of the night, when the victims are in their bedclothes. Where is Sherlock Holmes? Why in Scotland, on a fishing holiday with Watson. But from what he reads in the papers, the detective is sure the suicides are actually murders, for the police could find no notes which suicides invariably leave. "There's something uncanny about this—monstrous and horrible." But Holmes is no longer up to solving crimes; recently he's been subject to "the most alarming dizzy spells." Moments later he topples into a swiftly-moving stream and is carried away by the torrent. Watson must return to England with the news that Sherlock Holmes has drowned.

The grief of Watson, Mrs. Hudson and even Inspector Lestrade (in a very affecting moment) is moving, as the doctor packs his friend's belongings for shipment to the British Museum. A cranky, aged postman turns up to enrage Watson with slurs against the detective's memory; naturally it is Holmes himself in disguise, not dead after all. In the following incredible dialogue, we are given Sherlockian logic regarding the well-organized gang behind the suicides:

HOLMES:—Directing them is one of the most fiendishly clever minds in all Europe today. I suspect a woman.

WATSON: You amaze me, Holmes. Why a woman?

118

In the basement of the spider house, Holmes unmasks Radlik (Alec Craig) as being an imposter. The latter, releasing his store of deadly insects, manages to escape, however.

HOLMES: Because the method, whatever it is, is peculiarly subtle and cruel. Feline, not canine.

LESTRADE: Poppycock. When a bloke does himself in, that's suicide.

HOLMES: Unless a bloke is driven to suicide; in that case it's murder.

WATSON: Driven? That *sounds* like a woman, doesn't it?

HOLMES: Definitely—a female Moriarty. Clever. Ruthless. And above all, cautious. Therefore, my first step was to give her enough rope by passing out of the picture. . . .

These eyebrow-raising conclusions might well provide ammunition for those who have read in Holmes an underlying hostility towards women. It did not escape Archer Winsten, movie critic of the New York *Post,* that though lacking motive, method or any idea of the culprit Holmes is able to link the crimes to a diabolic femme fatale: he says "if that appeals to your sense of inescapable logic, perhaps the rest of the picture will not seem too childish."

Because Holmes has learned that all the suicides liked to gamble, he disguises himself as an Indian officer, Raja Singh, dark-skinned and turbaned, with a paralyzed arm and a "devotion to the goddess of chance." At a posh London casino he meets the fascinating Adrea Spedding. His losses are heavy. She prevents him from putting a gun to his temple in the shadows of the garden outside. He confesses that he is desperate for money; she tells him how he can borrow the sum he needs on his insurance policy simply by making a new beneficiary.

So far so good. But in the very next scene— Singh is taking tea with Adrea in her flat—the sinister lady has, thanks to a newspaper photo, penetrated Holmes's disguise, and some delicious fencing begins. She spills hot tea on the supposedly paralyzed arm; noting as well the fluid has washed some of the dark-stained skin. Clearly Holmes has been outfoxed; he gamely leaves while he still can. Later, Adrea shares her suspicions with her amiable half-brother Norman (played by Vernon Downing, a series regular always cast in kinky

Adrea Spedding gloats at Holmes, trussed behind the moving target of Hitler at a shooting gallery.

In fine disguise, Holmes tries to extract Adrea's fingerprints.

roles). When he protests that the detective is dead, she replies: "*Is* he? I think not. But if you were to say to me *tomorrow* Sherlock Holmes is dead. . . ."

That night Holmes learns the method of the murders, as a spider is released in the air shaft to Singh's flat. "The bite of the creature drove these pajama suicides to kill themselves." But on the roof he and Lestrade discover a large carrying case with air-holes—and the footprints of a child.

In the days that pass the London press reports the happy news of Holmes's return from the dead. At Baker Street, the detective receives a surprising visitor: Adrea Spedding. She is accompanied by an odd young child, a mute given to quirky hops and movements, whom she identifies as her nephew ("I'm playing nurse today"—"I'm sure you'll give an exceptional performance," fences Holmes). Miss Spedding is there ostensibly to engage Holmes to find Singh—a cunning move—but all

our attention is on the boy, barefootedly snatching at flies. (Raves McManus in *P.M. New York:* "Watch for the brief appearance of a youthful apprentice of the Spider Woman named Teddy Infuhr, aged about seven. The one scene he appears in he captures handily from three such redoubtable scene-stealers as Rathbone, Miss Sondergaard and Nigel Bruce, and all without saying a word.") As the woman and child leave, the boy tosses some candy wrappings in the fireplace. As the paper burns, billows of poisonous smoke fill the room, and Holmes and Watson nearly succumb. The detective barely manages to smash open a window. "What was it?" gasps Watson weakly. "*Death*, my dear fellow. We've been entertaining Miss Adrea Spedding!"

(Interestingly, the deadly fumes are identified by Holmes as from a rare vegetable poison originating in Central Africa, "*the devil's foot*," which Watson re-

Holmes fences with a gypsy fortune teller (Belle Mitchell) who is part of Adrea's gang at the amusement arcade.

122

Lestrade puts the cuffs on the remarkable Miss Spedding in the climactic arcade sequence; the crowd looks on.

members from the Cornish Horrors case—thereby ringing in another reference to the works of Conan Doyle.)

The trail of the spider Holmes has killed, the *lycosa carnivora,* leads the duo to the suburban home of Matthew Ordway, a specialist in rare and exotic insects, and to one of the best scenes in the film. They find Ordway an eccentric elderly man who is unable to distinguish between species of spiders kept in his hothouse basement. Holmes easily spots him for an imposter, but the surprisingly nimble fellow releases some deadly insects as a distraction and makes his escape. Exploring the house, Holmes finds the body of the real Ordway—the one link between the rare spiders and the gang which used them, and that link now gone. In a fireplace they spot the charred remains of what appears to have been a journal of the scientist's travels in Central Africa, with references to something "doglike," "faithful," "immune." What

could it be? Tucked away in a closet Watson makes a grisly discovery: a dangling small skeleton. The ensuing dialogue (here somewhat abridged) not only shows Watson not to be a buffon, but illuminates the great detective's clear-minded reasoning and even his humanity.

HOLMES: That's curious. Ordway's main interest was *in*vertebrates, not vertebrates. And why the skeleton of a child?

WATSON: But it isn't.

WATSON: What?

WATSON: It isn't a child.

HOLMES: Are you sure?

WATSON: Look at all its teeth. And the skull of a normal child of this size—five or six years old— would be much larger than the proportion of the circumference of its chest.

HOLMES: Watson, I've got it! That devil of a woman! Bringing that child to Baker Street to throw

123

me off the track. She knew I had found that tiny footprint; she wanted me to think it was the footprint of a child. Watson, I've been blind—a mole, an owl, a bat! Look here: "poison," "little," "doglike," "faithful to their masters"; able to creep through the smallest openings, the perfect instrument for the spider murders! If you ever see me too cocksure again, fancying myself more clever than Adrea Spedding, just whisper one word to me.

WATSON: What word, Holmes?

HOLMES: *Pygmy!*

Unfortunately, after this dazzling exchange, the film hurtles speedily downhill to a poor climax. Holmes traces the pygmy to the High Holburn Arcade—inspired no doubt by a similarly transplanted pygmy in *The Sign of Four* who also put in time as a sideshow display—but very carelessly finds himself trapped by Adrea and her gang, who tie him behind a moving life-sized cutout of Hitler being used as a shooting gallery target. Conveniently, the patrons are allowed *real bullets* (incredibly, during munitions-scarce wartime!), and it is sure-aimed Watson who raises a rifle. In the nick of time, though, Holmes frees himself, and the gang is rounded up. Inspector Lestrade leads a smiling, unhandcuffed Adrea Spedding out of the arcade.

"A remarkable woman," says Holmes after her, "as audacious and deadly as one of her own spiders." But fancy trying to commit murder in a place like this, Watson sniffs. Holmes disagrees: Adrea Spedding has picked the most logical spot in the world to commit murder—in the middle of a crowd.

The *Spider Woman* character was fairly well received both by the critics and theater audiences, and therefore Universal studios did not long abandon it. After all, she was not eliminated by Holmes at the end of the film, just carted presumably to prison. (Not that being killed in the finale seriously perturbed some master villains; the evil Moriarty was resurrected from certain death *twice* to battle Rathbone on screen.) Three years later Gale Sondergaard returned in *The Spider Woman Strikes Back,* trading on memories of Adrea but a different character entirely, and with Holmes nowhere in sight. This time Miss Sondegaard is the supposedly blind owner of an American ranch, draining blood from young hired companions whom she drugs and kills. The blood is used to feed a carnivorous plant from which she distills a deadly cattle poison. There are no spiders, but interestingly her grotesquely deformed servant (also mute!) is played by the popular horror-film actor Rondo Hatton, Sherlock Holmes's menace in *Pearl of Death.*

The less than satisfying conclusion to the current adventure was not, however, the start of a trend. The very next film in the series, released six months later, was the best mystery Rathbone was to unravel on the screen.

The Scarlet Claw

Holmes and Watson consult with the local police, in the
person of Sergeant Thompson (David Clyde).

*Universal Pictures, June 1944. Screenplay by Edmund L.
Hartmann and Roy William Neill. Original story by Paul
Gangelin and Brenda Weisberg, based on the characters created
by Sir Arthur Conan Doyle. Produced and directed by Roy
William Neill.*

CAST

Sherlock Holmes, Basil Rathbone; *Dr. Watson,* Nigel Bruce;
Potts/Tanner/Ramson, Gerald Hamer; *Lord Penrose,* Paul
Cavanagh; *Emile Journet,* Arthur Hohl; *Judge Brisson,*
Miles Mander; *Marie Journet,* Kay Harding; *Sergeant
Thompson,* David Clyde; *Drake,* Ian Wolfe; *Nora,* Victoria
Horne.

Perhaps it was the singular contribution of
producer-director Roy William Neill, that genius
of mood and atmospheres, who for the first time in
the series co-authored the screenplay. Without
question, in retrospect, *The Scarlet Claw* with its
eerie suspense and expert construction was the
best entry in the entire Universal Holmesian ros-
ter.

At the time, however, it was curiously neglected.
When the film premiered at New York's Rialto
theater, the critics slammed it. For Howard Barnes
in the *Herald Tribune* (5/20/44), "Basil Rathbone
plays Holmes with a rather tired approach to the
project of solving several murders in a village near
Quebec. Nigel Bruce, whose fine talents are
rapidly being buried under the weight of this assignment, does almost nothing to enliven the pro-
ceedings." Bosley Crowther of the *Times*—"our old
friend Sherlock Holmes is snooping around the

"THE RED-DEATH STRIKES."

BASIL RATHBONE AS SHERLOCK HOLMES

NIGEL BRUCE AS DR. WATSON

THE SCARLET CLAW

KAY HARDING · GERALD HAMER
PAUL CAVANAGH
ARTHUR HOHL
MILES MANDER

Poster high art—certainly getting its message across.

misty marshes again"—called the production merely adequate. But actually the film was far more. Michael Druxman in *Basil Rathbone: His Life and His Films* quotes the movie's editor, Paul Landres: "Everybody involved was very excited about this film because we all knew that it was far superior to anything else in the series." The enthusiasm shows.

The superiority of the entry is even more astonishing when one considers these three facts: the story is completely original, it is set not in England but completely in Canada, and it begins with Holmes attending an occult convention!

The only other Universal film to transport the detective to the American continent—*Sherlock Holmes in Washington* (one cannot really count the cameo Hollywood appearance in *Crazy House*)—was a hybrid drama with the setting forced. In *Scarlet Claw* the gloomy Canadian village life which forms the backdrop to the deaths (the Universal

backlot again doing admirable service) seems a perfectly natural milieu for the great detective. He and Watson are at home.

The villagers of the tiny hamlet of La Morte Rouge are terrified; a legendary glowing monster has reappeared, flitting through the nearby fog-shrouded marshes, and sheep have been found dead, their throats cut. The body of Lady Penrose is discovered in the village church, her hand clutching the bell-pull, her neck ripped open. Lord Penrose is quickly contacted: he's addressing a meeting of the Royal Canadian Occult Society in Quebec, some miles away, and to our surprise Holmes and Watson are also in attendance. The detective appears openly skeptical of most supernatural phenomena, while during a seminar Watson recounts the naturalistic explanations for those supposedly psychic manifestations, the Baskerville hound and the Sussex vampire; but when Penrose learns of his wife's murder the conference is ad-

126

The parish priest (George Kirby) of the Canadian village called La Morte Rouge discovers the body of Lady Penrose. She has crawled in from the marsh into the church and, dying, clutched at the bell-pull.

journed and he hurries away, refusing Holmes's offer of help. But a letter is delivered to Holmes, written by Lady Penrose before her death, expressing a vague fear for her life and pleading with him to come to the village. Holmes and Watson cancel their plans to return to London. "Consider the tragic irony: we've accepted a commission from a victim to find her murderer. For the first time we've been retained by a corpse."

Holmes soon realizes that Lady Penrose was once Lillian Gentry, an American actress who came to Canada some years before and disappeared. He and Watson book rooms at the local inn run by Emile Journet, a stern outsider, and his pretty daughter Marie. From local characters like a wispy postman, Potts, they learn about the village, its inhabitants, and the "ghosts and monsters" rumored lurking in the marshes. But Holmes does not believe in monsters. Instead he thinks the murder was committed by a five-pound garden weeder—

heavy enough to rip open a throat. That night, as Watson mingles with the locals at the hotel bar, Holmes begins a solo exploration of the treacherous marsh, and hears the church bells toll like they did last night as Lady Penrose lay dying. Out of the mist a glowing figure runs toward him, only to vanish again as Holmes fires his revolver. (The apparition is actually the work of Academy-Award-winning special effects wizard John P. Fulton, who across the years was a major contributor to the Universal studio's onscreen magic, and who in this film is credited for "Special Photography.") Holmes pockets a shred of phosphorescent cloth caught on a branch.

The cloth—from an expensive shirt—leads Holmes to the barricaded home of a supposedly crippled recluse, the retired Judge Brisson— shotgun in hand, obviously in fear of his life. (His servant Nora carefully screens all visitors from behind locked doors.) A year before he had given a shirt to a limping yard-laborer. That worker is said now to live in an abandoned boathouse by the village docks; Holmes, Watson and the local police sergeant pay a visit to the ancient building, and hear shuffling sounds above them. ("To the trained ear, footsteps have a characteristic rhythm as identifiable as fingerprints," Holmes lectures.) Searching the effects of the limping, bearded Tanner, they find a glowing shirt; he is the marsh monster! Holmes's sharp eyes also spot an old torn photograph with the inscription: "To Alastair Ramson—a great actor."

More digging brings to the surface a strange tale of vengeance. Alastair Ramson was an actor in Lady Penrose's company. Five years ago in Quebec, madly in love with her, he had killed another actor; three years ago he had been thought killed while escaping prison. Now he is in the village, and as his first act has turned upon the woman who spurned him. He was Tanner, but has abandoned that identity when it was discovered. But "Ramson has undoubtedly established another character for himself—perhaps several others—by now familiar to the people of La Morte Rouge and quite above suspicion. He could be almost anyone . . . ."

Judge Brisson, Holmes learns, was the magis-trate who sentenced Ramson, and in a chilling, macabre sequence we watch the actor, disguised as the housekeeper Nora, rip open the judge's throat while the detective knocks in vain at the locked door. Holmes rushes to the docks, hoping to catch the actor before he changes into the trappings of another personality. He is nearly killed by the actor—we cannot see Ramson's face in the darkness—saved only by the fortuitous arrival of Watson. There is yet to be one more victim in Ramson's orgy of crime, Holmes reasons. Journet was a guard at Tanner's prison, and now the hotel-keeper has disappeared, obviously in fear of his life. But the killer is to have his revenge. In a back room of the hotel Holmes discovers the body of Journet's daughter Marie.

The detective uncovers Journet's hideaway and persuades the grief-stricken man to return to the hotel so that a trap can be set for the murderer. "We know who the killer is. It's just his disguise we haven't penetrated." That night Holmes and Watson make a noisy show of leaving for London . . . and Journet declares he is going to church to offer a prayer for Marie's soul. On a footpath leading through the foggy marshes, the diminutive postman Potts hurries up to the cloaked figure of Journet: "Do you mind if I walk with you? It's a bit

Lord Penrose (Paul Cavanagh) with the body of his wife (Gertrude Astor); she is laid out in his dark manor house.

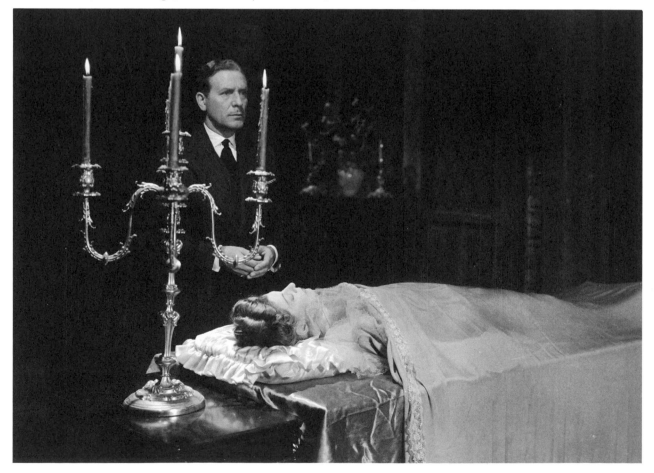

The investigator and friend enter Penrose Manor.

Watson testifies as a small, informal autopsy is held—in a scene not in the final cut of the film.

Innkeeper Emile Journet (Arthur Hohl) tries to comfort his nervous daughter Marie (Kay Harding).

130

Holmes and Watson are witness as Lord Penrose's butler Drake (Ian Wolfe)—afraid—tenders his resignation.

The supposedly harmless postman Potts (Gerald Hamer) looks terrifying evil as he is about to kill Marie. Naturally, this scene was never filmed, and it's unfair for the publicity pose to have been made, for it gives away the murderer.

131

Villagers and Watson look on as a distraught Emil announces he is going out into the night to offer prayers in church for his dead daughter. Holmes will take his place in the fog as he crosses the marshes.

The crazed Potts—actually an actor named Ramson—tries with his clawlike murder weapon to kill the man he thinks is Emile, actually a detective named Holmes.

Emile has managed to kill Potts, who has left scars. Note that the French Canadian police are the very unlikely wearers of curved bobby helmets.

frightening out here. Three deaths in three days. And still one more to be accounted for." Potts reaches into his pocket for a garden weeder; he is the murderer. But Holmes, who has taken Journet's place on the footpath, is ready for him.

Later, we see Holmes and Watson driving through a picturesque lakeside forest (the terrain looks somewhat like Lake Louise, and if so would make their return to England by way of the Pacific!), voicing another of those stirring speeches we have come to expect from the finish of all Universal Holmes films. Watson confesses that he would have liked to have seen a bit more of Canada before they sailed, and Holmes agrees, lauding the nation's "relations of friendly intimacy with the United States on the one hand and their unswerving fidelity to the British commonwealth and the motherland on the other. Canada, the link which joins together these great branches of the human family." Did Churchill say that? "Yes, Watson, Churchill. . . ."

We do not witness the detective's return to London in this film; as has been noted, it all takes place on Canadian soil, and Holmes's Churchillian speech is evidence of how much he welcomed the change of setting. Despite the alien geography, however, it remains the most characteristically *Holmesian* of mystery dramas, helped a great deal by a cunning, well thought-out plot and the quite superior acting of series regular Gerald Hamer, who is billed directly under Rathbone and Bruce and is credited in the closing with all three parts he played, and played well: Potts, Tanner, Ramson.

A somewhat strange publicity shot finds Holmes and Watson in front of a California fieldstone impersonation of their home. This very false setting is even more bizarre since no scene of the film takes place in England, let alone 221 Baker Street.

134

The Pearl of Death

Universal Pictures, August 1944. Screenplay by Bertram Millhauser. Based on "The Six Napoleons" by Sir Arthur Conan Doyle. Produced and directed by Roy William Neill.

CAST

Sherlock Holmes, Basil Rathbone; *Dr. Watson,* Nigel Bruce; *Naomi Drake,* Evelyn Ankers; *Giles Conover,* Miles Mander; *Lestrade,* Dennis Hoey; *Bates,* Richard Nugent; *Mrs. Hudson,* Mary Gordon; *Amos Hodder,* Ian Wolfe; *James Goodram,* Holmes Herbert; *Digby,* Charles Francis; *The Creeper,* Rondo Hatton.

This interesting film, based four-square on a Doyle story, has garnered critical acclaim in some circles—especially Universal studio itself—as among the very best in the series, but it is not en-tirely satisfying. The basic plot is almost too simple: the pursuit of six statuettes much in the manner in which Holmes chased down the matchbook in *In Washington*—pure MacGuffin. True, in this case the reason behind the smashing of the six wet-plaster Napoleons (something of value is hidden in one of them) comes straight out of the Sacred Writings, but across the years since "The Six Napoleons" was first published the novelty of the solution has rather worn away. What *is* superb about the film is its fine and murky atmosphere, and the sinisterness of its three kinky villains, particularly the grotesque "Creeper."

The mood was especially gripping to the New York *Herald Tribune* reviewer, Bert McCord, who was moved to say (8/26/44): "Motion picture titles for the most part suggest far more excitement than

Holmes interrogates master jewel thief Giles Conover disguised as a workman. Behind the group we see a corner of the elaborate museum setting.

is contained in the film itself, and many dull and uninspired pictures have particularly provoking labels. Occasionally a film comes along with an innocuous title tending to discourage you from the outset, but which if you chance to see it anyway proves a pleasant surprise. This is true of the latest Sherlock Holmes episode. . . ." The *Times,* slightly less enthusiastic, felt the film "holds a good share of thrills and horror-chills." The word *horror* was especially apt, for *Pearl of Death,* though less menacingly titled than the monster-suggesting *Spider Woman,* was because of the homicidal Creeper the first Universal Holmes film to stray into the horror as well as the mystery genre. In previous entries in the series, the murderers were always calculating. Here he was a mindless brute, a simple killing machine. For Rondo Hatton, who played the killer, the role was to transform him into a horror star.

Hatton, who unfortunately suffered from ac-

romegaly, a progressive glandular deformity which causes enlargement of the extremities, had played bits in movies for years—wrestlers and toughs, whenever a non-pretty face was needed. Cast as the Oxton Creeper, however he was for the first time the pivotal terror in a fairly prestigious and literate film, playing a genuine, first-class monster for a studio which took its monsters seriously. Opined McCord of Hatton: "if he goes to the right Hollywood parties with the right people, Boris Karloff had better look to his horrors." Evidently Hatton managed to attend a few influential parties, for in the next few years he enjoyed something of a terror stardom, all as a result of the Holmes film. In 1946 he was first Gale Sondergaard's deadly servant in *The Spider Woman Strikes Back,* and then was "introduced" as the Creeper in *House of Horrors,* this time as an American brutish maniac sent by a vengeful sculptor he befriends out to kill hostile critics. He was the Creeper again in *The Brute Man,*

The six Napoleons all lined up in a row, in the plaster statue works of Harry Cording.

a football player horribly scarred in a lab accident becoming a psychopathic killer. "He's big and ugly and mean," the *Times* said of him in *Pearl of Death*, and so he continued to be until his death in 1946.

Contrasting with the mindless death-dealing of Hatton is the intellectual villainy of Miles Mander, who had played the hapless judge in *Scarlet Claw* but here gives a fine-honed portrayal of sadistic evil, with some surprisingly quirky dialogue. He is aided by a coolly wicked Evelyn Ankers (the ill-fated, patriotic Kitty of *Voice of Terror*). One must note as well that in the original Doyle story only one death litters the trail of the statuettes, while the film multiplies the murders by five. And the deaths are ghastly: the Creeper delights in breaking his victims' backs, always at the third vertebra!

On a Channel crossing the patrician thief Naomi Drake steals the fabled Borgia pearl from a courier and enlists an elderly clergyman's innocent aid in smuggling the jewel through customs. Naturally the white-haired prelate is a disguised Holmes, who easily outwits her and sees to it that the pearl gets to its proper destination, the Royal Regent Museum. Naomi with some fear confesses her failure to her sinister associate Giles Conover, who snarls that an old friend of hers is back in town, moaning and whimpering for her: the Creeper. The girl shudders, but Giles assures her silkily that he has the friend under control.

Meanwhile, this is the description of Conover Holmes gives to Watson: "This man pervades Europe like a plague, yet no one has heard of him. That's what puts him on the pinnacle in the records of crime. In his whole diabolical career, the police have never been able to pin anything on him. And yet, if there be a crime without a motive, robbery without a clue, murder without a trace, I'll show you Giles Conover!" Reaching for tobacco in a fine-looking Persian slipper (the Baker Street rooms seem to add delightful touches with each

The Creeper has been at work. A corpse is found amid a litter of broken china.

Rondo Hatton as the murderous Creeper—three characteristic poses in the role which was to make the player a star.

Holmes tracks down Naomi in one of her disguises—as *she* is on the track of one of the Napoleon statues in the antique shop of Ian Wolfe.

film in the series), Holmes declares, "If I could free society of this sinister creature, I should feel my own career had reached its summit." The sentiments make Conover's infamy sound comparable to Moriarty's, at least.

But Giles's evil is not understated. The pearl is placed on display at the museum; Holmes, however, is dissatisfied with the protective alarms surrounding it, for to him electricity is "the high priest of false security." To demonstrate his point, he secretly disconnects the wires leading to the alarms, and a lurking Giles, dressed as a workman, sensing the jewel's vulnerability, makes off with it! Holmes is discredited.

Holmes is despondent, and Watson is forced to punch newspapermen for attacks against the detective in the press. Then a series of pecular murders begin, and Holmes senses a link to the theft of the Borgia pearl. The victims all have their backs broken, always at the third vertebra—grisly

trademark of the Oxton Creeper, "a monster with the chest of a buffalo and the arms of a gorilla," and Giles Conover's right hand. Why the murders? Holmes surmises that Conover has had to abandon the pearl somewhere, and is desperately trying to retrieve it, much as is the detective himself.

All the victims are discovered in a litter of broken china. Because no bric-a-brac can be found under the corpses, Holmes reasons the china was smashed after the deaths in each case. Bits of identical plaster busts of Napoleon are found—busts made at a pottery shop on the route along which Conover fled the day he grabbed the pearl from the museum. He undoubtedly hid the jewel in the wet plaster of one of the busts, and Holmes traces the last of the six Napoleons cast that day to a surgeon in private practice in a London suburb. In the darkness of night Conover in a van drives the Creeper to the doctor's home, finding him in surgical mask and gown. Naturally it is Holmes, and

Into the arms of the law and the world's greatest detective: the apprehending of Naomi Drake.

Sadistic Giles Conover (Miles Mander) bursts in on a doctor while in surgery. Why is the doctor in mask and gown? Because—you've guessed it—he is actually Holmes, who has been waiting.

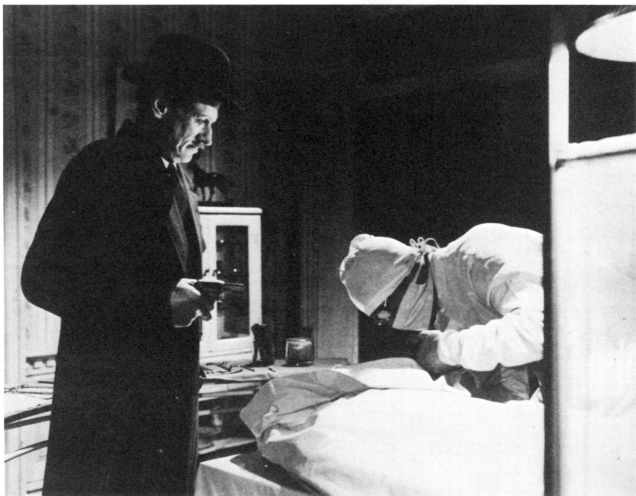

The climax of the film: the Creeper, goaded by Holmes, turns upon his master.

there is a confrontation. His berating of Giles is classic.

"I don't like the smell of you," Holmes thrusts, "an underground smell, the sick sweetness of decay. You haven't robbed and killed merely for the game like any ordinary halfway decent thug. No, you're in love with cruelty for its own sake." Conover, however, has his gun on Holmes, and urges the Creeper to break his back. Holmes plays up the brute's beauty-and-the-beast feelings for Naomi Drake, making him think Conover has betrayed the girl to the police. The Creeper thereupon kills his master, and when he turns upon Holmes the detective fires three bullets into him—the first time in the Universal series Sherlock Holmes personally ends a major villain's life.

Giles Conover dead at his feet, the Creeper turns upon Holmes—who is reaching for a revolver. Seconds later the Creeper will be dead. Photographed on the set by an uninspired publicity department, this still gives no hint of the shadows and atmosphere in which Director Neill would bathe the scene.

A better than average ad for the series, though misleading. Most of the twenty deaths promised occur before the film opens—part of the Borgia pearl's unsavory reputation. And the girl who risks her life is a thief out to steal the gem.

We first meet Naomi Drake (Evelyn Ankers) on a channel crossing as she attempts to hoodwink an old priest (Holmes, actually, hoodwinking *her*).

Naomi Drake in disguise as a matchgirl.

It is now time to find the Borgia pearl. Holmes and Watson smash open the final Napoleonic bust—"if it's not here I shall retire to Sussex and keep bees"—but it *is* there; Holmes's career is intact. His curtain speech this time is not specifically patriotic, but with heavy utopian overtones, as he comments on the jewel's evil history and hopes for the time when "the greed and cruelty has been burned out of every one of us, and when that time comes even the pearl will be washed clean again."

The film has any number of good touches, and Roy Neill's atmospheric controls are sure. The Royal Regent Museum set, although used in only one sequence, is magnificent in its clutter and in the rightness of the extras (artists, scholarly types, schoolgirls) mingling about as the alarms go off. There are a goodly number of disguises used in the film, starting with Holmes's elderly clergyman, and we see the detective actually remove the complex layers of makeup once he is safely in Baker Street. Interestingly, Universal provided the Baker Street rooms with a makeup table tucked in a corner, complete with wig-stand, which Holmes put into service in several films. Later, not only does Holmes stand in for the doctor who is to be the Creeper's last victim, he also does an expert imitation of Giles Conover's voice over the telephone, good enough to fool Naomi on the other end.

(Contrary to the practice of the day, Rathbone actually *does* mimic Miles Mander's voice, and quite creditably, without any resorting to dubbing.) As well, Miles Mander is allowed two disguises of his own, and Evelyn Ankers gamely tackles three impersonations: a kitchen helper, a match-seller of the streets, and a shop assistant. At one point Giles impersonates an old bibliophile and former Holmes client (the detective uncovers the disguise because of his well-known familiarity with tobacco ash) to leave for Holmes a first folio Samuel Johnson which actually has a springing knife concealed inside. Interestingly, Johnson memorabilia also play a hand in the last film in the Universal series.

But the most interesting element of the film, aside from its Krafft-Ebing outlook, is the lurking menace of the Creeper. The beauty-and-the-beast relationship between him and Naomi was a Quasimodo–Esmeralda construction of scripter Millhauser, but the shuddery, brooding visuals was the talented work, once again, of director Neill, the supreme shadow-master. We *never* see Rondo Hatton's full face clearly until just before Holmes kills him at the end; throughout the film he moves in the dark, an only partially observed, lumbering, terrifying silhouette. Small wonder this film was to make him a star.

A publicity pose; certainly the scene is not in the film. Bad-girl Naomi Drake cringes with horror along with Holmes and Watson at (we must suppose) the lurking menace of the Creeper.

House of Fear

Universal Pictures, March 1945. Screenplay by Roy Chanslor. Based on "The Adventure of the Five Orange Pips" by Sir Arthur Conan Doyle. Produced and Directed by Roy William Neill.

CAST

Sherlock Holmes, Basil Rathbone; *Dr. Watson,* Nigel Bruce; *Alastair,* Aubrey Mather; *Lestrade,* Dennis Hoey; *Simon Merrivale,* Paul Cavanagh; *Alan Cosgrave,* Holmes Herbert; *John Simpson,* Harry Cording; *Mrs. Monteith,* Sally Shepherd; *Chaimers,* Gavin Muir; *Alison MacGregor,* Fiorette Hillier; *Alex MacGregor,* David Clyde; *Bessie,* Doris Lloyd; *Stanley Raeburn,* Cyril Delevanti; *Guy Davies,* Wilson Benge; *Ralph King,* Dick Alexander.

After an exhausting pace of a new film every few months, the unit producing the Holmes films on the Universal lot was the steadiest-working unit at the studio, and it was suggested that perhaps the series was flagging. "Sherlock Holmes has certainly gone to the bow-wows in Hollywood," moaned Bosley Crowther in *The Times* (3/17/45), and the *Herald Tribune* cautioned that both the scriptwriting and directing of the series would have to improve. Not that Rathbone was flagging (even though Crowther ungallantly called his performance "as pedestrian as a cop's on patrol"); he was grafted to the role, portraying the detective almost constantly both at the film studio and on his weekly radio series. And the films themselves, churned out though they were, had in all of them moments to cherish. But *The House of Fear* was perhaps the last fully satisfying entry in the series.

Sherlock Holmes and Dr. Watson arrive at the remote Scottish manor house occupied by the Good Comrades—being murdered one by one. Simon Merrivale (at far left) welcomes them soberly, while the elflike Bruce Alastair stands, center, in a tartan shawl.

A new scriptwriter, the veteran Roy Chanslor, had been added to the unit, and it was vigorously decided to return the "timeless" Holmes stories more firmly into a Victorian atmosphere. A Universal press release confessed that attempts of a modern Holmes "to solve problems of the current war, in Canada and Washington, did not meet with the expected response from devotees of the Conan Doyle mysteries. Film fans seem to want their Holmes and Watson in typical Doyle plots and in the English settings where they belong." Telephones and automobiles notwithstanding, Holmes was being moved back into the past.

The familiar past obviously included a standard old-dark-house ("*Death stalking its halls! Horror seeping from its walls!*") plot, handsomely fashioned from a Conan Doyle story which had no old dark house in it at all. Interestingly, in most of the film's print advertising the Doyle source story is misspelled as "The Adventures of the Five Orange Pips," the plural making the title sound more like a musical or lighthearted romp, rather than the grim story of vengeance it actually was. The film uses little beyond the orange pips, or pits, themselves; the story is set in Scotland and the menace of the Ku Klux Klan which Doyle envisioned is forgotten. But the film—lashed with Roy Neill's more than generous fogs and atmospheres—is good. As is the advertising copy, which with pulpish glee calls the film's six victims "six guests of death!", continuing with the eloquent line: "Walls of hate, holding an orgy of murder—as crime's Master Minds crack their weirdest case!!"

The story begins in a remote coastal corner of West Scotland, where the middle-aged members of a club, "The Good Comrades," have six months earlier bought a gloomy cliffside manor appropriately named Drearcliff. The seven clubmen, all from London and all with no near kin, have taken out heavy insurance policies with each other as beneficiaries. Two have suddenly died horribly—after receiving an envelope containing orange seeds. Chalmers, an insurance company representative, worriedly brings the case to Sherlock Holmes, who agrees to take it on after learning one of the Comrades is Simon Merrivale, a doctor who some years ago had been disagreeably involved in the death of a young girl, though acquitted. "Murder is an insidious thing. Once a man has dipped his fingers in blood, sooner or later he'll feel the urge to kill again."

Staying at the village inn, Holmes and Watson learn of the local legend that no inhabitant of

Inspector Lestrade examines a sailor's knot with Holmes as Captain Simpson (right) looks on.

Drearcliff "goes whole to his grave"; no ghost haunts the house, "only the memory of evil" and brutal death. However, the current owner, Good Comrade Bruce Alastair, is a bubbly, ebullient old elf who welcomes the detective with open arms when a third member is found dead, burnt to a crisp in the furnace, identifiable only by his cuff links. He too had received an envelope of orange pips. Alastair cheerfully contributes the odd fact that for an obscure African tribe orange seeds represent death.

The remaining comrades grow rather suspicious of one another as other murder attempts (poisoned needles, drinks) are uncovered. Alone, staring into a blazing fireplace in the cheerless house, Holmes and Watson have another of those exchanges of dialogue which so delighted audiences . . .

HOLMES: I don't know, Watson. This is a most unique case. Instead of too few we have too many clues and too many suspects. The main pattern of the puzzle seems to be forming, but the pieces don't fit in.

WATSON: Muddy waters, eh, Holmes?

HOLMES: Too muddy. As if someone were constantly stirring them up.

WATSON: Why should they stir them up?

150

There are rumors of ghosts and emptied graves in the wild coastal country around Drearcliff; Holmes and Watson investigate. The cemetery and ruined church are familiar Universal backlot sights.

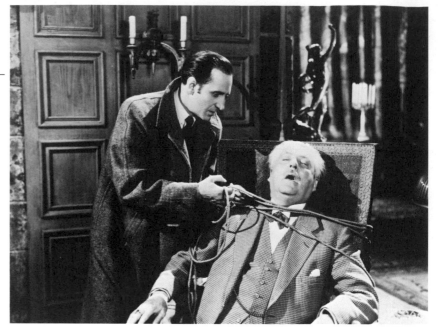

Watson has fallen asleep on the job—
and someone has trussed him up.

HOLMES: To confuse me. There's intelligence behind this business, Watson. Cold, calculating, ruthless intelligence.

Another Good Comrade meets a nasty death—blown to bits in a dynamite-laden garden shed—and Scotland Yard arrives on the scene. It's Lestrade, rather annoyed to find Holmes and Watson already there. Then the grim housekeeper silently brings yet another envelope, this time to the seafaring comrade, Captain Simpson, who bolts in terror. He's found on the beach, his head, arms and legs chopped away, his identity ascertained only by the ship's tattoo on his chest. The Drearcliff legend about no resident going intact to his grave still seems to hold.

The club is reduced to two members, and when the village tobacconist is found shot after sending a note to Inspector Lestrade, Holmes discovers the solution to the grisly crimes. The tobacconist's daughter tells the detective that her father, who "naught believed in ghosts," had seen one of the dead men on the beach late at night. Holmes rushes back to Drearcliff to learn that Merrivale has been crushed to death under a falling rock, Lestrade has arrested fey old Alastair—the last surviving comrade—for murder and Watson has disappeared.

Holmes explores the main room of Drearcliff

inch by inch (the set, even down to the chessboard floor, is the same one used for Musgrave Manor in *Faces Death*) and in the great fireplace discovers a passageway leading, Alastair remembers, to "an old smuggler's cave." There they find the six murdered Good Comrades all alive, and Watson a prisoner. It was a murder scheme for the insurance, using mutilated bodies of recently deceased villagers (even adding tattoos), with Alastair as the lone innocent dupe.

Interestingly, it is *Watson* who discovers a most important clue, when he notices that Simpson's favorite tobacco has conveniently disappeared when Simpson himself "dies." This leads to Watson's own disappearance, and when Alastair mentions Watson's discovery to Holmes it leads him to the solution. It also leads Holmes to a rather novel curtain line, this time differing much from the patriotic speeches established in previous films, and a rare demonstration of the deep, warm affection between the two men. Holmes turns the insurance reward over to Alastair, for this reason:

HOLMES: It was your timely warning, when you drew our attention to the empty tobacco jar and saved the life of my dear friend and colleague Dr. John H. Watson—
WATSON *(muttering)*:   . . . Very nice of you, old boy . . .

152

(Opposite page) An interesting studio pose, framed in a keyhole.

HOLMES: —thereby enabling us to continue our long and happy association together!

The House of Fear was an interesting film in the series, owing perhaps some debt to Agatha Christie's *And Then There Were None,* which though released three months later had been in preparation much longer and had been based on a hit Broadway play of the year before. Watson's clinching deduction, charming though it seemed to most, did not win over all the critics. Otis Guernsey, Jr., writing (5/17/45) in the New York *Herald Tribune,* had this bone to pick: "To be constructively critical of Hollywood's treatment of the great Conan Doyle detective, Sherlock is not as clever at crime prevention or crime detection as he should be. Vindictiveness always outfaces him until the final reel; in *The House of Fear* he lets the guilty get away with too much crime before he levels the final revolver. And then his solution, when it finally comes, is attained more by good luck and opponents' blunders than by good and artful management on his part."

It was time to put more dash into the series. The next film was to resurrect Moriarty.

Footprints by the coastline.

Insurance agent Chalmers first brings the problem to the detective, and we are treated to a view of cozy, cluttered Baker Street.

Discussing the case. Note the gasogene lamp and pipes strewn about the fireplace top.

Woman in Green

Universal Pictures, June 1945. Screenplay by Bertram Millhauser based on the characters created by Sir Arthur Conan Doyle. Produced and directed by Roy William Neill.

CAST

Sherlock Holmes, Basil Rathbone; *Dr. Watson,* Nigel Bruce; *Lydia,* Hillary Brooke; *Professor Moriarty,* Henry Daniell; *Inspector Gregson,* Matthew Boulton; *Maude,* Eve Amber; *Onslow,* Frederic Worlock; *Williams,* Tom Bryson; *Crandon,* Sally Shepherd; *Mrs. Hudson,* Mary Gordon.

Radical steps were to be taken to pump new life into the Sherlock Holmes series. The next film was to have not one, but two adversaries worthy of Holmes's mettle: a supreme master villain and a seductive femme fatale. The first was to be Professor Moriarty himself—even though in two previous encounters with Rathbone's Holmes he had been securely put to death, first at Twentieth Century-Fox and then at Universal. Bringing him back this way, without even an explanation of how he cheated the grave, seemed to prove him an awesome force of terrible evil.

But even Moriarty was to be crowded by the female of the species. Universal had great hopes for the sexual lures of a lady criminal, especially as enacted by the coolly patrician Hillary Brooke, an actress then in the best years of her career (she was the driver, Jill, in *Voice of Terror,* as well as the compassionate Sally Musgrave, and in 1944 conducted a sinister seance in Fritz Lang's adaptation of

157

Moriarty and his gang study their handiwork: a hypnotized Holmes. Henry Daniell is Moriarty (second from left), and Hillary Brooke to the right is the notorious woman in green.

Graham Greene's *Ministry of Fear*). Not only is her character the title role of the film, she also corners all the attention in the film's ad posters—"*ONCE IN HER ARMS no man could refuse her love . . . or his LIFE!*"—with Moriarty mentioned hardly at all.

But for the wicked Professor a good character actor had been chosen. The diabolic Henry Daniell, so suavely saturnine, had been badly used in previous entries, playing a glum red herring in *Voice of Terror* and what amounted to a bit in *Secret Weapon,* while a few months earlier over at RKO he had done the plum role of the doctor for whom Burke and Hare supply corpses in *The Body-Snatcher.* He was excellent as Moriarty; indeed Basil Rathbone, dismissing such fine actors as George Zucco and Lionel Atwill, sang the praises in his autobiography of "Henry Daniel's masterly Moriarty. There were other Moriartys, but none so delectably dangerous as was that of Henry Daniel." (Note that Daniell's name is twice misspelled;

Rathbone was a terrible proofreader, and in his reminiscences also while lavishing admiration on Roy William Neill manages to drop the final "l" of that name as well.) It's a pity that he was surrounded with a pedestrian film.

The reviews, however, were not uniformly bad. While the *New York Times* (6/16/45) was to say "A Hollywood scriptwriter named Bertram Millhauser takes full responsibility for what transpires on the screen, and it's just as well, for Sir Arthur never perpetrated a disappointment such as *The Woman in Green*" (significantly it was the last Holmes screenplay Millhauser was to write). Otis Guernsey, Jr. in the *Herald Tribune* was to take the completely opposite view: "Because it presents a little more of Baker Street and of the detective's philosophy than has been usual lately, *The Woman in Green* is one of the better Sherlock Holmes mystery thrillers . . . Rathbone's performance is always equal to the breadth of the script, which in this case allows

Sir George Fenwick's worried daughter stands in front of his study door; beyond it he lies dead. A serious Inspector Gregson is to the left, hat in hand.

him to approach very near to the character of the Sir Arthur Conan Doyle detective."

Interestingly, Dennis Hoey's Inspector Lestrade—who had been so much a part of the Scottish investigations in the previous film—was not a part of this program and was only once seen in the series again, replaced this time by an altogether more serious (as he was in the Doyle source) Inspector Gregson. Hoey was a character actor of the highest skills, and succeeded in investing a good deal into his part beyond the surface bluster, but the role was becoming impossible. Scholar Michael Pointer in his *The Public Life of Sherlock Holmes* rightly commented that "nothing was added to Holmes's stature by his solution of problems which an idiot of a policeman bungled." His arrogant stupidity in the handling of an investigation appeared to reach new heights in *The House of Fear;* his comic exchanges with an equally buffoonish Watson made it seem as if Holmes were

being trailed by a parade of clowns. In *Woman in Green*, the comedy nonsense was left at least to Watson alone.

"We're confronted with a series of the most atrocious murders since Jack the Ripper," announces the Commissioner of Scotland Yard to his assembled men—"finger murders," where in each case the victim is a young woman whose right thumb has been hacked off!

Gregson consults Holmes, visibly affected by the four murders to date: "I don't turn a hair when it's a bloke who can look after himself, but when it's a little slip of a thing . . ." Holmes promises to help.

In another part of London the distinguished Sir George Fenwick pays a discreet visit to the flat of a new friend, Lydia Marlowe ("a very handsome woman, not born to the purple, but giving an excellent imitation," Holmes was to comment); together over drinks in the dim light they look at flowers floating in a shallow dish; clearly the man is being

A sniper has made an attempt on Holmes's life—an assassination similar to the method used by Colonel Moran in Doyle's "Adventure of the Empty House"— but, questioned, the man appears in deep trance.

hypnotized. Later Fenwick wakes up in a cheap hovel off the Edgeware Road, just after another finger killing has occurred. He can remember nothing. In his pocket he finds a severed finger.

An attractive client drives up to Baker Street to consult Holmes. (Amazingly, the glimpse we have of the street shows it as the straight, modern thoroughfare it is in actuality, rather than the crooked lane of previous screen portrayals.) It is Sir George's worried daughter Maude, who has seen him bury a finger in their garden at night. They find Sir George dead, "obviously murdered to keep him from telling me what he knew," Holmes surmises.

The detective immediately guesses the motive for the multiple murders: a blackmail ring. "If my assumptions are correct, this little scheme has behind it one of the most brilliant and ruthless minds the world has ever known"—Professor Moriarty. Watson snorts that Moriarty was hanged in Montevideo over a year before (!), but Holmes is not so sure. The doctor is called out on an emergency case, and as Holmes, alone, plays "Clair de Lune" on his violin, a visitor steps out of the shadows. The confrontation between Holmes and his ancient enemy is brilliant. The dialogue is inspired largely by Doyle's "The Final Problem," but it is expertly enlarged, and moves to a marvelous climax.

MORIARTY: We've had many encounters in the past. You hope to place me on the gallows. I tell you I will never stand upon the gallows. But, if you are instrumental in any way in bringing about my destruction, you will not be alive to enjoy your satisfaction.

HOLMES: Then we shall walk together through the gates of Eternity hand in hand.

MORIARTY: What a charming picture that would make.

HOLMES: Yes, wouldn't it. I really think it might be worth it.

Just before leaving the Baker Street summit meeting, Moriarty unobtrusively pushes Holmes's

160

easy chair closer to a window overlooking an empty house across the street, and we can guess we are in for a reworking of Doyle's "The Adventure of the Empty House." A marksman fires at what seems like Holmes's silhouette, but is actually a bust of Julius Caesar ("through the ages, prominent men have had prominent noses," the detective advises Watson). The sniper, a war veteran, appears under hypnosis.

Holmes hopes the sniper will lead them to the murder ring, but later he is found dead on the Baker Street doorstep. Holmes and Watson repair to the Mesmer Club, "meeting place of the top hypnotists in London," where, curiously, and presumably in addition to his Diogenes Club sanctuary, brother Mycroft is "a valued member." Watson, the medical traditionalist, brands hypnosis as poppycock for the weak-willed, but during an experimental session is quickly brought under. ("Anyone with an ounce of character," scoffs Wat-

son, but he is soon under a spell removing shoes and socks before an open fire—and indeed, just to add a distinctly British touch many of the sets in the film featured blazing fireplaces.) Suddenly Holmes spots Lydia Marlowe—a few nights previously he had seen her with Sir George Fenwick—and assumes a role new to us in this film series, that of amorous swain. They discuss hypnosis, and Lydia invites the detective to her penthouse flat. He stares into the pool of floating flowers, and accepts a "harmless" drug to heighten his hypnotic potential. His eyes are soon glassy and vacant. Professor Moriarty enters. He had Lydia lure Holmes to her apartment, playing on his one great weakness: his insatiable curiosity.

Certain that the detective is in a state of "profound hypnosis"—Moriarty has a sadistic doctor henchman prick Holmes's neck with a scalpel, noting that "he could not fake insensitivity to the knife"—the Professor dictates a suicide note ("I

Lydia Marlowe and Professor Moriarty are solemnly watchful as Sherlock Holmes walks to his death—they hope—off the ledge of a London penthouse terrace.

161

At the Mesmer Club, Dr. Watson demonstrates how anyone with an ounce of character can resist hypnosis. (Frederic Worlock, a series regular who here plays a club official, is holding Watson's shoe and sock.)

have at last found a case which I cannot solve") and instructs him to walk over the edge of a terrace parapet, high above the London streets.

Watson and Gregson lead police to the scene in time, though it is hardly necessary to "save" Holmes; he has not actually been hypnotized, having substituted for Lydia's drug one which causes insensitivity to pain. The disgruntled Moriarty, in a futile attempt to get away, plunges headlong from the roof and is killed.

The female of the species must indeed be deadlier: in this poster for *The Woman in Green*, evil Moriarty is not mentioned.

ONCE IN HER ARMS—
no man could refuse her love—or his LIFE!

THE WOMAN IN GREEN

Starring
BASIL RATHBONE
NIGEL BRUCE

with
Hillary BROOKE   Paul CAVANAGH
Henry DANIELL   Eve AMBER
Sally SHEPHERD   Matthew BOULTON

Based on the Characters created by SIR ARTHUR CONAN DOYLE

WATSON: An evil man, Holmes, but . . . what a horrible death!

HOLMES: Better than he deserved.

WATSON: What are you thinking of?

HOLMES: I'm thinking of all the women who can come and go in safety in the streets of London tonight. The stars keep watch in the heavens, and in our own little way, we too, old friend, are privileged to keep watch over our city.

Otis Guernsey, Jr., in his *Herald Tribune* critique, has the kindest words to say about actor Daniell (interestingly, *no* review mentions Hillary Brooke's title contribution at all): "Henry Daniell makes a perfect Professor Moriarty—suave, self-possessed and confronting Holmes in Baker Street in a coolly audacious duel of wits. No doubt the series would benefit from Daniell's continued presence as an opponent for the Rathbone character." He notes that Moriarty has been thoroughly killed at the end of the picture, but rightly implies this has not constrained Universal before and that public credibility has been stretched in such cases.

However, *Woman in Green* represented Moriarty's screen twilight. He was not to appear again—in an American theatrical film, at any rate—for three decades. And then, in *The Seven-Per-Cent Solution*, the demon professor's portrayal was altered and whitewashed, his most serious crime being adultery.

Inspector Gregson (Matthew Boulton) places a restraining hand on Moriarty; his game is finished. A moment later the crime genius would—in an escape attempt—fall to his death from the parapet. Note the painted diorama of London rooftops stretched across the background.

Pursuit to Algiers

Holmes advises Sheila to trust him.

Universal Pictures, October 1945. Original screenplay by Leonard Lee. Based on the characters created by Sir Arthur Conan Doyle. Executive producer, Howard Benedict. Produced and directed by Roy William Neill.

CAST

Sherlock Holmes, Basil Rathbone; *Dr. Watson,* Nigel Bruce; *Sheila,* Marjorie Riordan; *Agatha Dunham,* Rosalind Ivan; *Sanford,* Morton Lowry; *Nikolas,* Leslie Vincent; *Mirko,* Martin Kosleck; *Gregor,* Rex Evans; *Jodri,* John Abbott; *Kingston,* Gerald Hamer; *Gubec,* Wee Willie Davis; *Prime Minister,* Fredric Worlock.

Ever interested in freshening the series, Universal decided to give Holmes and Watson a change of locale, this time not westward to the American con-

tinent, but along southern sea routes to Graustarkian destinations. "Sherlock Holmes enters Europe's political underworld," a press release promised somewhat less than truthfully, while ad posters showed a luxury liner plying through fog with captions like "5,000 miles of terror" and "the port of a thousand intrigues!"

The film marked Executive Producer Howard Benedict's official return to the credit billing, and other shifts and changes as well. Character actress Rosalind Ivan, who had scored such a great success as Charles Laughton's nagging wife (and victim) the previous year in *The Suspect,* was given a generous eccentric's role and outstanding billing—a part, too, in which she was allowed to pull out all the stops, and play against Nigel Bruce, stealing scenes outrageously. Morton Lowry, who was the

Out for a stroll, Holmes and Watson learn of missing emeralds. Although not the basic problem of the film, the jewels are almost effortlessly recovered by the detective during the adventure.

villainous Stapleton in Rathbone's very first Holmes, returns herein an interesting impersonation. And Nigel Bruce is allowed to make his screen vocal debut, singing *"Loch Lomond."*

The shipboard setting of the film was from a melodrama standpoint very promising, now that the war in Europe was over and civilian travel could be freely indulged. The critics on the whole found the film novel and fun. Bosley Crowther, in the *New York Times* (10/27/45), applauded the way Holmes "stalks calmly and precisely through a bewildering maze of plot and has the exact countermeasure for every incipient threat." But the compliment is backhanded, for he continues: "Indeed, this unerring accuracy of Holmes—Basil Rathbone, that is—has now become so dependable that his pictures have virtually no suspense. All that's left is to sit there and chuckle at Dr. Watson's wretched jokes and sniff at the upstart presumptions of the sleuth's transient enemies."

The film begins with Holmes and Watson encountering some extremely odd types in a foggy nighttime London, each passerby cryptically directing the pair to a dockside alley. There the Prime Minister of the European monarchy of Rovenia hires Holmes to safeguard the young heir, Nikolas, on his journey from London to his homeland after his father, the king, has been assassinated ("a great loss to the whole democratic world," murmurs Holmes). The detective is to fly alone with the prince, but arrangements have been made to meet Watson in the Mediterranean; the doctor is to sail aboard a ship ominously named S.S. *Friesland*—a sinister vessel in one of Doyle's untold stories.

Watson easily makes friends with his fellow passengers—including a charming young singer from Brooklyn, Sheila Woodbury. "Perhaps some day you'll allow me to give you an insight into some of our most interesting cases," he presses warmly, and we are reminded that the Irene Adler who so

Still out on that stroll, the pair stop for some fish and chips—and find a message in their menu directing them to a dockside alley.

intrigued Holmes was an operatic singer from New Jersey. He notes suspiciously that rugged mannish spinster Agatha Dunham carries a revolver in her handbag. There is a wireless report of a light plane crashing in the Pyrenees, and Watson is distraught. The captain asks him to look in on a sick patient in the cabin next to his; of course it is Holmes, and with him is the young heir to the throne. For the rest of the voyage he is to pose as Watson's nephew.

As the liner moves through the fogbound sea, Sheila begins to act very oddly, especially when first learning Holmes is aboard. Watson also distrusts a lurking young steward, Sanford. The ship makes an unscheduled stop at Lisbon, and is boarded by a trio of sinister characters: the deceptively jovial Gregor, the mute giant Gubec, and the lithe Mirko.

There is a poison attempt on the young king's life. Mirko is about to hurl a knife through the king's stateroom when Holmes drops a porthole

cover on him and says affably: "Why, I'm afraid you've broken your wrist. You shouldn't have played shuffleboard today, you know. When I saw that skillful hand and unerring eye of yours I remembered the Circus Medrano in Paris and your amazing exhibition of knife-throwing. Good night."

On the day before they are to land in Algiers, Holmes uncovers the reason for Sheila's nervousness: she is an unwilling courier for an international jewel thief. He promises to help her. That night the fierce Miss Dunham, formidably sporting a monocle, throws a party at which a florid Watson recites the adventure of the giant rat of Sumatra. (Just as tantalizing as Doyle, the film only gives us brief glimpses of the case and its epilogue: ". . . the freighter was towed out to sea and blown up, and London, and all England for that matter, was saved from the terrible menace.") A bomb is concealed in a party favor, but Holmes tosses it into the ocean.

More clues, as the night becomes progressively more foggy and sinister.

Behind that door the detective is to meet young Prince Nikolas—and the drama proper (on ship) is to begin.

A suspicious Watson eyes two sinister fellow passengers, Gerald Hamer (left) and John Abbott, who later turn out to be merely red herrings.

Nighttime aboard the S.S. *Friesland*, as Mirko listens in to Holmes's edgy chat. Note that the knife-thrower's arm is out of commission, thanks to the detective.

The detective's cleverness is not sustained, however. As the ship docks at Algiers he is surprised, bound and gagged, and Nikolas kidnapped. But it is the wrong victim—the real young king is revealed to be Stanford the steward, a curious plan on Holmes's part, since during the entire voyage the busy steward, though disguised by his uniform, was both highly visible and vulnerable. Says Holmes, on leavetaking: "Dr. Watson and I shall not forget we've had the unusual distinction of having our breakfasts served in bed by a king!"

Guernsey in the *Herald Tribune* again served up sage commentary when he noted that the twentieth century adventures seemed to favor melodrama more than keen mental conflict. "Holmes himself seems to sense this deterioration from time to time in the excellent Rathbone characterization, and one of the lines in *Pursuit to Algiers* allows him to be positively nostalgic. He is explaining to Watson that musical talent is not necessarily an indication of good character. With a longing for the gaslit era in Baker Street evident in his eyes, he searches the past for an illustration of his point—and then finds it. 'The late Professor Moriarty,' remarks Holmes in a tribute to his former adversary, 'was a virtuoso of the bassoon.' "

Perhaps it was time to revive Moriarty once more—or at least his right hand, the wicked Colonel Sebastian Moran.

A very amiable encounter in the ship's dining salon with the three villains (from left to right: Wee Willie Davis, Rex Evans, Martin Kosleck). Standing with Holmes is "Watson's nephew" (Leslie Vincent).

172

The brisk sea air is conducive to romance, especially as Holmes has solved a particularly worrisome problem for Sheila (Marjorie Riordan).

Terror By Night

Holmes and Watson examine the Star of Rhodesia.

Universal Pictures, February 1946. Screenplay by Frank Gruber. Based on a story by Sir Arthur Conan Doyle. Executive producer, Howard Benedict. Produced and directed by Roy William Neill.

CAST

Sherlock Holmes, Basil Rathbone; *Dr. Watson,* Nigel Bruce; *Major Duncan-Bleek,* Alan Mowbray; *Inspector Lestrade,* Dennis Hoey; *Vivian Vedder,* Renee Godfrey; *Lady Margaret,* Mary Forbes; *Train Attendant,* Billy Bevan; *Professor Kilbane,* Frderic Worlock; *Conductor,* Leland Hodgson; *Ronald Carstairs,* Geoffrey Steele; *McDonald,* Boyd Davis; *Mrs. Shallcross,* Janet Murdoch; *Sands,* Skelton Knaggs.

The major innovation in the latest film in the series, the first Holmes effort for 1946, was its set-ting: trains had been a melodramatic movie background since the silent *Hazards of Helen* days, and *Terror by Night* is laid nearly completely aboard a crack express heading from London to Scotland (*"murder . . . at 90 miles an hour!"*). It was a far more claustrophobic setting than the expansive ship-board decks of *Pursuit to Algiers,* and the mystery played against it is no simple assassination attempt; it is a complex and convoluted crime involving several deaths and intricate deceptions. The menace is of a high order, too: the late Professor Moriarty's trusted lieutenant, Colonel Moran, portrayed, for the first time at Universal, by the very British character actor Alan Mowbray, who in the previous decade had played Scotland Yard inspectors (including Lestrade) in two Holmes series. Perhaps it is his familiar look which allows him to deceive

Watson into thinking him an old school pal. Lestrade is back in the film, too, scarcely restrained.

Reviews were mixed. The ordinarily kind Otis Guernsey, Jr. complained in the *Herald Tribune* (2/9/1946) that the film was "poorly conceived and only loosely put together . . . the plot is nearly suspenseless . . . the modern Sherlock Holmes has rarely sunk to lower levels of excitement." However, over at the *New York Times* the hypercritical Bosley Crowther had for this entry very much pulled in his claws: "This episode in the famous detective's career is told in a tight continuity and with flavorsome atmosphere." He reaches back to a 1938 classic to point up a source. "Obviously, Hitchcock's *The Lady Vanishes* inspired the author of the script, but that's not a bad inspiration. And the action has been handled well."

The author of the script, indeed, was quite new to the series, but a veteran writer who since 1927 had churned out a massive amount of popular fiction. Frank Gruber had become the king of cheap-magazine writing during the Depression—a career he wrote about at length in the autobiographical *The Pulp Jungle*—and in the forties began an assault on Hollywood. He eventually became one of the industry's most prolific screenwriters ("in Hollywood I have written sixty-five motion picture screenplays. . . ."). Among his first tasks was the screen version—*Mask of Dimitrios* (1944)—of an Eric Ambler novel, and *Terror by Night*. His enthusiastic handling of the plot's mysterious elements make for an interesting journey, but the overriding dramatic force is the train itself. It is an appeal which especially works if one responds to the train mystique. As Bill Pronzini writes in his recent anthology of train mysteries, *Midnight Specials,* "If to you a train is not just a mode of transportation (and a nearly outdated one in the eyes of many) but a symbol of adventure, intrigue, suspense. . . ."

Terror by Night begins with Holmes being commissioned by young Ronald Carstairs to accompany him and his mother by train to Edinburgh, to protect the diamond known as the Star of Rhodesia which they are carrying with them ("all those who possessed it came to sudden and violent deaths"). Inspector Lestrade is also on the train, pretending to be heading for a fishing holiday, and Watson boards with an old friend he has just run into, the retired Major Duncan-Bleek of the Twelfth Indian Lancers. Ronald's mother, the aristocratic Lady Margaret, is quite haughty as she allows Holmes a glimpse of the gem. Later, while Holmes and Watson dine in the restaurant car, Carstairs is murdered in his compartment. The jewel has vanished.

The train roars through the night carrying an eccentric group of passengers as suspects. (Interestingly, Universal ran through a good deal of stock train footage as transitions during the film, and while these quick shots are darkened to simulate the nighttime in which the story occurs, any reasonably astute train buff can discern they are of wildly differing engine and carriage models!) A sultry young lady named Vivian Vedder is grieflessly transporting the body of her mother to Scotland for burial; the coffin is in the baggage compartment. An arrogant Professor Kilbane turns on Watson savagely when he attempts to question the man. A timid, middle-aged Scottish couple confess to being thieves—but they have only made off with a London hotel teapot (the man is played by an unbilled Gerald Hamer, giving another deft characterization). Holmes senses an evil presence aboard. "Colonel Sebastian Moran was the most sinister, ruthless, and diabolically clever henchman of our late and unlamented friend, Professor Moriarty. I've never seen him, but I've been unpleasantly conscious of his presence more than once. As a matter of fact, he was directly responsible for what nearly turned out to be my premature death on three separate occasions. His speciality was

An elaborate, realistically detailed British Railways train interior was used throughout the film.

Holmes questions the owners of the jewel, one of whom will shortly be dead.

spectacular jewel robberies." Later, there is an attempt on Holmes's life, and it is only the detective's sinewy agility which enables him to hoist himself back on the speeding train. (I've been observing the landscape—from the outside, he comments to Watson drily).

In a discovery which reminds us of the case of Lady Frances Carfax, the coffin in the luggage compartment is found to have a secret bottom, where the killer of Ronald Carstairs had hidden himself. The baggage guard is found murdered. Holmes reveals to Lestrade that only an imitation diamond was stolen, Holmes having cleverly palmed the real Star of Rhodesia when Lady Carstairs first showed the stone to him. (And on reviewing the first scene, we actually can *see* Basil Rathbone approximate the sleight-of-hand.) In the meantime, however, the killer, played by the skull-faced Skelton Knaggs, is stalking the train, his hands twitching with a life of their own, a diminutive variant on the Creeper theme. The death weapon is that Doyle favorite, an air-pistol, but it is turned against the no longer useful murderer (he has knocked out Lestrade and retrieved the actual diamond) by the crime's real mastermind, Watson's supposed old chum, the amiable Colonel "Duncan-Bleep."

The train makes an unscheduled stop and a stern Inspector McDonald of the Scottish police and two aides come aboard. Holmes unmasks Moran, and there is a brief tussle; finally, McDonald escorts the Colonel, subdued under a mackintosh, off the train. But it is actually Lestrade under the cloth—an alert, armed Lestrade—for McDonald is an imposter, and Holmes has managed to keep both a handcuffed Moran and the real Star of Rhodesia safe aboard the train.

Watson turns up an old school chum.

Holmes interrupts Watson at dinner for a hurried conference.

How did Sherlock Holmes uncover the deception? Simple.

HOLMES: . . . I happen to *know* the real Inspector McDonald of the Edinburgh Police.

WATSON: Oh. Was Lestrade in on all this?

HOLMES: Yes, and surprisingly enough, he grasped the situation immediately.

A kind word for Lestrade! Watson, too, is allowed to be more help than hindrance in the final struggle with Moran: when the Colonel has everyone covered, he manages to knock the gun from his hand. The series rarely permitted him to be this agile.

178

The detective with the notorious air-gun used as the murder weapon.

In the train's baggage compartment Holmes and Watson examine the coffin with the secret hiding place.

Major Duncan-Bleek, Watson's supposed school pal, reveals himself to be the notorious Colonel Moran (Alan Mowbray) by killing his accomplice, Sands (Skelton Knaggs).

Holmes gets his man—by train! Here he cuffs the false Inspector McDonald (Boyd Davis).

Dressed to Kill
...AND EXIT BASIL RATHBONE

A publicity pose released for *Dressed to Kill*, bearing no relationship to any scene in the film.

Universal Pictures, May 1946. Screenplay by Leonard Lee. Adaptation by Frank Gruber. Adapted from a story by Sir Arthur Conan Doyle. Executive Producer, Howard Benedict. Produced and Directed by Roy William Neill.

CAST

Sherlock Holmes, Basil Rathbone; *Dr. Watson,* Nigel Bruce; *Hilda Courtney,* Patricia Morison; *Julian Emery,* Edmond Breon; *Colonel Cavanaugh,* Frederic Worlock; *Inspector Hopkins,* Carl Harbord; *Evelyn Clifford,* Patricia Cameron; *Detective Sgt. Thompson,* Tom P. Dillon; *Hamid,* Harry Cording; *Kilgour child,* Topsy Glyn; *Mrs. Hudson,* Mary Gordon; *Scotland Yard Commissioner,* Ian Wolfe.

Whatever critics were still paying attention were divided in their comments on the twelfth Sherlock Holmes film in the Universal series. Some found to their surprise they liked it, while others were bored with the film and frankly bewildered with the title. The studio itself seemed not to be paying much attention; perhaps because of the influence of pulpman Frank Gruber who fashioned the story, the film sounded more like a pulp novel than a Holmes film (and actually, *Dressed to Kill* had been the title of a Michael Shayne screen whodunit in 1941). Even the *New York Times* (5/25/46) declared its puzzlement in print: "Heightened mystery is added by the fact that the title has nothing to do with the story and, though probably no great loss, [the title] remains inexplicable to the end." In every preceding Universal Holmes film with an action verb in the title (*Faces Death, Pursuit to Algiers*) the subject reference is always the detective

181

The body of Julian Emery lies on the floor, and Holmes (holding the murder weapon) tells the assembled police he has been killed for a music box.

himself—but it is definitely not Holmes who here is dressed to kill!

Interestingly, a press release for the film about Basil Rathbone's clothing is an inadvertent commentary on the entire series. "Basil Rathbone holds a record which no other screen player can approach. He's worn the same basic wardrobe in his twelve Sherlock Holmes films at Universal." This means a green tweed sack suit, tweed topcoat, modified fedora hat, and black woolen dressing gown. (Watson's only standard bit of dress is a Victorian bow tie, on the other hand.) "Authenticity, rather than economy, demands the same clothes in every Holmes film. Sherlock was dressed that way in fiction, somewhat on the untidy side, and that's the way his millions of fans expect to see him on the screen." Small wonder Rathbone was exasperated with the role!

Once again Universal had rather tiresomely resorted to pitting Holmes against a female an-

tagonist: it is she who is dressed to kill (*"A price on her lovely head! A dare on her luscious lips! Danger- -in her icy heart!"*). Patricia Morison, a singer-actress who had already handled several thrillers, had joined the usual band of Holmesian regulars. Even though the villainy seemed familiar, *Dressed to Kill* got some compliments from the press: grudgingly from the *Times* ("Although suspense is nil, the film contains enough novel twists and odd developments . . . .") but outright raves from Joe Pihodna in the New York *Herald Tribune*. "For a change the modernization of Sherlock Holmes and Doctor Watson is bearing fruit on the screen . . . *Dressed to Kill* stands out like a drum major," he enthuses. "Recommended highly to mystery fans."

The film starts at Dartmoor, where we learn a certain prisoner, for rehabilitation, is making music boxes. An outwardly respectable-looking Colonel Cavanaugh arrives at a London auction hall to bid on three music boxes but is too late; they have been sold. Then, at Baker Street, we find Holmes at his violin and Watson eagerly devouring the latest issue of the *Strand* containing one of his "slightly lurid stories"; it is "A Scandal in Bohemia," the exploits of Irene Adler, and Holmes drily observes, "I do hope you've given *the* woman a soul—she had one, you know."

An old school chum of Watson's, Julian "Stinky" Emery, an eccentric collector of music boxes, stops by to tell that a petty thief broke into his house and made off with a valueless, ordinary specimen. Holmes is intrigued, even though Scotland Yard had dismissed the robbery ("That's consistent, at any rate."). The stolen box was similar to the plain one Emery had just added to his collection that day, from a Knightsbridge auction gallery. Holmes notes that it plays a haunting melody (and although he hears the tune only once, he memorizes it note for note). That night Emery entertains a woman visitor, the patrician Hilda Courtney. (It is one of director Neill's deft touches of character to have the old collector, simpering with anticipation,

Watson amuses a young girl who has been locked in a closet by a woman who has made off with a music box.

Hot on the trail: Sherlock Holmes sniffs out a special kind of cigarette at a tobacconist's.

adjust his toupee.) The woman's hulking chauffeur, Hamid, kills the man.

Investigating Emery's death, Holmes soon surmises that the music box was the cause. From the auctioneer he learns of the two other boxes, and traces the owner of one. An ancient charwoman opens the door and disappears; they are too late. "What a fool I've been! She took that music box out of this house in a market basket, right under our very noses. She's a consummate actress, an extremely clever, unscrupulous woman who'll stop at nothing!"

A Scotland Yard detective is murdered when he comes too close to the trail of Hilda Courtney, and Holmes learns that the Dartmoor prisoner who made the music boxes was arrested just after stealing and hiding a set of Bank of England plates used in engraving five-pound notes. As the discovery by counterfeiters of these plates could ruin the nation's economy, the recovery of the music boxes is of paramount importance.

At a low cafe frequented by London's buskers (street-entertainers) Holmes seeks out a certain Joe Cisto, whom he had once cleared of a murder charge by proving he was blowing a safe elsewhere, and whistles for him the music-box tune. It is an Australian folksong, "The Swagman," but some of the notes are off. It is of course some sort of code. Back at Baker Street, thanks to Watson's reminiscing about a piano teacher in his childhood numbering the keys in a vain attempt to get him to play, Holmes breaks the code: the plates are hidden behind the books on the shelf of Doctor S——. The remaining missing music box still hides the name of the doctor.

While they are out, the Baker Street rooms are ransacked by a veiled woman who leaves behind a cigarette stub. Because it is composed of rare Egyptian tobacco blends, Holmes traces it to Hilda Courtney, at a fashionable address. His triumph is hollow, though, for actually she had used the cigarette as bait to lure him there, "having read with great interest your monograph on the ashes of 140 different varieties of tobacco." He is trapped by her men, and taken to a garage where, his mouth taped and manacled hands suspended from a hook in the ceiling, he is left to be overcome by the poisonous fumes of a running car motor. Fortunately, his agility permits him to escape. (Or, rather, the agility of a lean stunt man, for the "modified fedora hat" which never topples from his head in this scene allows for easy doubling.) In the meantime Hilda Courtney pays a visit to Watson, and, using the same duplicity employed by Holmes in "A Scandal in Bohemia"—a fake fire designed to flush out whatever valuable object is hidden in the room (and since Watson had previously told us he had just written up "Scandal" for the *Strand,* he really should have known better)—she manages to make off with their music box. Holmes, upon his return, is crestfallen.

WATSON: Cheer up, old fellow, cheer up. As Dr. Samuel Johnson once said, there is no problem that the mind of man can set that the mind of man cannot solve.
HOLMES: What's that, old fellow?
WATSON: I was just quoting Dr. Samuel Johnson. He said—
HOLMES (*thoughtful*): Thank you, Watson, thank you.

And with just that brief stimulus from Watson, the wondrously intuitive Sherlock Holmes divines that the hiding place of the bank plates is a bookshelf in the memorial home of Dr. Samuel Johnson!

(Interestingly, Johnson's house—where he had written his famous dictionary—had actually been maintained as a museum in Gough Square off Fleet Street. However, it had been mildly damaged by the wartime bombings and in 1946 was closed to the public. Restored, it was reopened two years later.)

Our climax is at the Johnson home, where a tour guide is showing about a splendidly eccentric collection of Roy William Neill characters: a clergyman, his gossipy companion whispering of Johnson's excesses; a spinster leading a few schoolgirls; and—insinuating themselves on the group—Hilda Courtney, Colonel Cavanaugh, and the sinister Hamid. The trio uncover the plates, but are apprehended by Holmes and the police. In an affable mood, the detective magnanimously claims his solving the case is "entirely due to Dr. Watson"—for pointing out the vital clue. Watson, who had done no such thing, grins broadly and foolishly: "I don't think I could have done it entirely without Mr. Holmes's help, you know." It is a warm, winning moment, these two old friends playing off their victory against one another. It is the last time we shall see them on the screen together.

After completing *Dressed to Kill,* Basil Rathbone seized upon the moment to kill Sherlock Holmes, much as Conan Doyle had—for nearly similar reasons—pushed him off Reichenbach Falls. The

Very proud of himself, Holmes demonstrates to the devilish Hilda Courtney (Patricia Morison) how he has traced her through her smokes—not realizing that she had dropped a cigarette to bait a trap for him!

185

Samuel Johnson's home as it looks in actuality. (The film, while reproducing the insides in some detail, never shows us the exterior.)

The entrance to Samuel Johnson's home, preserved—as it was in the film—as a National Landmark. In a case of life imitating art, the gathering shadows of night make the facade look almost like a Hollywood set.

The finale at Johnson's home, with the gang rounded up. To the left of Hilda is Colonel Cavanaugh (Frederic Worlock), and to the other side is Chauffeur Hamid (Harry Cording), holding his shoulder, for he has been winged by Holmes's revolver.

role had become too much for him: he had begun to find Holmes distasteful, even unpleasant, cruel in his friendships (so nasty and condescending to the worshipful Watson) and, more importantly, himself typed beyond belief. Rathbone felt himself strangled by the part. Children came up and asked him for autographs addressing him as Holmes (he would turn away, refusing). Holmes's infallibility, his interminable success, his ego, froze Rathbone into that one stance, ending his versatility as an actor. Then, in 1946, both his radio and studio contracts came to a nearly simultaneous end. Rathbone, against everyone's advice, decided not to renew them, and to run away from Sherlock Holmes forever.

It was a thunderclap decision. It threatened to disrupt his long friendship with Nigel Bruce. It dismayed his agent, MCA's famed Jules Stein. And naturally it was a blow to a nation of fans, not only of the films but also the long-running radio series.

(The impact of Rathbone's microphone image as Holmes was also strong, implementing his screen strength; indeed, Andrew Sarris was to recall years later in *The Village Voice:* "I remember the Holmes radio series with Rathbone and Bruce much more vividly than any of their movies.") Suddenly, the actor was through with the role most audiences thought he had been born to play. For many, it was very much like a royal abdication.

But the amputation was not quite total. Even though Rathbone fled to New York for a variety of stage successes *(The Heiress, J.B.),* he was to discover that while he could separate himself from the role he could not isolate himself from the image. In the heyday of early television he was to guest in a deerstalker with a trenchcoated Mickey Spillane in a mystery parody on "The Milton Berle Show." (This recalls earlier guest stints on radio: Frank Buxton tells in *The Big Broadcast* of Rathbone's visit to "The Bob Hope Show" where as Holmes he tracks down the mysterious Yehoodi—unveiled as the little man who pushes up the next piece of Kleenex.) In 1950, he appeared on NBC-TV as Sherlock Holmes, in a live pilot which did not sell. Three years later the CBS-TV *Suspense* series presented him as Holmes and Martyn Green as Watson in an adaptation of "The Adventure of the Black Baronet," one of a series of pastiches by John Dickson Carr and Adrian Conan Doyle (son of Arthur), then appearing in *Collier's.* That same year he appeared on Broadway in a play, *Sherlock Holmes,* written by his wife Ouida, and closely based on several of the stories.

Mrs. Rathbone claimed that all the dialogue Holmes had to say was taken straight from the Sacred Writings, and that the adaption had the blessings of the Doyle estate. A large supporting cast was headed by Jack Raine as Watson (Nigel Bruce was too ill to do the role, and died that year) and Thomas Gomez, the villain of *Voice of Terror,* as a corpulent, menacing Moriarty; the production was lavish, with the second act a Swiss hotel overlooking the Reichenbach Falls beyond the balcony, down which Holmes falls just before the curtain does. Spectacle could not fend off a lukewarm critical reception, and the play closed after three performances.

Rathbone was to touch on the Holmesian character again only briefly—a series of readings for spoken-word records; short introductions for the Universal films when they made their television debut over a local Chicago station. In June of 1967 he was dead. Some twenty years had passed since he last played Sherlock Holmes in motion pictures, and he would be the first to admit his attempts to wipe away his association with the role. But all the other people he had portrayed since—from Disraeli to Svengali—have done little to dim the world's conviction that Basil Rathbone was the man who *was* Sherlock Holmes.

The Hound of
the Baskervilles
PETER CUSHING

A Hammer Films Production (British; US release: United Artists), 1959. Screenplay by Peter Bryan. From the novel by Sir Arthur Conan Doyle. Produced by Anthony Hinds. Directed by Terence Fisher.

CAST

Sherlock Holmes, Peter Cushing; *Dr. Watson,* André Morell; *Sir Henry Baskerville,* Christopher Lee; *Cecile,* Maria Landi; *Sir Hugo Baskerville,* David Oxley; *Bishop Frankland,* Miles Malleson; *Dr. Mortimer,* Francis De Wolff; *Stapleton,* Ewen Solon; *Barrymore,* John Le Mesurier; *Perkins,* Sam Kydd; *Mrs. Barrymore,* Helen Goss; *Servant Girl,* Judi Moyens; *Servant,* David Birks; *Lord Caphill,* Michael Hawkins; *Lord Kingsblood,* Ian Hewitson; *Seldon,* Michael Mulcaster.

Nearly thirteen years passed after Basil Rathbone's final screen appearance as Sherlock Holmes before the character was tackled again. The new image was to come this time from the country which had cradled it originally—England—and was to be the first Holmes film in color, the enthusiastic effort of a vigorous new British film studio which had single-handedly started a brand new English horror film tradition, and was now attempting to do the same with the allied mystery genre.

Curiously, all through the 1940s the horror film cycle had been American in origin, specifically the product of the same studio which had spawned the Holmes series, Universal. The English were thought incapable of the form, and even to frown on it; indeed, many Universal titles were not given

Hi-jinks at Baskerville Hall back in the seventeenth century. The film begins with these events as a prologue.

general release certificates in England. But by the mid-fifties, thanks to the astuteness and drive of pioneer producer John Carreras and his son John, a tiny studio called Hammer began to attract international attention (and distribution) with lavishly mounted color remakes of such thrill classics as *Frankenstein* and *Dracula*. The studio even developed its own stars, making well-known names of excellent but previously unrecognized players like Peter Cushing (the scientist Frankenstein) and Christopher Lee (the vampiric Dracula). Flushed with happy success, Hammer sought about for other

190

(Overleaf) Sir Hugo leads a pack of hounds after the vanished girl. The manor house facade is actually part of the exterior of Bray (Hammer Studios was lodged in a country house) and can be seen in film after film from that studio.

properties in the period chiller vein . . . and made arrangements with the Doyle estate for the world's best-known mystery classic.

Of course Hammer was expected to give the story the studio touch—not a subtle one—and even the color was exploited (*"It's ten times the terror in Technicolor! The most horror-dripping tale ever written!"*) While the opening Baker Street sequences were acceptable and affectionate, once the story proceeded into the moors it veered far from the Doyle source, adding a Sir-Francis-Dashwood style Satanism, altering the character of Stapleton and changing Beryl completely, making her a hot-blooded, scheming Spanish beauty who is Stapleton's unlikely daughter and the true perpetrator of the horror of the hound.

Despite the irregularities of the adaptation, the choice of Peter Cushing as Holmes and Christopher Lee as a dashing Sir Henry were good ones. Cushing had previously made a wide impression as Professor Van Helsing in the Hammer *Dracula* success (1958); film critic David Pirie in his study of the English Gothic cinema, *A Heritage of Horror*, suggests that Sherlock Holmes and Van Helsing, Renaissance scholars with strong mystical overtones pitting the nominally rational Victorian milieu against dark, cruel legend, were not very far apart. Cushing was easily as eccentric and energetically nervous as Rathbone, and indeed at times seemed to positively out-twitch his immediate predecessor. Alas, he was nowhere near as tall, and appeared shorter than Sir Henry, Dr. Mortimer, and even Watson at times (well and scholarly played by Andrè Morell). Height aside, his Shakespearean training gave his Holmesian portrayal a good edge. Christopher Lee, cast against his type (vampires and monsters), was perfect as the Baskerville heir.

A suburban studio, actually a large house in Bray, Hammer was confined in the scope of its sets, and received criticism for the hemmed-in look it gave the story. But the period dress was accurate, some of the moorscapes chillingly eerie, and as it was the first Sherlock Holmes film to be done in color, the Hammer *Hound* was a landmark.

Hammer's eye-popping version of *The Hound* starts with the beginnings of the Baskerville curse told as a prologue and not as a flashback. "May the hounds of hell take me if I can't hunt her down," cries Sir Hugo as he sets a pack of hounds in pursuit of a local girl who has fled the nightly orgiastic revels at Baskerville Hall. Riding hard, and apparently into the dawn, Hugo traps the girl inside a ruined abbey, and in a savage frenzy stabs her to death. There is a terrible animal sound, and Hugo is killed by an unseen beast.

Immediately we are transported to Baker Street, where Doctor Mortimer is already relating to a musing, chess-playing Sherlock Holmes the death of Sir Charles Baskerville, a look of horror on his face. An only mildly intrigued Holmes agrees to meet the new heir, Sir Henry, fresh from Canada, at the Northumberland Hotel. "I believe your life is in some considerable danger," he tells the young man, and as if on cue an enormous tarantula creeps from a spare boot onto Sir Henry's shoulder; Holmes brushes the spider off with a stick. "The powers of evil can take many forms. Remember that while you're at Baskerville Hall. Do as the legend tells—and avoid the moor when the forces of darkness are exalted."

Watson accompanies Sir Henry to the moorland, for Holmes is detained in London. They learn of the murderer escaped from a local prison, and explore the dank corridors—lined with portraits—of the Hall. That night Watson sees a figure moving outside. His explorations lead him to the ruined abbey, where he meets—Holmes. The detective had taken the next train, and had been observing the house: "There is more evil around us here than I have ever encountered before." They discover the body of the escaped convict, as a spectral hound howls in the darkness.

The body disappears from the moors, and later is found on an altar in the ruined abbey, mutilated horribly—as if used in sacrifice. Holmes attempts to trace the tarantula which attacked Sir Henry by visiting a local resident, Frankland, changed by the film into a leading entomologist who is also a bishop (played by cherubic, elderly Miles Malleson, a Hammer favorite until his death). Holmes persuades the bishop to open up to him about a missing spider by confessing: "I am fighting evil—fighting it as surely as you do!" Meanwhile, Sir Henry begins a romantic entanglement with Cecile, the temperamental Spanish-born daughter of local farmer Stapleton, who has bought unyielding land in the district after some years abroad and is too poor and proud to pull up stakes. ("And so we are left with the moor and the mist," observes the girl bitterly.)

Holmes explores an abandoned tin mine nearby; there is an accident, and falling rocks injure his leg. On his return to Baskerville Hall, he discovers that the ornamental seventeenth century dagger he had found near the abbey altar has disappeared from

194

Sir Hugo (David Oxley) kills the girl.

The first day at Baskerville Hall, Watson (Andre Morell, left) meets Bishop Frankland (Miles Malleson) as Sir Henry (Christopher Lee) looks on.

Was there someone signaling from the window?

Farmer Stapleton (Ewen Solon) and his daughter Cecile (Maria Landi) come to call on Sir Henry.

Stapleton takes Watson on a tour of Grimpen Mire.

Watson outside the abandoned mine shaft with Perkins (Sam Kydd).

Sherlock Holmes points out to Watson Sir Hugo's webbed fingers among the family portraits.

Holmes has a talk with Stapleton as a huge Dr. Mortimer (Francis De Wolff) looks on holding a lantern.

Holmes finds a dagger bearing the Baskerville crest in the ruined abbey.

his room. Sir Henry tells Holmes that they have been invited to dine at Stapleton's farm cottage, but the detective uses his bruised leg as an excuse not to go. He is certain that Sir Henry is to die that night.

Events speed to a climax. We see Henry and Cecile embrace in the moor twilight. Holmes surmises that a missing portrait at the Hall shows Sir Hugo with webbed fingers on his right hand, and as Stapleton also has a webbed hand he is the "illegitimate descendant of Sir Hugo . . . next in line for the Baskerville fortune." He and his daughter dabble in the black arts as well.

Cecile leads the amorous Sir Henry to the dark abbey, then turns on him suddenly, savagely. "*Swine!* You thought it was going to be easy, didn't you? you won't be the first one in your family to think that—and you won't be the first one to die because of it." She gloats of Sir Charles's death, changing somewhat Conan Doyle's structure of the events leading up to it: "Your dear uncle died here—died because he wanted me—like you . . . He died screaming. I know. I watched him." Henry looks on horrified as the girl spits out her motive: "I too am a Baskerville, descended from Sir Hugo—descended from those who died in poverty while you scum ruled the moor! We've waited and prayed for this moment, my father and I. Now our time has come—*and yours.* The curse of the Hound is on *you!*" A great dog (nonphosphorescent) leaps on the astonished heir.

Fortunately, Holmes and Watson arrive in time. A bullet dispatches the animal, and another shot fells Stapleton, who has lunged at Sir Henry with a knife. Cecile flees from the abbey only to be caught in moor quicksand. Holmes and Watson, helping Sir Henry back to the Hall, manage to come upon the girl just as she is going under.

WATSON: So the Curse has claimed its last victim.

HOLMES: Yes, no more will be heard of the Hound of the Baskervilles.

We take leave of the detective and his friend back at Baker Street, amiably discussing the finished case (Sir Henry has sent a generous check *and,* as a souvenir, the missing portrait of his ancestor, since uncovered at the Stapleton farm).

Reaction to the new *Hound of the Baskervilles,* despite its radical changes from the basic Doyle plot, was essentially favorable. Lingering Rathbonian memories made this new interpretation rather audacious, but on the whole critics were kind to Cush-

Holmes pays a visit to Bishop Frankland, who observes the neighborhood with his upstairs telescope. Note his collection of spiders, left.

Holmes makes an observation regarding boots to the butler, Barrymore (John Le Mesurier).

Watson loses his footing in the mire.

Cecile caught in the quicksand.

ing. Although perhaps too small or nervous for the role, he *was* an actor; despite his Hammer stardom, he *did* have solid Shakespearean training and background. Reviewers appreciated that.

"There is a great deal less of the hound" to be seen, observed Paul V. Beckley in the New York *Herald Tribune* when the film opened at Broadway's prestige theater, the Victoria (7/4/59). He noted that when first seen at the climax the hound might appear somewhat disappointing to those whose imaginations were stirred by the book. Nevertheless, the film "should be a pleasant introduction to the adventure for those who may never before have gasped at the howl of the hound in the dark of the moon." The *Times,* however, was quite surly about the film, savaging it completely; Bosley Crowther called it a "garish excuse for what should be a fog-wreathed and ghost-haunted vehicle," criticizing its well-lit, obvious studio sets as a complete miscalculation, missing the atmosphere and

the vanished menace of the hound. "Outside of a little baying once in a while, we get no image whatsoever of this creature, until pretty near the end. Then we're given a glimpse of a Great Dane, looking somewhat like somebody's pet, except that he's wearing a false-face, making a playful lunge at Christopher Lee."

The film was financially successful for Hammer Studios (United Artists released it in the U.S.), but although the motion picture company was to frequently exploit period thrills, it was never again to tackle another Holmes story. (The Conan Doyle estate, then entering a difficult era, could not be brought to terms.) Peter Cushing, however, whose energetic, forceful portrayals of dynamic character types have intrigued audiences from *Curse of Frankenstein* to *Star Wars*, was to play Sherlock Holmes, and even the Holmes of *Hound of the Baskervilles,* once again on British television, in versions just as controversial and even more violent.

The case is solved; Holmes and Watson share tea and muffins at Baker Street.

Sherlock Holmes und Das Halsband Des Todes
SHERLOCK HOLMES AND THE NECKLACE OF DEATH

Edith Schultze-Westrum as a Germanic Mrs. Hudson whose supper of mutton has just gotten in the way of Sherlock's knife practice. One never knows what to expect at Baker Street!

Constantin-Film, (Germany), 1962. Screenplay by Curt Siodmak. Freely adapted from "the novels of Sir Arthur Conan Doyle, with the permission of the estate of Sir Arthur Conan Doyle." Produced by Artur Brauner. Directed by Terence Fisher (with Frank Winterstein).

CAST

Sherlock Holmes, Christopher Lee; *Ellen Blackburn,* Senta Berger; *Professor Moriarty,* Hans Söhnker; *Inspektor Cooper,* Hans Nielson; *Paul King,* Ivan Desny; *Chauffeur Charles,* Leon Askin; *Peter Blackburn,* Wolfgang Lukschy; *Mrs. Hudson,* Edith Schultze-Westrum; *French Policeinspektor,* Bernard Lajarrige; *Light girl,* Linda Sini; *Auctioneer,* Bruno W. Pantel; *American,* Heinrich Gies; *Doctor,* Roland Armontel; *Johnny,* Max Strassberg; *Librarian,* Danielle Argence; und *Dr. Watson,* Thorley Walters.

The next Holmesian epic was to appear, not in England or America, but in Germany.

Of all postwar moviemaking in Europe, German films were the most melodramatic and the least successful. They were not able to claim a large share of the foreign market, and relied mainly on their own internal audiences. However, tastes in Germany run strong, and they run toward melodrama. Both Father Brown and Raffles were postwar movie heroes in Germany, and the revival of Fritz Lang's sinister master criminal Dr. Mabuse (who owes, as do all masterminds, much to Moriarty) has been startling, as well as the impact of Edgar Wallace on the German screen. This English mystery writer, who died in 1932, began in the fifties a fantastic revival, with a half-dozen or so slick,

A superb portrait of Christopher Lee as Holmes. The
false nose is virtually undetectable.

well-made stories being made into films each year. All are in German, and all have English locales: a strangely Teutonic London, sinister haunts along a fogbound Thames, remote country houses. With the traditional English mystery story finding such favor, it seemed only a question of time that the German film industry—rich in mysterioso traditions, where during its golden age before the war Caligari, Nosferatu, Jack the Ripper and even the Baskerville Hound stalked—should return to Sherlock.

One of Germany's biggest studios, Constantin Film Verleih of Berlin took that basic step, contacting the Doyle estate. (All advertising and the film itself states: "Freely based on the literary creations of Sir Arthur Conan Doyle, with the permission of the estate of Sir Arthur Conan Doyle.") Three international film figures of some prominence were assigned to the project: director Terence Fisher, writer Curt Siodmak, and star Christopher Lee. Fisher was certainly among those responsible for the success of the lavishly mounted Technicolor horror films spawned by the English Hammer company—he directed *Horror of Dracula* and *Curse of Frankenstein* for them, as well as, just a few short years before, their *Hound* version. Curt Siodmak had a long screenwriting career in both Europe and Hollywood, generally in science fiction (*Floating Platform One Does Not Answer*) and terror (*Son of Dracula*) moods. An able workman in more than one language, Siodmak created the story, *Donovan's Brain,* which has been an enduring favorite across the years and become something of a classic of the genre.

English actor Christopher Lee was chosen to play Holmes in order to widen the film's potential—especially in whatever international markets it could invade—and therefore became the only player to impersonate both Holmes and Sir Henry Baskerville on the screen (as well as Mycroft Holmes, some years later). Even though fluent in German, he was nonetheless dubbed by a German-speaking actor on the film's sound track (and by yet another anonymous voice in the later English-language version!), so that an evaluation of Lee's performance can be only partial. Certainly his appearance—and the look of the film altogether—were a trifle bizarre. The settings seemed straight out of Brecht, and Holmes's costuming—the Germans wanted to give the detective a familiar look of checkered greatcoats—exaggerated. Even Lee's lean, imposing profile was given a more impressive rubber-and-wax nose!

The terror star who had played the title role in both *Horror of Dracula* and *Curse of Frankenstein,* who had been evil Chinese mandarin, revived Egyptian mummy and even hound-haunted young lord, plays Sherlock throughout in a false nose.

The only other English actor in the cast is Thorley Walters, who specialized in the sort of florid, blustering comedy roles which remind one of Nigel Bruce. It is far from subtle, but must have been satisfying enough to cinema audiences: he was to play Watson several times afterwards, to a variety of different Holmeses. He too is dubbed for German film and his voice is also not used for the English-language release.

Because of the dubbing, it's difficult to make a qualitative judgement on Lee's performance. Certainly he looked the part, and *gestured* it, at times brooding and withdrawn, but quivering when the scent is up. Too, like Shakespeare, the Canon sounds first-rate in German once one gets used to it. The script sounded less first-rate. Although drawing heavily from incidents in and even the solution of *The Valley of Fear,* it has very little other basis in the Canon, and is pedestrian. The direction is similarly inspired.

The film opens on a curiously Germanic vision of the London docks, an almost Victorian panorama. This nineteenth-century mood is only somewhat dispelled when Professor Moriarty (solidly played by German "Godfather" type Hans Söhnker) drives up in a shiny Rolls Royce (like the Universal series, this film is set in vaguely contemporary times but overlays the setting with a subtle turn-of-the-century feeling). In a rather clumsy maneuver Moriarty exchanges a note with a dockhand, and is observed in this by a tattered, evil-looking sailor. The sailor makes his way to Baker Street, and frightens the wits out of Doctor Watson, who does not recognize our Sherlock so disguised. But right at this moment, an informant of Holmes—a thief named Jenkins—is found knifed on the doorstep of 221-B, and, dying, whispers the words "Hare and Eagle," the name of a notorious Soho pub. Holmes immediately attaches the blame for this murder on Professor Moriarty.

But Scotland Yard Inspector Cooper is not convinced, and here is one of the few good points of the film. This is the first Holmes screenplay in many decades in which—as was the case in life—Sherlock alone suspects Moriarty of being a king of the underworld, a Napoleon of crime. To everyone else, including the Yard, Moriarty is thought of merely as an honorable, harmless, distinguished

Horseplay at Baker Street.

archaeologist. Indeed, Inspector Cooper repeats verbatim Alec MacDonald's little speech about visiting the professor's office from "Valley of Fear," in a careful attempt to show Holmes the error of his suspicions (This comes off quite well in German, and in the film.)

Holmes, heedless, rushes off to the Hare and Eagle, a pub straight out of the Threepenny Opera, where gross and bumbling Watson must fight off the advances of a doxy while Holmes eavesdrops on a conversation between Moriarty and a henchman. Their plot is faintly reminiscent of "The Sign of the Four." Long ago Moriarty uncovered a Pharaoh's tomb in Egypt, and from it stole a necklace of immense value—the necklace of Cleopatra (!). Two conspirators were involved with him in this scheme, and both went to prison after. One is now dead and the other has become troublesome, and must be put out of the way. His name is Blackburn, and he lives at Birlstone Manor.

Holmes has overheard all this while on the roof of the pub (the professor's voice has carried through the chimney), but at this point Watson clumsily dislodges some bricks and gives the game away. Holmes rushes to Birlstone Manor, but it is too late. Peter Blackburn lies dead, his face blasted away with a shotgun. His beautiful young wife Ellen is being comforted by family friend Paul King (overly comforted, one might add, in a curious scene thrown in merely to give the film a touch of romance), and Ellen reveals that her husband had long lived under the shadow of a death threat. Holmes speedily deduces—from the absence of a wedding ring on the corpse—that it is not Blackburn's body, but that of his attacker, sent by Moriarty. Blackburn had killed him in self-defense, and dressed the body in his clothes, so that at last he could free himself from his enemies. Their secret discovered, Ellen and Paul readily take Holmes to the priest's-hole where Blackburn has been hiding . . . but again it is too late.

Holmes and Watson look remarkably out of place in a low pub.

Blackburn tumbles out, a knife buried in his back. Leaving Paul King to comfort Ellen anew, Holmes and Watson rush back to London.

Holmes is certain Moriarty is behind the murders, but has no proof. Through a trick—really a mild comedy sequence in which Watson ties up traffic in a London street—Holmes obtains the keys to Moriarty's ostentatious villa. Breaking into the professor's office (which looks scarcely the way Alec MacDonald described it, but rather as Sax Rohmer might), Holmes makes his way through a variety of traps and alarms to ferret the necklace from its secret hiding place in a sarcophagus, one of Moriarty's many sinister relics.

He confronts Moriarty with this evidence in Inspector Cooper's office at Scotland Yard, but the professor merely laughs—Holmes has no witness that he actually found the necklace in Moriarty's home. The detective is beaten, and there follows a strange and somehow quite Germanic scene.

Holmes and Moriarty walk together to the Thames. Moriarty, in the gathering dusk, reveals all. He wants Holmes to join him, become his partner. Holmes refuses, and the professor tries to kill him with a knife blade that springs from the handle of his walking stick. When Holmes wards this off with a rolled-up newspaper, Moriarty waves one hand and a dozen of his men appear out of the darkness and slowly advance on the detective. But Watson, who has just come upon the scene, imitates a police siren and the gang, plus its leader, disappear.

The necklace is now to be sold at public auction, and Holmes rightfully suspects that Moriarty will make an attempt to reclaim it as Scotland Yard, in an armored truck, delivers it to the auction gallery. This armored car robbery, which serves as the climax of the film, is too absurd for detailed description. In brief, Holmes—disguised as the sailor again—manages to worm his way into Moriarty's

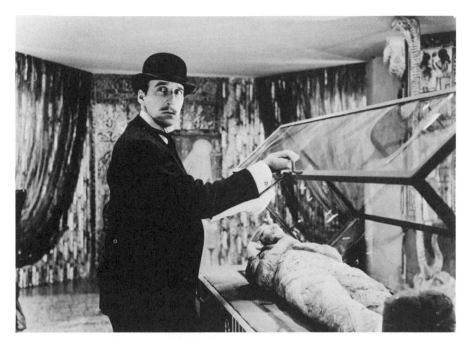

In disguise, the detective furtively examines Moriarty's pet mummy-case.

Holmes surprises Watson—in an effort to keep him from blundering.

gang by saving the life of a henchman at the Hare and Eagle. On the day of the auction, the armored truck leaves Scotland Yard with Inspector Cooper and the necklace inside. The former is soon overcome by some gas fumes, while the truck itself is stopped on a sidestreet by a traffic accident manufactured by Moriarty. The truck has been stopped exactly over a manhole cover, and from the sewer underneath Moriarty quickly slices into the bottom of the car body, reaches up and simply takes his treasure. The fiendish ingenuity of his plan is somewhat spoiled, though, when Holmes—who as the sailor has become a trusted member of the gang—snatches the necklace and runs off through the sewer passages.

The epilogue, however, is genuinely fine. We are at the auction gallery. Holmes, shorn of his disguise, has delivered the necklace, and Inspector Cooper, recovered from the effects of the gas, is there as well. So are Ellen Blackburn and Paul King, looking radiant, for Ellen apparently will share in whatever the necklace brings. Also in attendance is Professor Moriarty, looking far from radiant. The necklace is sold to a rich American for a high figure. Afterwards, Holmes, Watson, Moriarty and the Inspector meet in the lobby, and a cool, calculating, and quite stunningly achieved cat-and-mouse game is played by the two archenemies. This is delightful, and razor sharp. Extraordinarily, Moriarty wins. In a desperate last-ditch attempt to save face before the Inspector, Holmes insists that Cooper examine the professor's walking stick: "You'll find it contains a springknife

with which he tried to kill me just the other night!" smiling, Moriarty unscrews the top of the stick to reveal a glass vial filled with a dark liquid. Brandy for damp nights, he explains, and offers each in turn a sip from it. (All refuse.) Whereupon Moriarty smiles, bids all farewell, and walks out the door—a free man.

Holmes's failure to entrap the Professor certainly indicated a sequel in the works: especially as the steely-eyed detective watches Moriarty's limousine giving a lift to the necklace's new owner, a wealthy Texan. Will a Sherlockian film once more venture to America? And as a second tantalizer, in the German film it is mentioned that Jack the Ripper is again at work in London!

With all the indication of a follow-up film, it is surprising that Christopher Lee did not play Sherlock Holmes once more, although he starred in many other films shot on the Continent, including a German Edgar Wallace-type thriller. He was even announced for a German Holmes film involving a missing train; Conan Doyle had written a mystery story called "The Lost Special," but the detective in it was *not* Sherlock. Lee, however, was not to don the false nose again, and was not to be involved with a Conan Doyle character for nearly a decade, when he portrayed an all too lean Mycroft Holmes.

(*Note:* while more accurately translated into English as *Sherlock Holmes and the Necklace of Death,* the English-language version of the film was titled *. . . and the Deadly Necklace.*)

A distinguished Professor Moriarty (second from left, Hans Söhnker) offers Inspektor Cooper (right, Hans Nielson) a drink from his flask-concealing cane, as Holmes and Watson look on—in the puzzling climax of this film.

A Study in Terror

A Compton-Tekli-Sir Nigel Films Production (British; U.S. release: Columbia Pictures), 1965. Screenplay by Donald and Derek Ford. Based on characters created by Sir Arthur Conan Doyle. Executive Producer, Herman Cohen. Produced by Henry E. Lester. Directed by James Hill.

CAST

Sherlock Holmes, John Neville; Dr. Watson, Donald Houston; Lord Carfax, John Fraser; Dr. Murray, Anthony Quayle; Mycroft Holmes, Robert Morley; Annie Chapman, Barbara Windsor; Angela, Adrienne Corri; Inspector Lestrade, Frank Finlay; Sally, Judi Dench; Prime Minister, Cecil Parker; Saloon Singer, Georgia Brown; Duke of Shires, Barry Jones; Max Steiner, Peter Carsten; Home Secretary, Dudley Foster; Michael, John Cairney; Mrs. Hudson, Barbara Leake.

The second Sherlock Holmes film to be made in color represented an innovative step forward on a number of counts. A Study in Terror not only took the fictional detective and challenged him with a real crime from his own period in history, it also gave us a younger Holmes with a pronounced flair for action in a film more sexually explicit than any Holmesian cinematic adventure had been before it. It was an excellent contribution to the genre.

Much of the credit must go to executive producer Herman Cohen, an American whose work ranged from I Was a Teenage Werewolf in this country to, in London, Konga and Horrors of the Black Museum. It is to his credit that he rose from the level of these low-budget chillers to tackle the intriguing concept of Sherlock Holmes solving the

Sherlock Holmes (John Neville, right) discusses the Ripper murders with Lord Carfax (John Fraser) and Dr. Murray's niece.

Angela (Adrienne Corri), the pubman's wife, reveals her scarred face.

case of Jack the Ripper, for the detective and the murderer coexisted in London and in history. Originally he called the treatment *Fog,* and not only did he receive the blessing of the Conan Doyle estate, he also involved the new family production company—Sir Nigel Films (named after another Doyle hero)—as coproducers.

A lavish color film was the result, realistically re-creating the sordid East End, setting of the Ripper murders, in detail, sparing neither the depravity of the period nor the sadistic horror of the times. That this was done both with excitement and taste is due to the skill of British director James Hill, who in a long career had worked in every style of film including documentaries. An intelligent script by brothers Donald and Derek Ford presented a surprisingly accurate solution to the Ripper mystery, pointing, as does more recently uncovered evidence, to the involvement of a titled family.

But the true joy of the film was in its casting. Young, blond John Neville was a dashing Holmes, absolutely superb, proving once again that the most exciting Sherlocks (Rathbone, Cushing, Barrymore) have had solid Shakespearean training. Crisp, cool, prone to action, this new Holmes is not above trading blows with ruffians, *and* using a swordstick *("Spell his name excitement!");* a *mod* Holmes, the press marveled—a change partially influenced by the advent and success of another British hero, James Bond, a few years before, but in no way altering the Conan Doyle original beyond recognition. A good cast of English star players helped recreate the times (saloon singer Georgia Brown is especially remembered for her raucous period songs), headed by Donald Houston as a solid, wonderful Watson—perhaps the best Watson on the screen—and Robert Morley in the unique role of Sherlock's brother Mycroft—the first time the corpulent, wise older Holmes had been presented on the talking screen.

(Curiously enough, actors Robert Morley and John Neville, here portraying brothers, appeared five years earlier in the film *Oscar Wilde,* in the roles of Wilde and young friend Lord Alfred Douglas!)

Even before the opening credits a scarlet-dressed prostitute is stalked down the dark London streets, and a knife flashes. Her body is discovered *("Police! Help! Murder!"),* and the credits form in swirling fog, accompanied by a haunting, seductive, melancholy musical theme by John Scott. The sense of East End depravity and squalor is quite strong, as we wander through Whitechapel saloons and alleys, mingling with pickpockets, addicts and whores—and watch Jack the Ripper carve once again from the shadows.

After the third death, all London is in an uproar, and a surgical kit is sent anonymously to Baker Street. Holmes goes into his deductive act (the kit has recently been in a pawnshop window, which "faces south in a narrow street . . . and I might also add that the pawnbroker is a foreigner"). A concealed coat-of-arms on the kit leads Holmes and Watson to the stately home of the elderly Duke of Shires, who has disowned his older son—who had trained for medicine—because he had married a prostitute. The younger son, the pleasant Lord Carfax (John Fraser), claims not not have seen his brother Michael in years. Holmes then heads for Whitechapel. (It is both interesting and laudable that both the stately homes and the cobblestoned East End streets are at least in part location shots, something of a change from the Hollywood London of the Rathbone films.)

Suspects abound in the sinister district: a brutal pub owner and his wife, mysteriously scarred; the seemingly kindly Dr. Murray (Anthony Quayle), who with a dim-witted, necrophilic assistant runs a clinic-cum-soup-kitchen. In a well-done scene a marvelously disguised derelict Holmes leaves the revivalist soup kitchen—a grateful, starved-looking child grabs the remains of his food—and follows the doctor's niece ("I saw no one!"—"That is what people may expect to see when I follow them.") She has become romantically involved with young Lord Carfax, and it is his money which has kept her uncle's hospice operating.

A very dashing Holmes in full evening dress then takes a nonplussed Watson for a night at the low tavern called the Angel and Crown, but it is actually to harass the place's brutish owner ("My name would alarm you . . ."). As they leave, Holmes senses they are being followed: "Watch your back; I saw a movement in the shadow." It is a splendid opportunity to display his agility against three thugs—happily his walking stick has a steel-blade tip!

There are other deaths, and in the streets of East End an impassioned Dr. Murray tries to rouse the rabble: "Thanks to Jack the Ripper, thanks to this brutal killer, the world is watching Whitechapel. But it's not the killings by a demented hand the world finds horrible. It's the murder by poverty, the murder by misery, the murder by hunger—the cry of the starving, the moan of the sick!" And there are repercussions even in Parliament, where a worried Prime Minister asks Mycroft Holmes,

one of Her Majesty's most valued subjects, to intercede with his brother in finding the murderer. Mycroft, played to perfection by Robert Morley as a careful mix of pompous government official and shrewd ratiocinator (for, after all, he is a Holmes!), descends upon Baker Street.

HOLMES: My dear Mycroft, this is a surprise! Watson, some sherry. . . . Is this a social call?

MYCROFT: Yes, yes, oh yes, purely social. (pause) How are you?

HOLMES: Very well. (pause) Well, now that the social call is over, hadn't we better get down to business?

Even though it is of little concern to him whether, as Mycroft claims, public outcry may topple the government, Holmes assures his brother that he is investigating the case.

(The interplay between the two is the film's delicious high point. The bickering of the tempermental Mycroft gives us insight into both intellects, and also a rare glimpse of the brothers' childhoods as a brooding Sherlock attacks his violin, cello-style between his knees and Mycroft screams: "For Heaven's sake, stop sawing away on that infernal instrument! It was a sad day when Mother gave it to you, a sad day for her, a sad day for you, a sad day for us all . . . What I cannot understand is why, since you've had that violin with you so long, you have never learned to play!")

Another gruesome murder occurs, and Holmes unearths the vanished Michael, the Duke of Shires' elder son: he is now Dr. Murray's twisted, mindless assistant, his sanity gone when he accidentally spilled acid on his wife's face on discovering her with a lover. (The woman, Angela, is now the disfigured wife of the owner of the Angel and Crown.) He returns Michael to the home of his stern but ultimately forgiving father. Watson cannot understand where all this will lead.

HOLMES: There is work to be done before the final curtain can be brought down. That is what we have been doing this morning: setting the scene and rehearsing for the last act of Jack the Ripper.

WATSON (puzzled resignation): I wondered what we'd been doing. . . .

The final act is not long in starting. Holmes surmises that the Ripper will now attempt to kill Angela, and sets a trap for him in her bedroom upstairs in the chambers above the Angel and Crown. The killer is revealed to be Lord Carfax,

Holmes learns from Dr. Murray (Anthony Quayle) some startling information regarding the real identity of his halfwit assistant Michael (John Cairney).

Not terribly restrained poster art and copy for the film. Reference to "the original caped crusader" serves to compare Holmes with the then current popular success of Batman on television—another cape-carrying detective.

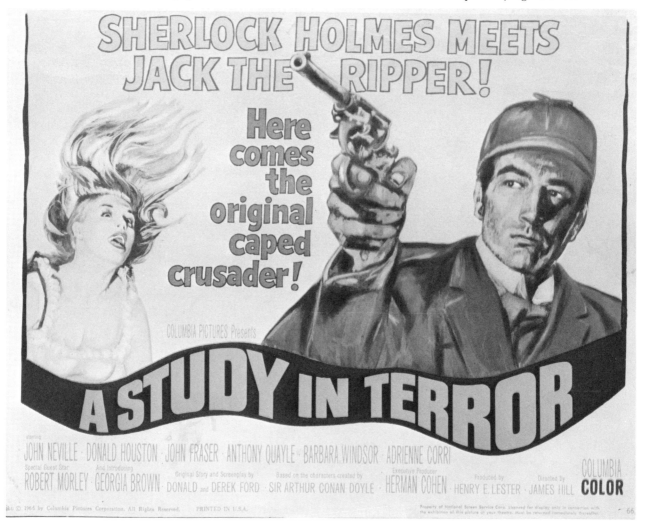

Holmes placidly saws away at his violin while brother Mycroft (Robert Morley) berates him.

In the slum doctor's grim backroom surgery.

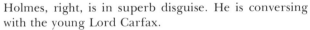
Holmes, right, is in superb disguise. He is conversing with the young Lord Carfax.

and the two engage in a fierce struggle. An oil lamp overturns, and the room is soon ablaze. Lord Carfax dies in the fire, but the agile detective escapes.

WATSON: But how on earth did you get out of it, Holmes?

HOLMES: You know my methods, Watson. I am well known to be indestructible.

Holmes will not reveal the identity of Jack the Ripper to the world, for "the family has suffered enough," and hopefully now will die out, for the detective has traced insanity back through four generations. Mrs. Hudson interrupts with a parcel (containing a bowler hat but with no message), and an elated, enthusiastic Holmes announces the game is once more afoot.

Holmes exposes the grim secret of Angela Osborne, whose scarred face is turned away.

B. Lee). The resultant paperback is more than just a prose retelling of the movie's plot; it is a small masterpiece: Ellery Queen, in contemporary time, comes upon an unpublished Watson manuscript about Jack the Ripper. Alternating chapters present Watson's story and Ellery's musing on the case; Ellery, from the vantage point of a half-century later, even elaborates and alters the Holmesian solution! The book is an ingenious work, two great detectives uniting across the barriers of time, and because it was only issued as a paperback and as a lowly movie tie-in, a scarce Sherlockian treasure.

Had the previous Anglo-American Sherlockian images, Rathbone and Cushing, been middle-aged and stuffy? John Neville, brash and youthful, was a new, striking, attention-getting Sherlock, showing filmmakers that there were still possibilities of freshness in dealing with the great detective. Sherlock Holmes was on the comeback trail.

In a blazing holocaust Holmes comes to grips with the real Jack the Ripper.

The critics, even though cringing somewhat at the necessary realism of the crimes depicted, lauded the film. "Sly and stylish," *Time* magazine called it (11/25/66), and rightly noted that "Bonds may come and Maigrets may go, but Sherlock Holmes goes on forever." The New York *Times* (11/3/66) praised the authentic Victorian flavor of a pleasant diversion: "the supersleuth and superkiller are well met now because a sense of humor and an unvarnished, old-fashioned melodrama raise the film several steps above the normal chiller."

There is a curious literary footnote to the film. Movie tie-in novelizations had been commonplace during the sixties, the work generally done by hack writers. But the agent contacted by Columbia Pictures (the American distributor), to create the book version of *A Study in Terror* happened to interest one of the greatest mystery writers of our time, Ellery Queen (actually the pseudonym of two Brooklyn cousins, Frederic Dannay and Manfred

214

The Private Life
of Sherlock Holmes

Robert Stephens as Sherlock Holmes, youthful and enthusiastic, discovers a clue in a canary feather.

United Artists, 1970. Written by Billy Wilder and I. A. L. Diamond "based on the characters created by Sir Arthur Conan Doyle." Produced and directed by Billy Wilder.

CAST

Sherlock Holmes, Robert Stephens; *Dr. John H. Watson,* Colin Blakely; *Mrs. Hudson,* Irene Handl; *First Gravedigger,* Stanley Halloway; *Mycroft Holmes,* Christopher Lee; *Gabrielle Valladon,* Genevieve Page; *Rogozhin,* Clive Reville; *Petrova,* Tamara Toumanova; *Old Lady,* Catherine Lacey; *Queen Victoria,* Mollie Maureen; *Inspector Lestrade,* George Benson.

The next cinematic Holmes was conceived by a man of extraordinary talent—as a comedy. Billy Wilder, the Austro-Hungarian writer-director, had emigrated to Hollywood in the early thirties and had been responsible for some of the most memorable achievements of the film medium in both drama and comedy: *The Lost Weekend, Sunset Boulevard, Some Like It Hot, The Apartment.* He had won six Academy Awards. For years he had wanted to film a Holmesian adventure, a *new* adventure giving fresh insight into the relationship between the detective and Watson. In 1970, having received financing from United Artists, Wilder began production at Pinewood Studios outside London on the most opulent Sherlock Holmes film to be made to that date, enigmatically titled *The Private Life of Sherlock Holmes,* "Being an account of some hitherto suppressed and thoroughly fascinating adventures of the greatest detective of all time as revealed by his friend John H. Watson, M.D.,

Colin Blakely as Dr. John H. Watson, Holmes's respectful biographer and devoted friend.

Holmes at Baker Street, working with his cigarette-smoking apparatus for a definitive study of tobacco ash. ("I'm sure there's a crying need for that," sniffs Mrs. Hudson, well played by character actress Irene Handl.)

late Indian Army." These "lost" stories were supposedly unearthed from Watson's dispatch box, opened at last after many long years in a London bank vault. The Sherlockian world, aware of Wilder's trenchant wit and bold humor, were somewhat nervous about the possibility of distortion and blasphemy.

Wilder's rebuttal was widely quoted. "We approached the characters and the Baker Street atmosphere in a straightforward manner, with warm-heartedness and good humor. I've loved the stories from boyhood, and the last thing I would want to do is parody them in any way. We treated Holmes and Watson with respect but not reverence. There's a certain amount of natural humor but the stories in our picture essentially show the relationship and friendship between the two men in their early years. And we hope the results will prove entertaining and maybe enlightening." All very well, but there were disquieting rumors that the impish Wilder (with his long-time collaborator, I. A. L. Diamond) had in his script *really* explored Holmes's private life—which Conan Doyle certainly did not—including his relationship with Watson and disdain of women, touching such "forbidden" topics as drugs and homosexuality!

Casting National Theatre Company actor Robert Stephens as Holmes underscored the possibility of offbeat currents; Stephens's master detective was only mutedly stern, his larkish superiority masking an obvious vulnerability which Wilder insisted was essential to the role. *His* Holmes could be hurt. And could also demonstrate affection: Wilder confided that his story was actually a love affair between two men. It is of course platonic and subconscious, for to trifle more with the traditional image would undoubtedly cause a public outrage, but Wilder at least wanted to illuminate facets of Holmes's makeup over which there had long been speculation.

Stephens was a superb performer; in 1965 he had been declared Great Britain's Best Stage Actor of the Year. In the pivotal co-starring role of Watson, Wilder chose talented English stage actor Colin Blakely, who had already appeared in several important films (*Saturday Night and Sunday Morning, This Sporting Life, A Man For All Seasons*) and had already worked comfortably with Stephens in several plays. Christopher Lee—adding to his Holmesian gallery—was given Mycroft's part, disregarding Doyle's description of Sherlock's brother as portly. Some of England's best players—as well as Continental beauty Genevieve Page and Russian ballerina Tamara Toumanova—were added to the cast.

Equally impressive were the spectacular sets and six-month shooting schedule. Production designer Alexander Trauner took pains with Holmes's rooms: masses of Victorian bric-a-brac, his littered chemistry bench, unanswered mail pinned to the mantelpiece with a knife, tobacco in a Persian slipper and cigars in the coal scuttle, initials *V. R.* shot in the wall. (Adrian Conan Doyle, who just before his death visited the set, declared delightedly, "If Sherlock Holmes were to enter this room he would immediately feel right at home—everything is exactly in its place.") Mycroft's Diogenes Club featured five hundred yards of books. Location work was filmed at Loch Ness in Scotland—where a sea monster was actually imported. But the most awesome set in the film was the recreation of Baker Street in the 1880s, built on the back lot—a fantastic street with more than a dozen horse-drawn carriages and nearly a hundred period extras (the street curved only slightly to give it forced perspective) which curiously was given only minimal use in the finished motion picture!

Indeed, this glittering film with all its careful attention to components and impressive contributors—Miklos Rozsa, for instance, composed a special score for the film and can be seen at one point conducting in the orchestra pit during a ballet sequence—was truncated before its general release. Wilder had created a work which ran well over two hours; a nervous United Artists decided its future was shaky and the distribution could be handled better if a half hour were trimmed. Continuity would not be too much damaged as *Private Life* was supposedly a composite of several new cases and some of them could be dropped. Alas, the illumination for which Wilder had been striving was now somewhat dimmed.

However, enough of this radical Holmesian image remains to merit our attention. In the first Baker Street scenes, Holmes takes Watson to task for distorting facts in his *Strand* stories:

HOLMES: You have taken my simple exercises in logic and embellished them, embroidered them, exaggerated them . . .

WATSON: I deny the accusation.

HOLMES: You have described me as six-foot-four, whereas I am barely six-foot-one.

WATSON: A bit of poetic license.

HOLMES: You have saddled me with this improbable costume, which the public now expects me to wear.

The fragile Gabrielle (Genevieve Page) is rescued from the Thames and brought to Baker Street.

Holmes, Gabrielle and Watson journey to Inverness, while above them file a procession of Trappist monks (who are actually a band of German agents).

WATSON: That's not my doing. Blame it on the illustrator.

HOLMES: You've made me out to be a violin virtuoso. Here's a request from the Birmingham Symphony to appear as soloist in the Mendelssohn Concerto.

WATSON: Oh, really?

HOLMES: The fact is that I could barely hold my own in the pit orchestra of a second-rate music hall!

There is an easy camaraderie between the two, and perhaps more. Watson's devotion to Holmes is best illustrated by a sequence unfortunately trimmed from the final film. The detective is pulled into investigating a bizarre murder by Inspector Lestrade (played by George Benson, a performance entirely missing from the final cut): a body is found in a room where all the furniture is hanging from the ceiling, upside down. It is a case to pull Holmes from his doldrums—and from a fascination with drugs which has a worried Watson already suggesting such alternatives, curiously enough, as clinics in Switzerland and work in hyponosis being done in Paris and Vienna, suggesting faintly the plot of *The Seven-Per-Cent Solution* to come.

It does not take Holmes long—about ten minutes—to determine the corpse has been supplied from the morgue and the upside-room has been a puzzle devised by his roommate to wean him from cocaine. Holmes is amused, but a bitter quarrel ensues.

WATSON: I guess I'm not very bright.

HOLMES: No, but you're most endearing. No one could ask for a better friend.

WATSON: Friend, indeed! The only reason you moved in with me is to have a steady supply of stimulants.

HOLMES: Now, now, Watson—you mustn't underestimate your many other charms.

Watson threatens to move out of Baker Street (a sobbing Mrs. Hudson commiserates with him; "I know how it feels—I once went through a divorce myself"), but a resigned Holmes smashes his narcotics bottles with a pistol.

WATSON: Thank you, Holmes. I know how difficult it must've been for you—

HOLMES: Not really. It was a simple choice between a bad habit and a good companion.

WATSON: You've made me very happy.

HOLMES: I've often been accused of being cold and unemotional. I admit to it. And yet, in my own cold, unemotional way, I'm very fond of you, Watson.

WATSON: I know that. But one likes to hear these things occasionally.

This remarkable exchange fell to the drastic shears of anxious United Artists executives; the film is the poorer for it.

Having dismissed the issue of drugs, however, the film moves on to other vices. Holmes is summoned by the famed Russian ballerina Petrova to be the father of her child. In an effort to extricate himself from this situation, the detective points out that he is a bachelor who has spent five happy years living with another bachelor, that "through a cruel caprice of Mother Nature . . ." He leaves the sentence unfinished.

For Holmes it was merely a way to escape the attentions of a madwoman; Watson, though, is incensed at the stain on his reputation.

WATSON: Let somebody start a rumor—just one ugly word—and we'll sue them for libel.

HOLMES: Nobody would dare. After all, you have an enviable record with the fair sex.

WATSON: Damn right. I can get women from three continents to testify for me. And you can get women to vouch for you, too, can't you, Holmes? *(pause)* Can you, Holmes?

HOLMES: Good night, Watson.

WATSON: Holmes, let me ask you a question—I hope I'm not being presumptuous—but there *have* been women in your life?

HOLMES: The answer is yes—you're being presumptuous. Good night.

And on this conversation the entire remainder of the film turns, for Sherlock Holmes is to meet the woman who will soften his heart. As Watson puts it, in the narrative: "The time has come to reveal the most intimate aspect of Holmes's life: his one and only involvement with a woman. Though I may be accused of sensationalism, I do it solely to prove Holmes was not just a thinking machine, but subject to the same temptations and human failings as the rest of us."

A frail, beautiful girl is brought to Baker Street by a cabbie who claims to have fished her out of the Embankment with Holmes's address in her purse. Gabrielle Valladon had come to London (she is Belgian) looking for her husband, a missing mining engineer who had invented a new kind of air pump. She had been writing him in care of his London employer, Jonah, Ltd., but Holmes discovers it is merely an accommodation address, a shop filled with caged canaries. And the detective learns to his surprise as well that his brother Mycroft (Christopher Lee, balding and thin) is also aware of the vanished engineer. In the hallowed, forbidding library of the Diogenes Club, Mycroft warns his brother to pursue the investigation no further, as "it involves the national security."

HOLMES: I have always suspected that there was some underground connection between this stodgy and seemingly calcified establishment and the Foreign Office in Whitehall.

MYCROFT: That's neither here nor there.

HOLMES: It seems to me the Diogenes Club is here, there and everywhere. When there are rumblings of revolt in the Sudan, an expedition subsidized by your Club conveniently shows up to study the source of the Nile. When there is trouble along the Indian frontier, some of your fellow members pop up in the Himalayas, allegedly looking for the Abominable Snowman.

MYCROFT (drily, to Watson): What a fertile imagination my brother has. At the age of five, by carefully observing a neighbor's house, he deduced that babies were brought not by the stork, but by the midwife in her satchel.

Defying Mycroft's direct order—which is virtually defying the British government—Holmes continues the case. A very slim clue points to Scotland; Holmes and the lovely Gabrielle, calling themselves Mr. and Mrs. Ashdown, with Watson accompanying them as their valet John, board the Highland Express to Inverness.

On the train, Holmes and Gabrielle are alone in their compartment, and the detective reveals an incident from his past, the reason why he is "not a wholehearted admirer of womankind." It is an illuminating reminiscence, but alas also cut from the film. During his student days at Oxford, the young Holmes falls madly in love with a stunning girl he sees only at a distance. Later, he is the winning rower in a boat race against Cambridge, and as prize his teammates smuggle a prostitute into the school. Somewhat uneagerly ("I felt that I was betraying my beloved, whose name I didn't even know"), and braced with whiskey, the young man joins the prostitute—and freezes. It is the girl he has worshipped from afar. He bolts, and observes drily in retrospect on the valuable lesson he had learned: "Any emotional involvement warps your

judgement and clouds your reason." In his profession, sentiment is fatal.

(In this excised scene there is another example, too, of Wilder's pawky humor, as Holmes casually reveals that Watson's account of a case involving 121 concubines in Constantinople, as written in the *Strand* magazine, caused that issue to be confiscated and the publisher fined! A rare number, indeed!)

In a Scottish village cemetary they find the interred body of Gabrielle's husband, his copper wedding ring turned green and dead white canaries buried with him. ("There is only one substance that can turn a copper ring green and bleach the color out of canaries: chlorine gas," Holmes deduces; M.

"Mr. and Mrs. Ashdown" in a romantic moment; Watson is frowning.

Valladon was asphyxiated.) Near him two midgets have also been buried; indeed, "boys with the faces of old men" have been the only mourners at the cemetery. Later, intuition takes the trio to a "closed" castle on the shores of the Loch—a castle to which shipments of sulfuric acid (which, mixed with salt water, produces chlorine gas) and canary cages have recently been made!

By night, Holmes, Watson and Gabrielle row out into the Loch to view the castle from the water side, and an incredible sea monster rears out of the lake and capsizes them before disappearing into the mist. Holmes rightly guesses that the "monster" has a mechanical heart, when brother Mycroft invites him alone to view the secret from inside the castle. The "Diogenes Club" (read here British Government) has been experimenting with an early submarine, using Valladon's air pumps, sulfuric acid batteries, canaries to detect escaping gas, midgets to run the craft, and a sea serpent disguise to fool the townsfolk. Valladon's death was accidental. All this Holmes had easily surmised, but Mycroft's next revelation is a bombshell: the fragile Gabrielle Valladon is an impostor, actually Ilse von Hofmannsthal, one of the most skillful agents of the Imperial German Government, sent to capture the air pump by enlisting (and duping) Sherlock Holmes. "You, my dear brother, have been working for the Wilhelmstrasse."

There is another visitor to the castle, Queen Victoria herself (played by Mollie Maureen, somewhat shorter than the historical image but just as imposing). She has come up from Balmoral to view the launching of the "submersible." Her meeting with Holmes, though unregal, is a delight and a high point of the film.

VICTORIA: Ah, yes. Sherlock Holmes. We have been following your exploits with great interest.
HOLMES: Thank you, Ma'am.
VICTORIA: Are you engaged in one of your fascinating cases at the moment?
HOLMES: In a manner of speaking, Ma'am.
VICTORIA: When can we expect to read Dr. Watson's account of the case?
HOLMES: I hope never, Ma'am. It has not been one of my more successful endeavors.

In the end, Mycroft takes Ilse into custody and she is exchanged for a captured British agent at the Swiss-German border. The defeated girl proudly reveals to Holmes she had asked for the assignment: "I couldn't resist the challenge of coming up against the best. I'm sorry I didn't give you a closer game." Despite her defiance, there is an unspoken tenderness in their parting. With her parasol—she had been using it as a Morse code transmitter—she signals him "auf Wiedersehen."

Six months later a message from Mycroft arrives at Baker Street: Fraulein Ilse von Hofmannsthal was arrested by the Japanese for spying on Yokohama Harbor naval installations, and executed by firing squad. "It might interest you to know," the note continues, "she had been living in Japan these last few months under the name of Mrs. Ashdown" (the name Holmes and she assumed as husband and wife in Scotland). "Where is it, Watson?", a distraught Holmes begs, and Watson shows him where in his files he has hidden a bottle of cocaine. The detective retires to his bedroom as the Miklos Rozsa music score soars over the end credits, a tragic love story coming to a completely melancholy finish.

Interestingly, an epilogue was prepared which was not in the final film. Inspector Lestrade—who, as noted, is completely eliminated in the ultimate cut—stops by Baker Street to enlist Holmes's help in solving the murder of three prostitutes in Whitechapel, the work of a killer the newspapers are calling Jack the Ripper. Holmes is too grief-stricken to be of use, so Watson proffers some excuse. "Well," Lestrade retorts, "I daresay we can solve it without his help." An ingenious explanation as to why Holmes never apprehended London's most notorious criminal!

For the record, the only major sequence cut from the film involves a sea journey on the Mediterranean and is unrelated to the main plot. Two bodies are discovered aboard ship, and Holmes and Watson go below deck to investigate. They find the bodies in bed—an undressed young honeymoon couple—and Watson deduces they have been poisoned by a swizzle stick. Then the "corpses" stir; they have been only overcome by champagne, and actually the detectives have entered the wrong stateroom. There is also a dropped prologue in which young Canadian Dr. Watson, grandson of the original and a veterinarian, opens up the tin dispatch box brought from the vaults of Barclay's Bank and begins the new adventures.

Critical reception of *The Private Life of Sherlock Holmes* was reasonably favorable; Vincent Canby in the *New York Times* (10/30/70) was clearly amused: "There is simply no reason to cavil with Billy

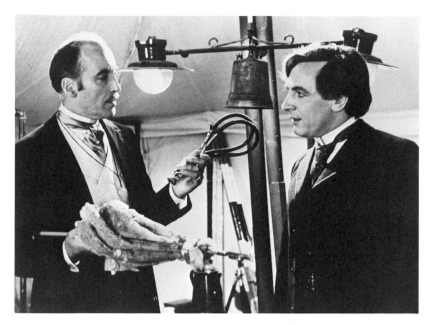

Holmes's brother Mycroft (Christopher Lee without hairpiece) shows the detective how he has been duped by German agent Ilse von Hofmannsthal, who has used her parasol to flash Morse code messages.

Two differing moods shared between Sherlock Holmes and Gabrielle.

Wilder's mostly comic, charming psychosexual analysis . . . I suspect that only Wilder would have the nerve to raise such a question [were Holmes and Watson lovers?] and then to dispatch it in a movie that is gentle enough to become the Thanksgiving holiday attraction at the Music Hall." For Canby the film is "comparatively mild Billy Wilder and rather daring Sherlock Holmes, not a perfect mix, but a fond and entertaining one."

Other critics were also favorable, but some were less impressed. Certainly the decision by United Artists executives to mercilessly, unforgivably mutilate the film before release—slashing it by nearly thirty minutes—did not help characterizations, mood, or critical acceptance. Appearing just a few years too soon, somewhat before the immense renewal of interest in Holmes (and before the emergence of what was later to be called the "buddy" vogue of movies depicting easy camaraderie between male friends), *Private Life* pioneered a portrait of Sherlock the man—faulted, human, no mere brain machine—that was only some years away from being accepted.

Robert Stephens's unconventional portrayal of the detective—by turns elegant, affected, sensitive, misogynistic, and in some few scenes almost priggish and bizarre—challenges our own images of Holmes and is beneath the surface amazingly busy and complex. It is a good one, and ultimately as illuminating as the character Wilder has liberally redesigned. Despite the "daring" premise of the film, the Sherlock Holmes we discover in the film—eccentric, arrogant, drug user, mistrusting women ("a twinkle in the eye, a pinch of arsenic in the soup"), comfortable with Watson and devoted to him—is stretched no further really from the portrait originally given us in the Conan Doyle stories.

Watson says in the opening of the film, in a message intended for his heirs: *In my lifetime, I have recorded some sixty cases, demonstrating the singular gift of my friend Sherlock Holmes, dealing with everything from the Hound of the Baskervilles to his mysterious brother Mycroft and the devilish Professor Moriarty. But there were other adventures which, for reason of discretion, I have decided to withhold from the public until this much later date. They involve matters of a—delicate and sometimes scandalous nature . . . .* But the disclosures are more human than scandalous. Despite a somewhat comic treatment of the Conan Doyle source, the film is Wilder's loving homage to "the man who elevated the science of deduction to an art, the world's first—and undeniably most famous—Consulting Detective" . . . and his good friend. *The Private Life of Sherlock Holmes* is among the very best Holmesian appearances on the screen, and—as Billy Wilder freely admits—a personal valentine.

They Might Be Giants

A Holmesian figure and his earnest Watson.

A Universal Picture, 1971. A Jennings Lang presentation. Screenplay by James Goldman, based on his play. Produced by John Foreman. Directed by Anthony Harvey.

CAST

Dr. Mildred Watson, Joanne Woodward; *Justin Playfair,* George C. Scott; *Wilbur Peabody,* Jack Gilford; *Blevins Playfair,* Lester Rawlins; *Daisy,* Rue McClanahan; *Dr. Strauss,* Ron Weyand; *Grace,* Kitty Winn; *Grace's boyfriend,* Peter Fredericks; *Maud,* Sudie Bond; *Miss Finch,* Jenny Egan.

Not *exactly* a Sherlockian film, but enough within the genre to qualify for our inspection, *They Might Be Giants* presents us with a madman who only *thinks* he is Sherlock Holmes. Because this is only a fancy, our standards can be minimal, but the acting involved is extraordinarily adept: George C. Scott, an American player, registers much of the authority and crispness of the genuine Holmes, in sharp contrast to the weaknesses displayed only a few years previously in *Private Life.* And, since in this encounter "Watson" turns out to be a woman, Holmes can permit his affections full rein without raising an eyebrow.

In truth, *They Might Be Giants* is every bit as fragile and tender as its immediate cinematic predecessor, and indeed, like *Private Life,* was misunderstood, mutilated, and a box-office failure. The ambitious project represented a collaboration between director Anthony Harvey and writer James Goldman, who had three years before teamed for the extremely successful historical tableau, *The Lion*

223

in Winter. Goldman's gossamer romantic fantasy was drawn from a play which had never been presented on Broadway, and is as fanciful and philosophic and pure at heart as anything done in earlier decades by Frank Capra. But as a Sherlockian fancy, it fell flat.

The cast, however, contained many amiable eccentrics to help along its fairy-tale elements, and was headed by George C. Scott, who as a Holmes figure was a tower of strength, just as he was two years previously in his award-winning performance as *Patton.* Interestingly, in 1963 he had the opportunity also to unravel a mystery as the crime-solver, retired British Secret Serviceman Anthony Gethryn, in the film made from Philip MacDonald's *The List of Adrian Messenger,* playing some scenes opposite Clive Brook; one wonders if the two discussed Holmes? Playing with Scott is Joanne Woodward (who actually receives top billing), whose portrayal of Dr. Mildred Watson—fascinated by the mad Scott, who uses Holmesian deductive skills to make accurate diagnoses about her patients—is first-rate and (even though she is of course not really a Watson figure) even Canonically appealing.

To sum up the peripherally Sherlockian plot briefly, Justin Playfair (Scott) is a widowed former New York judge who believes he is Holmes, dressing in deerstalker, setting up his townhouse as a crime laboratory, making deductions. His brother Blevins, quite unlike him and indeed a wicked schemer who is being blackmailed by the underworld, is trying desperately to have Justin committed to an insane asylum so that he can control the family fortune. To have Justin certified, Blevins enlists a specialist in abnormal psychology, a woman who unfortunately for Blevin's plot is named Watson. She is fascinated by Justin's "classic paranoia," and he in turn has found his companion-ally for the struggle against an unseen archfiend, Moriarty. Together they scour the city chasing down clues—actually evidences of the blackmailing vice ring—and meet a parade of Justin's outrageously eccentric friends, including a librarian who fancies himself as the Scarlet Pimpernel (Jack Gilford). At first Dr. Mildred Watson accompanies Justin only to study him firsthand, but soon finds herself drawn into his world, believing in him.

The climax is both ambivalent and poignant. Fleeing the police (sent by his brother), Justin and Mildred make their way to Central Park. There, in the dusk, they hear the clatter of horses' hoofs. Justin knows it is the forces of evil—Moriarty—and it may mean their deaths. Mildred Watson by this time has "crossed over," and shares in all of Justin's fancies. Together they will resist the unseen foe hurtling towards them, or die—as the screen is wiped into color. We recall Justin's comment earlier, giving us the title of the film, that Don Quixote was mad because he thought *all* windmills were giants to be fought—but despite Quixote's madness, they *might* be giants.

It is a curious footnote that Universal Pictures (who had in an earlier decade fattened from the Rathbone Holmeses) had so little faith in the film as made that they excised its climax—a scene in a supermarket just before our pair escape into Central Park, where Justin inspires his eccentric friends into a Marx Brothers melee against the police pursuing him. They felt it gave too raucous a note to the film; instead they added a high-sounding prologue stating that good men have fought evil men down through history—comparing Holmes versus Moriarty to Faust's struggles against the devil—and closed the picture with a lofty platitude: *The human heart can see what is hidden to the eyes, and the heart knows things that the mind does not begin to understand.* Interestingly, because the motion picture was now a short 88 minutes, not long enough to fit comfortably in prime time television's two-hour movie slot (which demands 95 minutes of film before commercials), for its TV debut *They Might Be Giants* had the supermarket sequence restored!

But of course the restoration was too late. In the theaters the abridged film won over few of the New York critics, despite the fact it had largely been shot in New York and New Jersey. Vincent Canby in the *Times* called it "a mushy movie," and others felt repelled by the Tinkerbell-like declarations of the reality of fantasy: Peter Pan pleading that Moriarty lives. Judith Crist in *New York* magazine at least laid the blame for the film's failure (though she called it "a fine madness") to its being "mangled . . . with cutting and the insertion of simple-minded prologue and epilogue" by the studio.

Newsday, in its incisive putdown (6/10/71) by Joseph Gelmis, felt: "For Scott's unbalanced character, Moriarty represents a personal devil, a specific name and face and conspiracy for what would otherwise be merely meaningless random tragedy, death, crime and violence"; it called the film pretentious and muddled, overripe surreal romanticism. Molly Haskell in the *Village Voice* (6/24) was even more savage, lashing out against an overdosage of whimsy "culminating in a Fellini-esque chorus-line which marches through the streets of New York and, more than all the accumulated and encrusted dirt, dope, and dog-doo, makes you want to flee to the suburbs . . . In the last scene, Scott and Woodward stand side by side in Central Park, waiting for the forces of reality to mow them down. Their eyes are ablaze and an invisible halo surrounds them, as they translate their nemesis into the sound of hoofbeats, turn impending doom into the spiritual salvation of a white horse. (Give me the jingling bells and satanic appeal of *Belle de Jour*'s dark horse anytime.)"

The judge who believes he is the reincarnation of Holmes finds himself trapped in a meat locker with a female Dr. Watson. (George C. Scott with Joanne Woodward.)

The cop on the beat (Oliver Clark) greets Scott's Inverness-clad figure with a "How do you do, Mr. Rathbone," as Dr. Watson (Joanne Woodward) looks on.

A quizzical Lester Rawlins (at desk) watches the transaction between Scott and Al Lewis. Theresa Merritt is the transfixed lady.

225

Sherlock Holmes' Smarter Brother
GENE WILDER

Douglas Wilmer as Sherlock Holmes, clenching an enormous pipe between his teeth. Of Sigi, he observes: "He has spent most of the past thirty-five years getting hopelessly twisted in my shadow."

Twentieth Century-Fox, 1975. Original screenplay by Gene Wilder. Produced by Richard A. Roth. Directed by Gene Wilder.

CAST

Sigi Holmes, Gene Wilder; *Jenny*, Madeline Kahn; *Orville Sacker*, Marty Feldman; *Gambetti*, Dom DeLuise; *Moriarty*, Leo McKern; *Moriarty's Assistant*, Roy Kinnear; *Lord Redcliff*, John Le Mesurier; *Sherlock Holmes*, Douglas Wilmer; *Dr. Watson*, Thorley Walters; *Bruner*, George Silver; *Queen Victoria*, Susan Field.

By 1975 the spectacular success of William Gillette's stage play revival and Nick Meyer's novel, *The Seven-Per-Cent Solution*, made Sherlock Holmes ripe for affectionate parody, and in that good-natured spirit *The Adventure of Sherlock Holmes'*

Smarter Brother was born. It was the brainchild of the immensely talented Gene Wilder, a comedian with a rewarding creative association with Mel Brooks in such winning laugh-getters as *The Producers*, *Blazing Saddles* and *Young Frankenstein*. Wilder (in collaboration with Brooks) wrote the screenplay for *Young Frankenstein*—a send-up of Gothic science-terror—and shortly after its release he (with producer-friend Richard Roth) hit upon Holmes as the basis for a film comedy. Actually, they had discussed the idea briefly—the Conan Doyle stories had long been Wilder favorites—and a week later Roth asked if he had given further thought to Holmes. "No," Wilder replied, but I have given a great deal of thought to Sherlock Holmes's insanely jealous brother, Sigerson!" And a film was devised.

Because the Wilder creation deals not specifically with Sherlock but with his hitherto unrevealed brother Sigi (and not with brother Mycroft, whom Doyle implied *was* smarter), the film does not merit exhaustive attention. Yet Sherlock *does* play his part in the unfolding, and Wilder himself admitted "I'm not doing a spoof on Sherlock Holmes." In approaching the role of Sigi, he tried to create "a real and many-sided character" in a comedy in which one might also find "romance, intrigue, adventure . . . an undercurrent of seriousness and a little melancholy."

Wilder surrounded himself with many members of the Mel Brooks comedy stock company, including Madeline Kahn, Dom DeLuise and the wild-eyed Marty Feldman (portraying Sergeant Orville Sacker from the records bureau of Scotland Yard, who throws his lot with Sherlock's brother and who is a Sherlockian leg-pull—for "Orville Sacker" was Doyle's original name for Holmes's assistant). Very appropriately cast was superb British character actor Leo McKern as Professor Moriarty. Actually born in Australia, but an English stage and screen actor since the late forties, McKern had a massive presence which made him ideal for the role. "Although I'm often cast as the 'heavy,' I think I'm a better comedian than a straight actor. But when I'm allowed to combine the two, then I really can take off. I've never had a part like this . . . it's the part an actor prays for."

In addition to a well-cast Moriarty, the film includes several remarkable cameo appearances by Sherlock Holmes and Dr. Watson. Holmes is portrayed by Douglas Wilmer, who had already been familiar in the deerstalker in the first BBC-TV series on the great detective. Interestingly, he had also starred on ITV's *The Rivals of Sherlock Holmes* and had played Sax Rohmer's very Holmesian creation, Sir Denis Nayland Smith, opposite Christopher Lee as Dr. Fu Manchu. Thorley Walters as Watson showed again his particular flair for period comedy; he had already played the doctor opposite Christopher Lee in *Sherlock Holmes and the Deadly Necklace.* Together Wilmer and Walters had made a very quick Holmes–Watson walk-on in a smirky British comedy, *The Best House in London* (MGM), about the reclaiming of a brothel, in which such other historical personages appeared as Dickens, Tennyson, Wilde and Lord Alfred Douglas.

After a somewhat tasteless opening involving Queen Victoria and missing state papers, we see Holmes and Watson at home at Baker Street—through a keyhole at which a hulking killer is peering. Out of his sight, while drinking tea and conversing normally, Holmes holds up cue signs for

Watson to read: UGLY 6-FT. 3-IN. MURDERER AT KEYHOLE, and then, as Watson sputters, ACT NORMALLY. Holmes then reveals that the Queen believes unless the stolen document be returned by Thursday, the country will be involved in a devastating war.

HOLMES: We have two and a half days. You know my thinking, Watson. How would you proceed?
WATSON: Seven forty-five to Paris.
HOLMES: Bravo! I don't suppose you've figured out some ingenious plan for us to leave the country without tipping off every murderer and petty thief in England as soon as we set foot on the train?
WATSON: Well, that's the sticky part, isn't it?

Sigi Holmes (Gene Wilder) practices his swordsmanship—a cavalier pose.

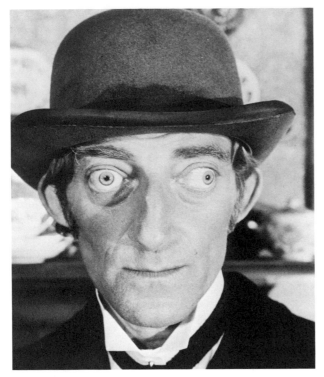

Marty Feldman is Orville Sacker of Scotland Yard, the man with the photographic sense of hearing. Says Sherlock: "For delivering messages exactly as they were given him, he has no peer in England."

Music-hall singer Jenny Hill (Madeline Kahn). She and Sigi will prance to a dance called "The Kangaroo Hop."

HOLMES: Quite simple! While Sherlock is gone, he shall pass on one or two of his less urgent assignments to his younger brother, Sigerson.

WATSON: Holmes! You never told me you had a brother Sigerson!

HOLMES: I never told you I had a brother Mycroft, until the occasion arose.

The "trifling" assignment Holmes passes onto his younger brother is the case of a young, beautiful music hall singer, Jenny Hill, who is being blackmailed. He passes the details of the case to his brother via Orville Stanley Sacker, sergeant of the Records Bureau of Scotland Yard, "not bright, but trustworthy," and the only man Holmes has ever met "who has a photographic sense of hearing." He can always be depended upon to deliver a message *exactly* as given. Orville finds Sigi insanely jealous of his older (by five years) brother, always ready to prove he can beat Sherlock at his own game. He is, however, an incurable romantic, and is soon involved in desperate situations—including Rathbone-like sword fights—in his efforts to aid the pretty singer, whose stories often contradict and who may not be all that she seems. Indeed, she may well be one of Moriarty's many pawns.

The evil Professor is extraordinarily well drawn, and the comic liberties taken with his insidiousness are all affectionate. (One notes with amusement that the sums chalked on his blackboard have mistakes in their totals!) In his secret laboratory, he gives a minion who has disappointed him the choice of leaving through a door behind which we hear a woman's alluring voice, or another door from which an animal snarls. Naturally, the victim chooses the first exit—and there are sounds of screams and a tiger's roar. A calm spreads over Moriarty's twitching face. He opens another door of his lab—where sits a priest in a confessional!

MORIARTY: Forgive me, Father, for I have sinned. It's the curse again, and I know you'll understand. Of course, it must be a great trial to your patience, Father, but just think of the burden it's been to me, ever since the day when my hereditary tendencies finally burst into the open and I felt this irrepressible desire to do something rotten every twenty-four minutes . . .

The priest nods benignly, and we discover it is a penny-arcade mechanical figure. Moriarty inserts a shilling into a slot: "If you could find it in your heart to forgive me, I'd be most grateful." The figure spits a card which reads "Absolved."

The most charming scenes of the film take place in the Tivoli Music Hall where Jenny Hill performs her songs ("If I'd known that love was like this/ Should I have kissed?"), an actual small theater re-created with perfect "Gay Nineties" fidelity at London's Shepperton Studios. Among the tarnished gold angels, giltwork and gas footlights Sherlock Holmes makes an appearance, disguised as an old man smoking an enormous pipe, in order to warn Sigi that an attempt was being made on Jenny's life. Alerting her to the danger forces Sigi to burst into song—and here Wilder joins Rathbone as a Sherlockian figure singing onscreen. There are many thrills in succeeding scenes, but Sigi and Orville find time to domesticate their new friendship . . .

SIGI: I suppose you call this tea???
ORVILLE: No, I call it hot water. I was just warming your cup when you grabbed it.

At the climax there is a wild, long parody of a comic Italian opera, (plus familiar film hints such

Sigi Holmes and Jenny Hill find love in what Gene Wilder has called "a romantic comedy thriller with music."

The fateful meeting between Sigi and Orville Sacker. Confusing him for his brother perhaps, the sergeant says: "May I say I've been an admirer of yours for many years, especially your handling of the case of 'The Three Testicles'."

The nefarious Professor Moriarty demonstrates his anguish at having to pay off an accomplice (the opera singer Gambetti, played by Dom DeLuise in heavy accent, who has just finished saying: "I love you face, I love you nose, where you keep you wallet?")

In an exciting highlight, Sigi and a Moriarty henchman (comedian Roy Kinnear) engage in what could be a to-the-death struggle atop giant Victorian advertising displays mounted on a speeding hansom cab.

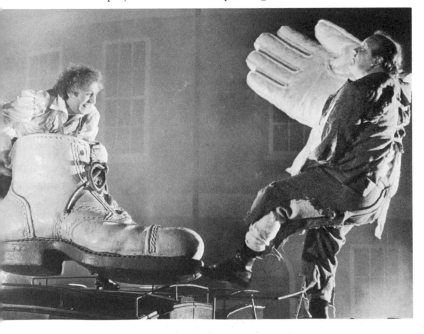

as the cymbal-crash from Hitchcock) and everyone seems at one point or another to have their hands on the sought-after Redcliff document or a counterfeit. (Just what world-shaking secret these papers contain is, in proper MacGuffin fashion, never revealed.) Sigi ultimately corners Moriarty in a storage prop room above the theater, but the Professor is carrying a sword and warns that he "used to be the sixteenth best fencer in Europe." A duel ensues.

MORIARTY: Where did you learn to fence? You have a peculiar style.
SIGI: Patricia Siddons Fencing Salon for Girls. I won the All-School Championship.

Finally, the two combatants find themselves on an outside ledge high above the Thames. Moriarty imparts a final wisdom: "It's very difficult to be a hero in real life; the villain usually doesn't behave the way he's supposed to. You were very good, son, but you should always, *always* be thinkin' two and three moves ahead. Your brother's a master at it." He lunges for the document, and falls with a scream, carrying with him a prop paper Sigi had substituted for the real thing. Moriarty was surely familiar with falling to his death—he had after all suffered this fate in at least three previous Holmesian cinematic tussles—but Gene Wilder's script provided this compassionate after-scene: a disgruntled Professor, rescued by a minion, floating down the Thames in a barge.

In an endearing epilogue, Sigi and Jenny meet in the lush greenery of a Victorian park. They kiss, sing ("But if you loved as I love . . ."), and dance away into the distance. Observing them benevolently is an old beggar playing a violin, accompanied by a stout male harpist. The pair are, of course, Holmes and Watson in disguise.

The Adventure of Sherlock Holmes' Smarter Brother is raffish comedy, and meant to be no more, but many touches display familiarity and love for the Conan Doyle writings. Even the name Sigerson was an alias Sherlock used in his roamings after the struggle at Reichenbach Falls. The critics were on the whole generous. "A comedy of wit and imagination," Judith Crist said in the *Saturday Review,* and *Time* called the film "the fastest escape from the blahs Hollywood is offering this season." But the most insightful commentary comes from Vincent Canby in the *New York Times* (12/15/75): ". . . a charming slapstick comedy that honors Sir Arthur Conan Doyle's original creation as much by what it

Jenny Hill on stage in a Victorian music hall. "I've got that 'won't you kiss me' wiggle in my style . . ."

Sherlock Holmes and Dr. Watson pretend to leave London by rail, under the watchful eye of a pie man who is actually Moriarty's minion Bruner (George Silver).

doesn't do as by what it does do. The film is a marvelously lowbrow caper but it makes no attempt to parody the great Sherlock himself, who is treated with cheerful if distant awe and respect, measured entirely in terms of Sigerson's ineptitude." Wilder's treatment "is full of affection and generous feelings for the genre it's having fun with."

At its base *Brother* is a tale of sibling fury and sibling rivalry: Sigi even has a sign saying "S. Holmes, Consulting Detective" on his door to trap the unwary client seeking out his more famous brother. He does not trap us, however; we know the film for what it is—just fun, merely tangentially Sherlockian, but still meriting our attention and our laughter.

Scenes from Gambetti's scrambled, frantic staging of Verdi's opera, "The Masked Ball," during which the Redcliff papers (on which hang the fate of the Empire) pass from hand to hand.

The Seven-Per-Cent Solution

United Artists, 1970. Screenplay by Nicholas Meyer. From his novel, "The Seven-Per-Cent Solution." Produced and directed by Herbert Ross.

CAST

Sigmund Freud, Alan Arkin; *Lola Deveraux,* Vanessa Redgrave; *Dr. Watson,* Robert Duvall; *Sherlock Holmes,* Nicol Williamson; *Professor Moriarty,* Laurence Olivier; *Lowenstein,* Joel Grey; *Mary Watson,* Samantha Eggar; *Baron Von Leinsdorf,* Jeremy Kemp; *Mycroft Holmes,* Charles Gray; *Mrs. Freud,* Georgia Brown; *Madam,* Regina; *Freda,* Anna Quayle; *Mrs. Holmes,* Jill Townsend; *Mrs. Hudson,* Alison Leggatt; *The Pasha,* Gertan Klauber; *Squire Holmes,* Leon Greene; *Young Holmes,* Michael Blagdon.

By the mid-seventies the Sherlock Holmes revival, sparked by the national preoccupation with the charms of the past which marked the start of the decade and as well by the wild success internationally of the Royal Shakespeare Company's well-timed staging of the old William Gillette play, was at its height. The renewal of interest in Sherlock and his world was fueled as well by an extraordinary work of fiction by a young Holmesian enthusiast, Nicholas Meyer, intriguingly and daringly called *The Seven-Per-Cent Solution* (the cocaine dosage the detective resorted to on dull days), which became a runaway bestseller.

Meyer took the pleasant game of Sherlockian speculation—on omissions in the Conan Doyle stories—and took it one giant step further: what if Holmes, after his encounter with Moriarty at Reichenbach falls and the erroneous reports of his

233

death, does not spend three years in hiding in Tibet and elsewhere, as Watson later tells us? What if, instead, Holmes travels to Vienna—at Watson's instigation—to undergo a drug cure at the hands of the father of psychoanalysis, Sigmund Freud? Further, what if Moriarty's terrible evil were actually the hallucination of Holmes's disordered mind?

To the Sherlockian purist this all was outright heresy; but to others it was a light-hearted, affectionate exposé which brought together two historical characters, one real and one fictional, for a highly dramatic conflict and a happy ending. (Actually, Meyer pioneered the contemporary use of this device for such later works as E. L. Doctorow's *Ragtime* and Tom Stoppard's *Travesties*.) The immensely successful account of the Holmes–Freud encounter was snapped up by Universal (the studio of the Rathbone series and the ill-fated *They Might Be Giants*) to be converted into a major motion picture.

The film, though not quite the record-breaking blockbuster the studio had hoped for, was a popular and important addition to the Holmesian cinema, aided by many extremely talented hands. Meyer provided the screen adaptation to his own book (even improving on the source by enlarging the mystery which the detective and the analyst come to solve together); he had actually written several movies and had begun the book when a long, drawn-out Writers' Guild strike in Hollywood gave him free time. Herbert Ross, the gifted producer-director, had worked on such period pieces as *Funny Girl* and the musical remake of *Goodbye Mr. Chips;* he looked upon *The Seven-Per-Cent Solution* as "a style piece . . . style that has taste and elegance, order and beauty."

The style was also innovative. For the first time in an actual Sherlockian film, Watson gets billing above Holmes (as, indeed, does Sigmund Freud), and—for the first time as well—we see Holmes *cry* on the screen. We know the movie is meant to tweak us from the very opening credits, which read: *In 1891, Sherlock Holmes disappeared and was presumed dead for three years thereafter. This is the true story of that disappearance. Only the facts have been made up.* But even though we know the events may be improbable, we are beguiled by the charm of the premise and its challenge. Although exploiting Holmes's most notorious weakness, it also gives him the strength to conquer it, giving us not only a fascinating character and an intriguing mystery (actually not much of one, confined as it is to the latter half of the film), but a very personal odyssey during which we ache for the protagonist. The film is much more than mere casebook; it is Holmes enlarged.

The Seven-Per-Cent Solution was also extraordinarily well cast. Robert Duvall, a young American whose greatest previous success had been in portraying a member of a ruling Mafia family in *The Godfather* and its sequel, was given the role of an athletic, courageous Watson, studiously avoiding the older Nigel Bruce image, and the very first Watson to noticeably limp on the screen from that old war wound. (Duvall's well-practiced British accent was impeccable.) His comments on the role are worth noting. "I saw Dr. Watson as a good, loyal and even protective friend and companion to Sherlock Holmes," no bumbling buffoon. "You have to remember that he was an ex-rugby football player, an ex-boxer, a brave ex-soldier, a highly skilled doctor of medicine and, of course, a practiced writer . . . He's also a quiet, rather self-effacing man, but a staunch one to have around in company." Duvall's thoughtful portrayal is worthy of the top billing the role receives; and indeed, Watson is the major focus of the first half of the film.

As Sigmund Freud, character actor–director Alan Arkin, known for such Broadway comedy hits as *Enter Laughing* and *Luv* as well as several films, plays the pioneer psychoanalyst—at the stage of his life when he is just beginning to be aware of his destiny—with deadly seriousness. The distinguished Sir Laurence Olivier, a peer of the realm, is seen briefly as Professor Moriarty, but a Moriarty not quite the Napoleonic criminal of Sherlock's nightmares. (Relishing the cameo part, Lord Olivier confessed: "I wouldn't want to have missed making *some* connection with Holmes in my career.") Vanessa Redgrave is an especially appealing woman in distress, rescued by both the detective *and* Freud. Cryptic brother Mycroft was portrayed by Charles Gray, who had been Blofeld of SMERSH in one of the James Bond films. British actor Jeremy Kemp crosses swords with Holmes in a very Graustarkian portrayal of the villain, Baron von Leinsdorf. Lesser roles were equally as carefully filled: Samantha Eggar as a beguiling Mrs. Watson (her first appearance in a feature film!); Georgia Brown as Freud's wife (quite a different role from her East End part in *A Study in Terror*); Jill Townsend as Holmes' mother; famed French entertainer Regine as a brothel madam, who elegantly sings a saloon ditty—about trying everything at least once but not twice—composed for the film

Poster art from *The Seven-Per-Cent Solution.*

Dr. Watson (Robert Duvall) has come to the study of mathematics professor Moriarty (Laurence Olivier) to enlist his aid in a plan to cure his friend Sherlock Holmes of drug addiction.

A classic confrontation: engineered by Watson, Sherlock Holmes (Nicol Williamson, right) meets Sigmund Freud (Alan Arkin, center).

Freud is about to defeat Baron von Leinsdorf (Jeremy Kemp) in a game of tennis.

by mystery buff Stephen Sondheim. The gifted Joel Grey, whose roles have ranged from George M. Cohan to the evil host of *Cabaret*, slinks about as an Austrian thug with the Canonical name of Lowenstein.

But the most challenging casting achievement was Holmes himself—and the dynamic stage actor Nicol Williamson was chosen. He gives an enormously rich performance in his portrait of a neurotic, driven genius. He is even more electric and theatrical than was Rathbone, but because he is crumbling before us he is also much more human, and when the tear falls from his eye he wins most of his audience. "Everyone has had a go at Holmes," he has said, "but my Holmes is different, a man in the grip of a terrible affliction, a man in a state of collapse. You will never have seen a Sherlock Holmes like mine." Williamson wanted to create a living man to whom things are happening, not just a hat and a pipe. As director Ross has put it, the film is neither farce nor spoof: "we have Holmes and Freud as nobody has ever had them, when they were young, when they were freshly felt, before they settled into clichés."

The Seven-Per-Cent Solution was the most lavish Sherlockian film yet made, filmed in both London—where many of the haunts, clubs, docks and hospitals of the time were used as actual locations—and Vienna, still much unchanged since Freud's time. For the climactic train chase, supposedly on an Istanbul-bound express, the film used the still workable steam railway in Severn Valley in the English midlands. Production designer Ken Adam of the James Bond films fame aided in the elegant period look, as did Bernard Herrmann's music. Bringing together Holmes and Freud with such care, Ross hoped, would make a rich mix, a dry martini of a film.

At the beginning of the film, a Spring day in 1891, Watson receives an urgent summons from Mrs. Hudson (Alison Leggatt) to return to Baker Street: Holmes is worsening, barricading himself in his rooms and refusing all meals. The doctor finds him raving, alternating between brief calms and sporadic harangues against a Professor Moriarty, a supposed "Napoleon of Crime."

HOLMES: . . . His agents may be caught and their crimes forestalled, but he—*he* is never so much as suspected! Until now, that is! Until I, his archenemy, managed to deduce his existence and penetrate his perimeters. And now his minions, having discovered my success, are on my track!

WATSON: Uh—but Holmes—what do you propose to do?
HOLMES (*sudden mood change*): Do? Why, for the moment, I think I shall nap.

Watson is alarmed by the evidence of cocaine usage: syringes, puncture marks. We, the audience, see flashes of Holmes's hallucinations: a small child climbing a darkened stair.

When the troubled Watson returns to his own home, he finds an unexpected visitor: Professor Moriarty, hardly the terrifying fiend of Holmes's rantings but a timid mathematics teacher who claims the detective is persecuting him.

MORIARTY: Doctor Watson, Mr. Holmes is convinced that I am some sort of criminal mastermind—of the most depraved order. I know he is a great and good man—all England resounds with his praise, but in my case he fosters a ghastly illusion and I come to you as his friend rather than turning the matter over to my solicitor—

Moriarty also reveals that he was Sherlock's childhood tutor at their father's estate in Sussex, and even hints at some long-ago tragedy, but refuses further details as "indiscreet."

Determined to save Holmes from himself, Watson decides only one man in all Europe can help—a Dr. Sigmund Freud of Vienna, who had written in *The Lancet* about cocaine addiction and its cure. But how to get Holmes to that city? To leave London would "generate unhealthy excitement in the criminal classes." Knowing how Holmes thinks, Watson devises a plan: he will provide him with an incentive he cannot resist, a false trail convincing him Moriarty has fled to the Continent. Enlisting the aid of a reluctant professor as well as Mycroft Holmes (we meet him first at his Pall Mall Diogenes Club), Watson bundles Holmes—who has brought with him old friend Toby, the bloodhound from *Sign of the Four*—on the express train leaving from Victoria Station for Vienna.

The confrontation with Freud is not an easy one; Holmes admits his illness but "my feet are on the inexorable path to destruction." No man can retrace his steps from drug addiction. Freud counters that *he* had taken cocaine and is now free of its power. "It is now my intention to help others. If you will allow me, I will help you." It will take time, and not be pleasant.

The long withdrawal process begins. Watson confides that the detective had started on the drug

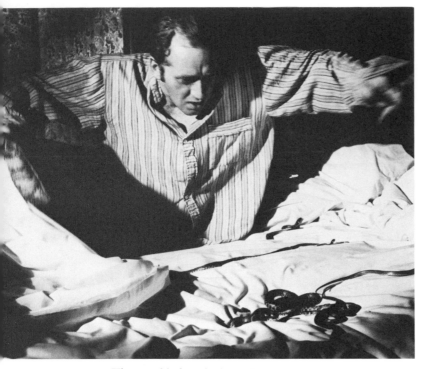

The speckled snake in Holmes's bed is actually a specter of his drug-disturbed mind in the film's nightmare sequence.

Holmes holds an Austrian thug (Joel Grey) at bay in a flashy bordello.

between cases to counter ennui. But the psychoanalyst feels the explanation may be different—and borrows from Holmes's own phraseology to explain.

FREUD: Herr Holmes's dependence on cocaine strikes me as a symptom—not an hysterical one, I grant you—but nevertheless, a symptom; an effect rather than a cause.

WATSON: What makes you say that?

FREUD: Elementary, my dear fellow. Knowing something—as I do—about drugs and drug addiction, I don't believe a man succumbs to their destructive appeal out of mere boredom.

Slowly, and racked with terrifying nightmares (the snake out of "The Speckled Band," for instance, changing into Moriarty), Holmes eases his dependence on the drug and begins the road to recovery. It is the most intensely dramatic section of the film. But having cured the detective, the second half of the motion picture—only slightly less gripping—provides him with something to do: solving a mystery. Freud becomes involved as well, but not so absorbed that he neglects to contribute pithy analytical commentary.

FREUD: Tell me something, Dr. Watson. Why have you taken so much trouble on your friend's behalf? You have left your practice, your wife—

WATSON: Because he *is* my friend.

FREUD: You have other friends, no doubt. Would you do as much for them?

WATSON (*after hesitating*): He is the best and wisest man I have ever known.

FREUD: And you have become his chronicler, his Boswell. Your place in the great scheme of things is to record his life, whatever happens. Your motives, then, for coming with him to Vienna, are not pure altrusim, but a sense of destiny that tells you to be at his side, always. Mixed motives.

These insights have more fascination than the unfolding case. At the Mauberg Tennis Club, an arrogant Prussian, Baron von Leinsdorf, resents Freud's presence because the latter is a Jew, and a duel results—a hotly played game of tennis in which Freud wins. The Baron storms away, but we know we have not seen the last of this bristling officer who supposedly will play an influential part in future European politics.

A woman now enters the case, the flame-haired Lola Deveraux, "not long ago the toast of four continents" and former addict, now hospitalized for again being on drugs. But not voluntarily, Holmes quickly deduces; the unconscious woman had been bound hand and foot and force-fed cocaine ("I think I have never seen anything so fiendish"). Investigation leads Holmes, Freud and Watson into great danger: riderless Lipizzan stallions are deliberately set on them, nearly trampling them to death. Soon after, Lola is spirited from the hospital, and the pursuit finds Holmes in a luxurious Viennese brothel, where he discovers (in addition to the body of the nun who also has disappeared from the hospital) that Lola has been abducted by the Baron so that he can pass her over to the wealthy Amin Pasha for his harem (he is an admirer of red hair). In return, the Pasha had promised to settle the Baron's debts at the gaming tables. The hapless girl has been whisked away by the Pasha on his special train with Istanbul as destination. Is all lost? Holmes, with Watson and Freud in tow, commandeers another train and a wild chase begins.

The railway pursuit is the climax of the adventure. In order to overtake the Pasha and his party, the Holmes group strip their own train, cannibalizing all but the locomotive for fuel in a desperate attempt to increase speed. (The situation is faintly reminiscent of Buster Keaton's *The General.*) Ultimately they catch up, Holmes manages to jump on the train ahead, and—as improbable as an Errol Flynn swashbuckler—crosses swords with the Baron atop speeding carriages. After some swordplay he runs the Baron through, and Lola is saved.

But the most important scene in the film is actually yet to come. It occurs in Freud's study, as a cured, grateful Holmes says goodbye.

HOLMES: Doctor, your hypnotic therapy has saved me from a terrible addiction, and beyond that, your judgement has saved my life—your judgement and Watson's, here. For him there will be a lifetime to repay the debt. What can I do for you?

FREUD: Let me hypnotize you once more before you leave.

HOLMES: What? But I tell you I am cured.

FREUD: I know; but there is another part of your mind to which I would like to say farewell.

Freud puts Holmes into deep hypnosis, and pulls up strange revelations. The patient had begun his cocaine addiction at twenty, because he was unhappy. He had become a detective to punish the

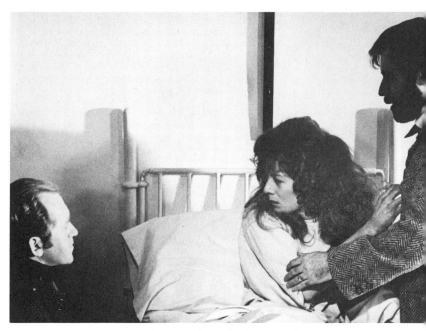

Holmes and Freud question the beautiful entertainer Lola Deveraux (Vanessa Redgrave), who may be the victim of a plot.

Sherlock Holmes has commandeered a steam locomotive to rescue a lady in distress.

wicked and see justice done. He had known injustice personally. His mother had taken a lover. . . .

Suddenly we know the meaning of those brief subconscious flashes of a child climbing a stair. It is Sherlock as a boy, witnessing his father shooting his mother to death after finding her with another man. And the fleeing lover was the child's tutor, Moriarty . . . It all becomes clear, Freud muses, borrowing Holmes's own methods and applying them to the detective, explaining not only his hatred of Moriarty but also his distrust of women and his choice of profession. Holmes will recover; he is a functioning human being who performs useful work and performs it well; within the framework of his work he is nevertheless successful and even beloved. Watson marvels at Freud's deductions: "You are the greatest detective of them all!"

Holmes is restored with no memory of what Freud has pulled from his unconscious. Holmes and Watson leave Vienna, but Watson is astonished when the detective declares that he is going away for a holiday alone—on a Danube steamer—and that his chronicler may make up any story he likes for his readers to explain his absence. ("Tell them I was murdered by my mathematics tutor! They'll never believe you in any case!") As the ship pulls from the docks, Holmes notices a certain red-haired lady in the deck chair next to his . . .

HOLMES: I was not aware that you were going abroad.

LOLA: It is an odd coincidence—but I am not sorry for it. Journeys alone are always so tedious—especially when they are long.

HOLMES: And will this be a long journey?

LOLA: It all depends, but I do think it will seem shorter if there are two of us. Don't you?

HOLMES (after pause): I hope it will not seem *too* short.

We have no more positive glimpse of Holmes the lover—in this case almost despite himself, but with certainty sailing towards a shipboard assignation—since Barrymore and Brook played the detective.

Author Meyer took great care with his screenplay, heightening both the visual and dramatic aspects of the mystery portion. In first drafts Baron von Leinsdorf is discovered dead—in a Moslem ritual slaying—on a bed in the brothel, and Holmes has his train-top swordfight with only the Pasha; wisely Meyer reworked his climax so

that the hero can confront the major villain. Despite Meyer's efforts, however, Universal had misgivings similar to those about the George C. Scott Holmes film. Perhaps the film would not be the towering blockbuster *Jaws* had been; it would demand special handling; it was actually too intellectual and would need trimming and "tightening": so reports came out of Hollywood. (Along the way an interesting prologue and epilogue were dropped: in an opening which did not make it to the final cut we first found an ancient Watson in a nursing home in 1939, dropping a newspaper and muttering, "He is dead!" He then begins this final revelation concerning his friend. But after the story is finished we ourselves see the obituary, and—the film holding true to Holmes's immortality—it is not the detective's death notice, but Sigmund Freud's.)

The film opened to surprisingly mixed reviews. Among some critics one felt an undercurrent of resentment, as if to lash out at tampering with a familiar mythos. "Some ideas are too good for the people who have them," John Simon wrote crustily in *New York* magazine (11/8/76), Nicol Williamson with "his querulous, high-pitched nasal twang" hardly suited Holmes's voice of reason, and Alan Arkin turns Freud "into a refugee from the movie *Hester Street,* too parochial and paltry to be at home in the uncharted vastnesses of the human psyche." The New Haven *Register* called Williamson's performance "cranky, quirky"—but nonetheless a well-realized portrait of "a man who has spent the better part of a lifetime carving his terrifying sexual ambivalence into a workable set of Victorian principles." Frank Rich in the New York *Post,* dismayed at the pedestrian mystery solved by brawn rather than brains, summed up his savage review of the film in this terse headline: '*Seven-Per-Cent' Is No Solution* (10/26/76).

The film did get its share of favorable reviews from important critics. Among them was the *Times's* Vincent Canby, always a Sherlockian partisan, who called the movie "simultaneously contemporary in its sensibility and faithful to the courtly mood and decent spirit of the Sir Arthur Conan Doyle originals. It's also one of the most handsome evocations of a vanished period . . . the most exhilarating entertainment of the film year to date." Pauline Kael in the *New Yorker* magazine, although not nearly as enthused as Canby (she cites hyperexcited Williamson's deductions as rattled off with "beserk velocity"), did class the film as "an ingeniously contrived spree . . . [with] one of the wittiest wrap-ups of any mystery movie." (11/1/76).

Freud, who, along with Holmes, has boarded the Pasha's harem train, tries to rouse the kidnapped Lola.

Sherlock Holmes, sword in hand, in the swashbuckling climax aboard a speeding train.

Holmes and Watson part in Vienna.

241

Universal had the good sense to book the film selectively in class houses in its initial release, carefully nurturing interest; the policy worked, and *The Seven-Per-Cent Solution* made a successful debut.

The film uses Holmes well, and matching him with Freud—whose analytic probings might indeed have been similar to the detective's—was brilliant. The movie reaches even deeper and with more detail into Holmes's psychoanalysis than does its book source—indeed, it improves it in many places, as by having Moriarty become the mother's *lover* instead of merely an informant (as did the original book), so that the whole subconscious reason for Holmes's hatred of his boyhood tutor is made more reasonable. And the inquiries into Holmes's psyche are fertile indeed, with much material for Sherlockian speculation!

The detective's neurotic flights are well limned by Nicol Williamson with almost hysterical enthusiasm, his bland-pudding face supercharged with the dramatic demands of the role. He plays the romantic Holmes well too, in that final scene on the Danube steamer as he struggles with his conflicting emotions in confronting the frankly seductive attentions of the courtesan Lola. We know that after the steamer sails and the film ends, Holmes will succumb—a different sexual liaison from the unconsumed and tragic love affair of *Private Life* (here Lola joins Ilse von Hofmannsthal in the ranks of Irene Adler look-alikes) and the respectable honeymoons of John Barrymore and Clive Brook.

But the really important relationship is not between Sherlock and Lola (can we wish them three years of clandestine bliss, and wonder at the events which brought Holmes alone back to public life in London?) or between Sherlock and Sigmund (may we wonder why Freud in later writings never acknowledged his debt to the detective's analytical methodology?), but between Holmes and John H. Watson. It is the core of the film, and it is Watson who is the most important person of the first half, plotting the scheme to bring Holmes and Freud together. It is not without justification that Watson receives top billing in the opening credits even before Holmes (credits, indeed, with *footnotes* of the kind dear to Sherlockian scholars, such as identifying Watson's first wife as his *only* Canonical one!). Watson's deep concern for his friend's well-being, the lengths to which he goes to cure him, his tears and his joy at Holmes's recovery—all tell us that the underlying twosome in this film is, after all, not Holmes–Freud nor Holmes–Deveraux but—as always—Holmes and Watson. It is a very human Holmes and Watson (as scripted, *both* men have occasion to shed tears on screen), and we sense, even more strongly than in the Billy Wilder film which explored the same feelings, the deep affection and love passing between them.

Sherlock Holmes is surprised to find a familiar and beautiful fellow passenger aboard the Danube steamer.

Sherlock Holmes on Television

A boyish Ronald Howard uses an early telephone as Sherlock Holmes.

Concurrently with Sherlock Holmes's cinematic appearances in feature films, shorter movies and television programs also attested to the popularity of the world's greatest detective. Actually, one of the first recorded experimental television shows was a dramatization of "The Three Garridebs"—a Conan Doyle short story in which Holmes traces the missing heir of an eccentric American millionaire who has left a fortune to any three persons of that name. The play was presented on the NBC system during field tests before the actual commencement of TV service, on November 27, 1937, in a performance from New York's Radio City studio. Louis Hector, who two years previously had done a season of Holmesian plays over WJZ-NBC radio, portrayed Sherlock. William Podmore was Watson in this historic event.

Because this places Sherlockian drama at the very beginnings of the television image, it is interesting to examine the program in some detail. Even though certainly primitive by any standards, the experimental drama tried to do justice to the power of the Canon. Two cameras were used, and a cluster of partial sets (a corner of the Baker Street rooms, Garrideb's study, etc.) interlinking within the confines of a tiny studio; these visuals were interestingly fleshed out with brief film clips to set the stage and bridge the scenes—Holmes and Watson traveling in a hansom cab, for instance, in footage specially shot in New York's Central Park. Although restricted in its presentation, the program offered a leisurely (commercial-free!), close version of a Doyle drama which Holmes himself within the show classed as "in all our explorations we have never come upon anything more singular." The show gave Holmes a good start in the new medium.

Radio had already made rich contributions to the saga; as early as 1930 William Gillette—on *Lux Radio Theater*—had starred in an audio adaptation of his famed stage play. In 1931 character actor Richard Gordon began a series of weekly Sherlockian impersonations which continued seasonally for several years; he became known as "Radio's Sherlock Holmes." In 1933 Universal released a theatrical short called *The Radio Murder Mystery,* written by H. O. Kusell and directed by Monte Brice, which featured what passed for typical studio activity in the then new medium, with Richard Gordon at work before the microphone along with such other on-air personalities of the day as Broadway columnist Louis Sobol, "Dream Girl" Alice Joy and Jack Fulton, "Golden Voice of the Air." Just as more than a decade later attempts were made to pass off Basil Rathbone as a real-life crime-solver (in the "Tales of Fatima" show), Gordon is acclaimed an "ace criminologist on and off the air," who blithely assists the police in solving the murder of the eccentric inventor of a war-gas, unmasking the killer in a studio roundup of suspects while reconstructing the crime during a live program *("I shall announce the murderer of Theodore Anson over the air!").* Actually, we never see a real radio play performed, just a middle-aged Gordon in deerstalker posturing flamboyantly before an NBC microphone.

Another rarely seen theatrical featurette (although made with an eye towards the early television industry) is the British *The Man Who Disappeared* of 1951, with John Longden as a wooden and somewhat rough-edged Holmes, but with actual London dockside streets—evidently unchanged in half a century—serving as authentic settings for a period retelling of "The Man With the Twisted Lip." The production is awkward and insensitive (Sherlock is called upon to engage in an opium-den brawl), but one brief scene—a murky Thames location where the detective finds the supposedly murdered Neville St. Clair's money-laden vest—conveys real power. Campbell Singer is Watson; Richard M. Grey directed.

As early as 1949 in America the *Story Theater* anthology series presented television audiences with a half-hour version of "The Speckled Band," a somewhat adulterated adaptation crammed into cheap sets and primitively filmed. As Sherlock Holmes, character actor Alan Napier (then in his mid-forties) is no doubt better remembered to a later generation of TV viewers as Alfred the butler in the *Batman* series. In 1953 Basil Rathbone—as reported in a previous chapter—ended his long boycott of the role by appearing as Holmes in the "live" CBS-TV *Suspense* half-hour presentation of the John Dickson Carr–Adrian Conan Doyle pastiche, "The Adventure of the Black Baronet," a story which had that year attracted national attention featured in *Collier's* magazine (heralded as a return of a Doyle to the Sherlockian grind). It was a pleasant enough story, well-suited to the half-hour television format (and was visual enough, for the plot turned on a secret spring-knife mechanical device), but no series spun from it.

The following year, however, a Sherlockian breakthrough occurred on television. An energetic TV programming pioneer, the legendary Sheldon Reynolds, who three years previously had made a series shot in Europe about a globe-trotting newspaperman, *Foreign Intrigue,* into the earliest syndication success, acquired rights to the Doyle character for thirty-nine episodes produced mainly in Paris, featuring Ronald Howard as the detective and H. Marion Crawford as a solid, earnest, beefy Watson. The show, thanks to its inherent appeal and to aggresive merchandising, was widely popular in the major American markets.

No small contribution to the series' success was Marion Crawford's truly impressive performance as Watson, among the very best in the Sherlockian cinema. Producer Reynolds wanted deliberately to move from the Nigel Bruce image of the previous decade: "Doyle didn't make Watson to be a buffoon. Dr. Watson was an intelligent man, and Holmes was a brilliant eccentric. They worked as a team. One would have never functioned without the other." The choice of Holmes, however, was less true. Ronald Howard, son of the deceased romantic idol Leslie Howard, appeared—although thirty-six at the time—boyish and far less razor-honed than his Rathbonian role model. A far from forceful Holmes seemed often overshadowed by a riveting, excellent Watson—and even an interestingly gross Lestrade played by Archie Duncan.

The stories, too, were weak. Only a few were drawn from Doyle; most of the rest were flawed dramatically, poor as mystery puzzles, and unmemorable. Happily, however, the very first episode, "The Case of the Cunningham Heritage," opened with an abridged account of how Holmes and Watson met and took up lodgings together, the first time this cosmic event was to be portrayed

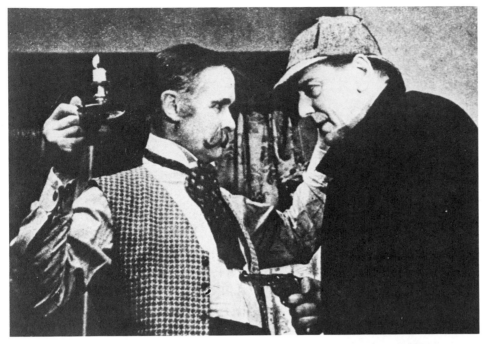

The very first television Holmes, Louis Hector.

H. Marion Crawford, one of the very best Watsons.

Occasionally Sir Arthur Conan Doyle himself has been portrayed on television (Peter Cushing played him in a TV biography of Harry Houdini). Here Nigel Davenport stars as the author in a PBS Masterpiece Theater drama showing how he provided solutions to some real-life cases.

on the sound screen. Indeed, there were fine touches throughout the series, and the critical reception was favorable in the trades. *Billboard* called it "polished, literate and an entertaining series ... The show is slick, commercial, and top-notch!" (10/30/54), while *Variety* hailed it as having "style, distinction and pace"; the *New York Times* called it "a winner."

Today the limited budgets and speed of filming the programs make the series seem hopelessly primitive; a recent biography, however, helps put this early television triumph into perspective. Nicole Milinaire, now the Duchess of Bedford, was for years closely associated with producer Sheldon Reynolds in *all* his ventures. In her just-published memoirs, *Nichole Nobody,* she reminisces fondly of the hectic period during which the show was assembled, and the fencing Reynolds engaged in with the Doyle heirs in his long campaign to negotiate rights for the characters. The recollections are merely amusing minutiae: Archie Duncan insisting that despite a feverish shooting schedule tea would be served promptly at four each day; Paulette Goddard (one of the few guest stars used), who had a horror of cemeteries, being driven on a three-mile detour on her way to the studios outside Paris—but give perhaps the most detailed written record of a Holmesian cinematic venture in the making.

The following year Boris Karloff appeared in a peripherally Sherlockian role as "Mr. Mycroft" in the TV play, *A Sting of Death,* based on H. F. Heard's *A Taste of Honey,* in which a retired detective in a remote village turns his own weapons of death against a farmer who has trained bees to murder. As in the source novel, we only suspect the aging hero of being Sherlock; it is never spelled out.

In 1957 CBS-TV's outstanding public affairs hour, *Odyssey,* devoted a loving hour to Holmes and his followers, affectionately probing—with Charles Collingwood as host and script by David Ebin—the membership and eccentricities of the Baker Street Irregulars. An actual yearly meeting was recreated at New York's Cavanaugh restaurant, with the traditional toasts to the Master given; among the participants on the program were Irregulars Red Smith, Edgar W. Smith, and Thomas L. Stix. Then Rex Stout made what was for him a typically outrageous pronouncement: that "The Red-Headed League" had actually occurred not in London but during a visit by Holmes to New York. The relocated story was then dramatized within the pro-

gram, with Michael Clarke Lawrence as Holmes, now living at 16B Gramercy Park—actually the address of New York's prestigious Players' Club, one of the city's most elegant corners.

Actually, television in England gave far more programming room to Sherlockian series. Alan Wheatley starred as Holmes in a number of 1951 adaptations from the Doyle stories over the BBC, making him the first series Holmes player in the visual medium (Raymond Francis was his Watson). In 1964 popular character actor Douglas Wilmer was Holmes in a BBC-TV version of "The Speckled Band" which expanded into a series the following year, with Nigel Stock as Watson. (Interestingly, Wilmer Was Sir Dennis Nayland Smith, along with H. Marion Crawford as his medical friend Dr. Petrie—characters Sax Rohmer clearly patterned after Holmes and Watson—in a Fu Manchu feature film, and has made cameo appearances as Sherlock in several features, as already noted.) Playing the "unusual, insufferable, fascinating" detective had long been an ambition of Wilmer's; *Punch* thought him "a fine Holmes, the Holmes we should all like to be—brilliant, cynical, cool and fearless." In 1968 BBC 1 again returned Doyle's creation to the British home screen, casting horror star Peter Cushing in elaborate hour-long adaptions of the sotires emphasizing that they were as much Victorian thrillers as studies in deduction. Locations for filming were chosen to most closely resemble the sites described in the Conan Doyle stories, and in *The Hound of the Baskervilles*—told in two parts—sequences were actually shot on Dartmoor. The series was surprisingly rich in violence, a dramatic device defended by the producers as merely reflecting the violent turmoil that was changing London at the turn of the century.

(A more recent British television series, *The Rivals of Sherlock Holmes,* dealt with the cases of *other* fictional detectives of Victorian times.)

In 1972 the most industrious of American film studios feeding television's insatiable need for programming, Universal, dusted off the detective who had served it so well in the forties, hoping to rotate him with two other "classic" sleuths, Stuart Palmer's spinster Hildegarde Withers and the dime novels' Nick Carter, in a thriller-oriented "Movie of the Weekend" series.

The vehicle was *The Hound of the Baskervilles*— surely a winner, as the best-loved mystery story ever written—and to play Holmes the dashing British leading man of countless adventure films, Stewart Granger, was chosen. Both the choice and

246

the adaptation somewhat misfired. Granger, who was then close on sixty but still—despite his un-Holmesian silver hair—a commanding, virile presence, had the stature of the detective but looked uncomfortably heavy-waisted for the role. His extensive stage and screen experience allowed him to give the part an acceptable richness. The telefilm itself was somewhat perfunctory, running a scant 73 minutes in order to fit with commercials into a ninety-minute TV show, it was a fairly hurried version of *The Hound*, lacking depth and detail. The casting, however, had some interesting character actors crowded into the ranks: William Shatner, the heroic captain of the *Star Trek* science fiction series, was a smoothly villainous Stapleton, with Jane Merrow as Beryl; John Williams and Sally Ann Howes played the Franklands, and Anthony Zerbe portrayed Dr. Mortimer. All were actors of distinction. As Watson, Bernard Fox resorted to a Nigel Bruce bluster, but was not overly trying, and evidenced real affection for his companion.

Speedily made on a television budget (and directed by Barry Crane), this first Hollywood color version of *The Hound of the Baskervilles* was totally shot on Universal's sound stages and extensive, familiar backlot. Even the old ramparts of Dracula's castle substituted for the ancestral home of the Baskervilles, and the studio moor landscape across which Holmes pursued the spectral beast seemed cramped. But the panoramic spires of Victorian London seen in the opening sequences, actually glass-shot art work provided under the direction of Universal's master matte artist Albert Whitlock, were stunning recreations of a city at the height of its glory, and set a luxurious standard which the rest of the skimpy, abbreviated telefeature had a hard time matching.

Stewart Granger, although he made a valiant attempt, could not quite submerge his own *persona* to the Holmesian dimensions. The audience ratings were not spectacular, and Universal abandoned its plans to use the great detective in a rotating weekend mystery series.

For television, and for theatrical release in Europe, the same studio which had unleashed Basil Rathbone upon the Sherlockian world, Twentieth Century-Fox, cast an actor well known as two great mystery figures—James Bond and the Saint—as Holmes in 1976. The suave, handsome Roger Moore (then 48) was certainly the prettiest actor to portray Sherlock: his unsettling good looks made it difficult to fully accept a talented actor bringing his best to a difficult role. Actually, it first

Boris Karloff as a man whom we suspect is Holmes in retirement examines a deadly killer bee in the television adaptation of H. F. Heard's *A Taste for Honey*.

At home with Watson in the comfortable Baker Street surroundings. (The set is certainly well appointed.)

247

Stewart Granger in a serious, probing expression as the great detective.

Universal's Grimpen Mire—not very big.

took a good deal of persuasion on producer Jack Haley, Jr.'s part to convince Moore to take up the deerstalker, but he was won over by the charms of the script. "Holmes comes to life in this story. I wear a number of different disguises and this appeals to me. I have a love affair with a beautiful actress who has a nine-year-old son named Scott and we learn that Holmes's middle name is Scott. And, of course, there is Moriarty threatening to steal all the gold in the world. But what I like *most* about playing Holmes is that there is more dialogue in this script than I ever had in 120 'Saint' episodes and two 'Bond' films." He plays the role absolutely straight. "And, most important, I do my own interpretation and don't copy any previous actors who have done the role."

Truthfully, the two-hour telefilm *Sherlock Holmes in New York* had actually been conceived as one further utilization of the extensive "period New York" sets Twentieth Century-Fox had originally built on its backlots for *Hello, Dolly*. Screenplay writer Alvin Sapinsley, well grounded in the Canon, had devised an endearing device to bring Holmes to the greatest metropolis of the New World in 1901, larding the events with many Sherlockian references from other stories.

The production also featured an interesting gallery of supporting players, helping to enrich the show's glamour. The alluring Charlotte Rampling played the actress Irene Adler with whom Holmes shares his heart. Patrick MacNee, the dapper male half of *The Avengers* team, patterned his Watson impersonation somewhat too closely to an unctuous Nigel Bruce model. But as the program's Moriarty John Huston gives the most interesting featured performance: leering, full of juicy lines ("I am going to crush you in such a way that your humiliation and downfall will be witnessed by the entire world!") spoken in an Irish brogue. He is a worthy addition to the villain's ranks of players.

Judith Crist, reviewing the show for *TV Guide* (10/18/76), felt herself pleased. "Moore and Patrick MacNee provide attractive variations on the familiar characters. Moore's Holmes, in fact, has a dash of the debonair and the worldly . . . that sits well on the great detective. After Moriarty, in his rococo lair, threatens Holmes with a trap door, flying daggers and a crashing chandelier, the great detective calmly remarks, 'A pity about the chandelier; it was the only item in the room that showed the merest modicum of style.' And when Sherlock and the lady in distress have their moments, there's an undertone of emotion new to Holmes

An odd group pose from *Sherlock Holmes in New York:* from left to right: Moriarty, Irene Adler, Watson and Holmes!

Holmes and Watson traveling by carriage down the streets of New York City.

sagas . . . Under Boris Sagal's direction, this is first-class entertainment."

The drama supposes that Irene Adler has borne Holmes an illegitimate son (Rex Stout had after all suggested that his Nero Wolfe was thus related to the detective) and that to lure Holmes to America Moriarty kidnaps the boy. Once in New York, Sherlock solves a very tricky puzzle regarding gold stocks vanished from a vault deep under lower Broadway—"The crime of the century." It is a caper that suggests the solution of "The Red-headed League," and is properly Doyle-like in style, but interests us not half so much as the dashing and masculine new Holmes, significantly different from the recent sexually ambivalent Holmes on the screen. Of course, *The Seven-Per-Cent Solution* was to end with the promise of healthy romance, but here we are happily presented with a liaison which is, to say the least, ongoing!

(*Sherlock Holmes in New York* was released abroad in movie theaters, and, curiously, its second network play was more complete than its first in this country. At the last moment a national political speech forced NBC to trim a few minutes from its premiere showing.)

There has been other Sherlockian activity on television. In 1964, on the animated *Mr. Magoo Storybook* series, surprisingly enough, a straight cartoon version of *A Study in Scarlet* was planned, but then (because of the copyright question, as well as the novel's scarcely being a children's tale) abandoned in favor of an original jewel heist melodrama with Star of Rhodesia overtones; radio voice Paul Frees—rich, deep and resonant—portrayed Holmes, with Mr. Magoo (Jim Backus) as his Watson. (Interestingly enough, an IBM industrial film the same year used an animated Holmes to explain the mysteries of computer workings.) In 1966, shortly after the death of Basil Rathbone, New York nostalgia host Joe Franklin over WOR-TV presented a warm tribute to "The Man Who Was Sherlock Holmes," in a television special using clips from all the Rathbone Holmesian contributions. A decade later producer Jack Haley, Jr. wove together a similar collage for an episode of his *That's Hollywood!* documentary series. The episode was called, without further subtitle, "The Great Detective"; it needed no more elaboration.

In 1975 Robert Shaw was announced as playing the title role in a TV special, *Timex Presents Sherlock Holmes,* to be filmed in England and taken from three short stories, the rights for which had been obtained from the Conan Doyle estate. Shaw (then

249

Larry Hagman dons the familiar dressing gown as Sherman Holmes in NBC-TV's *The Return of the World's Greatest Detective.*

Spoofs on the Holmesian image—most of them good-natured—go as far back as Buster Keaton's classic *Sherlock Junior.* Here the comedy team of Rowan and Martin portray the great detective and Watson for a series of skits on a *Laugh-In* TV program.

48) would have made a dynamic, excellent detective, but other commitments—and his success in *Jaws*—forced him to step out of the project, which then was abandoned.

The following year Larry Hagman, Mary Martin's son, was seen in *The Return of the World's Greatest Detective,* an NBC World Premiere comedy in which bumbling Los Angeles motorcycle cop Sherman Holmes, after a fall, wakes up assuming the personality of the fictional detective he most admires. He dons Inverness and deerstalker, takes lodging in a rooming house at 221B Baker Street run by a Mrs. Hudson, and attracts the professional attention and amorous sympathy of a young psychiatric social worker named Joan "Doc" Watson (!)—very akin to *They Might Be Giants,* although in this case the plot was created by veteran humorists Roland Kibee and Dean Hargrove (the latter directed). Actually, it was an affectionate parody, and the brainstruck investigator goes about making some fairly acceptable deductions with great Canonical flair; the mystery he solves in a surprise courtroom climax—a million dollar embezzlement—is interesting. There have been worse parodies on television. Paul Lynde played an irascible and fey Holmesian type in a burlesque pilot which did not sell; *Holmes and YoYo,* the brief comedy series in which a police detective is teamed with a human-seeming robot, contained nothing actually Sherlockian.

In 1977, *ABC Short Story Specials* presented a charming adaptation of Hugh Pentecost's "My Dear Uncle Sherlock," in which a twelve-year-old boy—using the powers of deductive reasoning he has developed playing Sherlock Holmes games with his uncle—solves a mystery in his own community, when the wrong man is arrested for robbing a wealthy old recluse. Robbie Rist played the boy, and Royal Dano (who, interestingly enough, had like Raymond Massey frequently been cast as Abraham Lincoln) was the uncle.

For children, as well, the popular and long-running *Sesame Street* educational series has presented to international audiences an inquisitive role-model, Sherlock Hemlock, as a continuing character since March of 1971.

Made in 1976, but as of this writing not yet sold to American television, is the British production of "The Silver Blaze" for the Highgate Associates series, *Classics Dark and Dangerous,* adapted by Julian Bond and directed by John Davis. A young-looking, dynamic Christopher Plummer (a vigorous Canadian then almost fifty) essayed an excellent Holmes, with Thorley Walters returning once more to the Watson role. The half-hour production was lavishly made on the real settngs of the story: old trains, great manor houses, the moors, and even a Victorian racetrack. The script is both literate and faithful, but with one regrettable lapse: the classic line about "the curious incident of the dog in the nighttime" is unnecessarily altered. Otherwise, the program is perfect.

The new permissiveness in theatrical films has allowed a strange cinematic offshoot: the use of Holmes in X-rated movies. Elaboration of the Holmes–Watson relationship has resulted in such pornography as *The American Adventures of Surelick Holmes* (A Hand-in-Hand release, 1975; directed by Bob Ell) in which the detective is flown to the United States to track down Maryarty, a transvestite killer, at the behest of a Thaddeus Sholto–like industrialist. David Chandler is Holmes; Frank Massey portrays his consenting Watson. At the film's end the detective and Maryarty go off together, certainly an unorthodox finish. (Interestingly, in the experimental stage play by Boston author Allen Sternfield, *Holmes and Moriarty*, the classic foes, assasinated together, die in each others' arms.)

Young Robbie Rist and his uncle Royal Dano use their wits in the ABC Short Story Special, *My Dear Uncle Sherlock.*

251

The Future

But at this writing several major Sherlockian theatrical productions have been delayed or abandoned. Plans to star Roger Moore in a follow-up to his *Sherlock Holmes in New York* seem to await the actor's availability; the new film was said to concern a number of ritual Thuggee murders, the thirteenth of which was to be the attempted assassination of Queen Victoria—an interesting idea. Nicholas Meyer's second Holmesian pastiche, *The West End Horror* in which the detective mingles with some of the foremost literary personages (Bram Stoker, Oscar Wilde among them) of his day, was purchased by Universal early, but the studio was cooled by *The Seven-Per-Cent Solution's* unspectacular reception in this country and in Europe. (In England the film was reportedly withdrawn and subjected to further "tightening.") Frank Saletri's 1975 screenplay, *Sherlock Holmes in "The Adventures of the Golden Vampire,"* in which Moriarty enlists the aid of Count Dracula to kill the detective, still awaits production. (Rock star Alice Cooper was asked to play the vampire.) However, a Canadian company is filming *Sherlock Holmes and Saucy Jack*—yet another confrontation with Jack the Ripper. *"Holmes and Watson become enmeshed in corruption and intrigue that rival Watergate—a scandal that leads right to the throne itself!"* The screenplay is by John Hopkins.

Parodies—either affectionate, outrageous or both—have recently been very much in vogue. As far back as 1972 pop artist Andy Warhol was reported to be teamed with critic Rex Reed in an "underground" [*sic*] variant of the Sherlock Holmes saga, with Reed also playing Watson; this has yet to reach the screen. On British commercial television in 1977, "London Weekend" presented an hour comedy called *The Strange Case of the End of Civilization as We Know It,* in which actor-author John Cleese plays Sherlock Holmes of Baker Street as a bumbling idiot, with Watson (Arthur Lowe) presented as "an absolute moron, the worst doctor ever qualified," who accidentally and unknowingly causes the murder which the detective investigates. A wild burlesque which tilts much of the Canon—instead of shouting "There's no time to lose," for instance, Holmes now says, "Hand me the crossword puzzle, Watson, there are several minutes to lose"—it was cheerfully received by the public. More recently—indeed, of this writing—Peter Cook and Dudley Moore are preparing a new and most unorthodox version of *The Hound of the Baskervilles.* The producer, Michael White, was most recently responsible for the medieval send-up, *Jabberwocky.* In this *Hound,* Watson (Moore) is a hysterical, rodentlike Welshman and Holmes (Cook) sports a strong East End Fagin-style accent, heading an outstanding cast of British comedy character players including Joan Greenwood, Terry-Thomas, Max Wall, Irene Handl, Hugh Griffith and Kenneth Williams, complemented by a large and amiable Irish wolfhound in the title role.

As the Holmesian cinematic image moves into the future and into the twenty-first century, the mood can no doubt be parody or straight, our detective romantically macho or sensitive, his methodology scientifically up-to-the-minute or quaintly Victorian. Each cinematic decade has perceived its Sherlock somewhat differently, and the traditional detective has been altered somewhat in the grip of our affectionate, yet awed, embrace.

However, as Holmes strides confidently to the year 2000, his popularity undiminished, his basic nature will not have changed that much. He will still represent to us, as he did to his chronicler Watson—our guide—the best and wisest man we have ever known, and—curiously, gratifyingly, unquestionably—a genuine superstar of the screen.